The Michaels
Book of Needlecrafts

The Michaels Book of Needlecrafts

knitting, crochet & embroidery

Edited by
Dawn Cusick
& Megan Kirby

LARK BOOKS

A Division of Sterling Publishing Co., Inc.
New York

Project Editor: Dawn Cusick
Art Director: Megan Kirby
Photographer: Steve Mann
Illustrator: Orrin Lundgren
Cover Designer: Barbara Zaretsky
Contributing Writers: Kelly Banner, Catherine Hamrick,
   Judi Kaufman, Linda Kopp, and Jane Woodside
Technical Editor: Marilyn Hastings
Technical Consultants: Catherine Ham, knitting; Jane Davis and Karen Manthey, crochet
Production Assistance: Shannon Yokeley
Makeup Artists: Diane Chambers, Dana McCoy
Art Interns: Sara House, Bradley Norris, and Myra Hester

Library of Congress Cataloging-in-Publication Data
The Michaels book of needlecrafts / [edited by] Megan Kirby, Dawn Cusick.--
1st ed.
   p. cm.
   Includes index.
   ISBN 1-57990-640-0 (hardcover)
   1. Knitting. 2. Crocheting. 3. Embroidery. I. Kirby, Megan. II. Cusick, Dawn.   III. Michaels (Firm)
   TT820.M53 2005
   746.4--dc22
2005012851
10 9 8 7 6 5 4 3 2 1
First Edition

Published by Lark Books, A Division of
Sterling Publishing Co., Inc.
387 Park Avenue South, New York, N.Y. 10016
© 2005, Lark Books
Distributed in Canada by Sterling Publishing, c/o Canadian Manda Group, 165 Dufferin Street, Toronto, Ontario, Canada M6K 3H6
Distributed in the U.K. by Guild of Master Craftsman Publications Ltd., Castle Place, 166 High Street, Lewes, East Sussex,
England BN7 1XU
Tel: (+ 44) 1273 477374, Fax: (+ 44) 1273 478606, e-mail: pubs@thegmcgroup.com, Web: www.gmcpublications.com
Distributed in Australia by Capricorn Link (Australia) Pty Ltd., P.O. Box 704, Windsor, NSW 2756 Australia

If you have questions or comments about this book, please contact:
Lark Books, 67 Broadway, Asheville, NC 28801, (828) 253-0467

For information about custom editions, special sales, premium and corporate purchases, please contact Sterling Special Sales Department at 800-805-5489 or specialsales@sterlingpub.com.

contents

introduction

Needlecrafters of the world, unite! Never has there been a better time to knit, crochet, or embroider. The recent surge in the popularity of needlecrafts has created a fabulous selection of materials and designs from manufacturers, as well as a culture of comraderie and creativity among crafters. Large numbers of young people have entered the field in droves, quickly becoming passionate about their work. Companies continue to develop one incredible new yarn after another, inspiring everyone from novices to retired crafters to pick up needles and hooks. Furs, chenniles, boucles, eyelashes, and dozens of novel fiber combinations beckon and inspire. These new yarns not only look great, but because individual stitches are difficult to see, they hide a world of flaws so they're perfect for beginners.

Today's needlecrafters demand interesting, fun patterns and designs. Even beginners want to make projects they can wear or display with pride. If you're making a gift, you want it to be valued and enjoyed, not stashed in the back of closet. You want to make something you will love, and that others will love, also. Today's needlecrafters demand that the process be fun, not frustrating or disappointing. Crafting groups are now as much about learning and having fun with friends as they are about making things.

This book features three project-packed chapters for knitters, crocheters, and embroiderers. Each chapter opens with an illustrated section of basic instructions, and then moves on to a hearty selection of projects. Beginning needlecrafters will be thrilled to discover dozens of projects that are both easy to make and look great, while more advanced needleworkers will find a great selection of challenges and inspirations.

Projects range from simple scarves, hats, and handbags that can be finished in a few evenings to sweaters, jackets, capelets, vests, and tops that may take a weekend or two. Bright, colorful kids' projects include mittens, hats, tops, sweaters, jackets, and even a toy; infant and toddler projects include blankets, booties, onesies, hats, and jackets. You'll also find a great selection of home dec projects, from pillows to afghans to decorative towels and sheets.

We hope *The Michaels Book of Needlecrafts* will become one of your favorite sources for projects, information, and inspiration. Enjoy!

knitting

Welcome to the knitting chapter! Here you'll find dozens of great projects using some of the newest, most interesting yarns on the market. You'll find simple projects that can be completed in an evening or two, as well as more challenging projects that may take a few weekends.

As you peruse the projects, keep in mind that many of them can easily be adapted into clever variations that may suit your fancy far more than the original. Even beginning knitters, for instance, can adapt a pattern to increase the width of a scarf or the length of a sweater.

Last, remember that while knitting patterns may mention specific yarns and colors, you are certainly free to make as many changes as you like. Page 21 provides detailed information on substituting yarns; a quick review of that text and a few sample gauge swatches will open up a world of possibilities.

Enjoy!

knitting basics

tools & supplies

needles

Knitting needles come in two basic types—circular and straight—and in a variety of materials. When buying needles for yourself, remember that there is no single, correct needle type or material. These are personal choices, and you'll find yourself tending to use one type more than another. Just use what feels most comfortable to you.

other tools

needle gauge

small pair of scissors or snips

tapestry needles for sewing up seams (these have large eyes and blunt tips)

knitter's pins

tape measure

stitch holders and safety pins

notebook and pen

yarn!!!

Yarns can be made from animal or plant fibers, commercially manufactured fibers, or a combination of both. Animal fibers include wool, mohair, alpaca, and angora, while plant fibers include cotton and linen. Natural fibers are often combined with synthetic yarns to create yarns with special characteristics. An acrylic/wool mixture, for example, will have some of the properties of a wool fiber, together with the easy-care qualities of a synthetic.

Yarns are spun in various ways to achieve a particular effect, giving the knitted fabric a distinctive look. For example, yarn may be very smooth or have loops or nubs twisted with it, resulting in a flat or highly textured surface. A yarn may be very fine or it may be bulky, in which case it will knit up very slowly or very quickly. Novelty yarns have the advantage of not requiring fancy stitches to showcase them, making it easy to create lovely fabrics with very plain knitting. Novelty yarns are also very forgiving of uneven gauge, making them a great choice for new knitters.

Knitting yarns are typically sold in skeins and balls and occasionally on cones. Always buy enough yarn to complete your project, as the yarn may not be available in the same dye lot later or may even be completely sold out. Unused balls can usually be returned to the yarn shop or put into your yarn stash for future use.

The labels found on commercially produced yarns provide a great deal of information. They'll tell you the fiber content and give you an indication of the gauge you can expect to obtain. Suggested needle sizes are usually given, as well as care instructions for the particular yarn.

winding yarns

Many yarns today need to be rewound into a ball before you begin to knit. Be sure to keep everything loose and relaxed during this process—and that includes you! If you pull, the yarn tightens up and may tangle. Even if this should happen, don't get frustrated: just keep it loose, wind slowly, and gently unravel the knots.

common abbreviations

Review the abbreviations in your pattern instructions to make sure you understand them. If you're unsure about a particular technique, refer to a basic knitting text or ask a knitting buddy to explain it to you.

*	repeat from * as many times as indicated		N	needle
()	alternate measurement(s)/ stitch counts		oz	ounces
			patt	pattern
alt	alternate		p	purl
approx	approximately		rem	remain or remaining
beg	begin or beginning		rev st st	reverse stockinette stitch
BO	bind off		RS	right side(s)
cm	centimeter(s)		SC	single crochet
CO	cast on		ssk	slip 1 st as if to knit, slip 1 st as if to knit, then knit these two sts tog, tbl
cont	continued or continuing			
dec	decrease or decreasing		st(s)	stitch(es)
dpn	double-pointed needles		St st	stockinette stitch
g	gram(s)		tbl	through back of loop(s)
g st	garter stitch		tog	together
inc	increase or increasing		WS	wrong sides
k	knit		yd	yards
k2tog	knit two sts together		yo	yarn over
m	meter(s)		yfd	yarn forward
MC	main color		yrn	yarn round needle
mm	millimeter(s)			

knit

Knit and purl are the two stitches on which all other stitches are based. Here's a refresher on the basics of each.

Position the yarn in the back of your work. Insert the right needle into the first stitch of the left needle, going from front to back.

Pass the yarn under and up the front of the right needle. Draw it through the stitch with the right needle.

Drop the stitch from the left needle. The stitch on the right needle is your knit stitch.

techniques

using patterns and schematics

Before you begin a project, it's a good idea to read through the pattern Instructions carefully to familiarize yourself with what you'll be doing.

Pattern instructions are usually given in a range of sizes. Determine which size you want to use, and mark it in some way to highlight your requirements. (If you don't want to mark the pattern itself, photocopy it, then mark it up. Photocopies are also useful so you don't have to carry the whole book around with you.) To determine your size, check the measurements given for the garment. For sweaters, vests, and tops, the pattern is accompanied by a schematic, which is a diagram of the finished piece with the measurements indicated. Do remember that even if your bust measurement is 34 inches (86 cm), the finished garment is unlikely to measure 34 inches (86 cm), unless you're knitting a second skin. Almost all patterns have ease added to them. This extra width, which often surprises new knitters, provides wearing comfort. Measure your favorite loose-fitting sweater, and you'll likely find that it actually measures quite a bit more than you are accustomed to thinking of as your "size."

The schematic also gives finished lengths, so you can decide in advance if you want to adjust the body or sleeve lengths. It's a good idea to keep a record of any changes you make in case you want to knit the item again later. You should also note what gauge you achieve with a particular yarn for future reference .

making and measuring a gauge swatch

This preparation step is the most important step you can take to ensure good results. Don't skip this step unless you enjoy unpleasant surprises. Making a gauge swatch is a lot like test-driving a car: You need to see how the yarn behaves, how it feels in your hands, and what results you can expect from it. Once you've selected the yarn and needles, cast on a minimum of 20 stitches—preferably more—and knit a swatch at least 4 inches (10 cm).

Before you measure it, handle the fabric to decide if it feels good enough against the skin to wear comfortably. Does it have the right "hand" for the item you're making? If you'll be washing the finished garment, you should ideally wash and dry the gauge swatch first. Then, lay your swatch down on a flat surface and place pins to indicate where you'll start measuring. Measure with a ruler, carefully counting the stitches in exactly 4 inches (10 cm). A clear plastic ruler can be very helpful.

As you measure, take care not to stretch the knitting. Also, do not include the edge stitches, which easily distort. If your gauge differs from that given in your pattern by even a fraction of an inch, your finished piece may be significantly larger or smaller than it should be, which, of course, can be devastating. If your gauge swatch is too big, try again on smaller needles. Use bigger needles if your swatch is smaller than it should be.

purl

Position the yarn in front of your work. Insert the right needle into the first stitch on the left needle, going from back to front.

Pass the yarn over, down the back, and under the right needle. Draw it through the stitch to the back.

Drop the stitch from the left needle. The stitch on the right is your purl stitch.

basic stitches

casting on

Casting on creates a foundation row for your knitting. There are many ways to cast on, and knitters soon develop favorites. Two that are used most are single and cable cast ons.

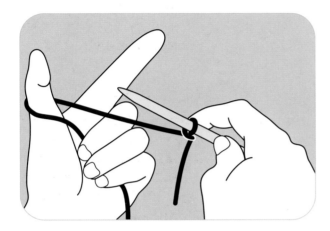

1 Make a slip knot on right needle. Wrap the yarn around your left thumb and secure it with your fingers.

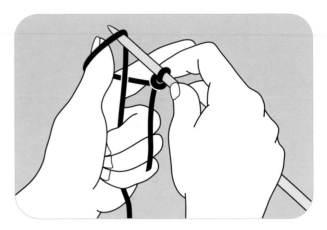

2 Insert needle under the strand on the front of your thumb.

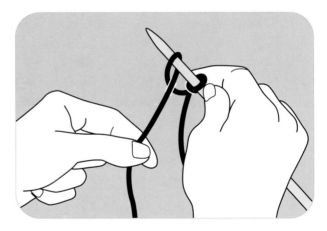

3 Slip this loop onto the needle and pull the yarn to tighten. Continue for as many stitches as needed.

decreasing tip

When working increases and decreases, work these one or two stitches in from the edge(s) of the knitting. This gives a nice smooth edge to the work and makes seaming much easier.

cable cast on

Place a slipknot onto the left needle, and knit one stitch into it. Place the stitch on the left needle.

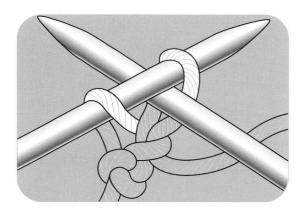

1 Next, insert the right needle between these two stitches, knit a stitch, and place it on the left needle.

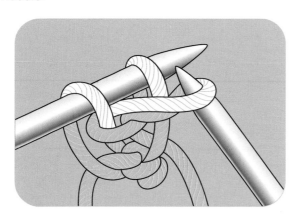

2 Continue for the required number of stitches.

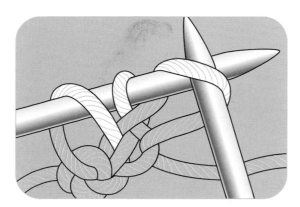

3 This cast on creates a firm edge with the look of a tiny cable, but it is not very elastic. This is a good cast on to use when you must add several stitches at the edge of a piece of knitting.

stockinette stitch

You form this stitch by knitting alternate rows of knit and purl stitches (see pages 12 and 13). Stockinette stitch does not lie flat, but curls on all edges, which can be a great way to enhance a design. This stitch has a very distinct right and wrong side, but the wrong side can sometimes be more attractive, especially if you're using a highly textured yarn, where the bumps are thrown to the back of the knitting. If the back of the knitting is the right side, it's called reverse stockinette stitch.

garter stitch

This is a knitter-friendly stitch! Every row in garter stitch is a knit row, and for every two rows knitted, one garter stitch ridge is formed, so it's easy to count the rows. It's a fully reversible stitch that doesn't curl at the edges, and its ability to lie flat makes it very useful.

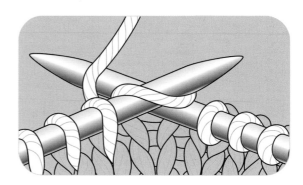

circular knitting

Knitting around a circle can produce a seamless tube of knitted fabric, which you can work on a circular needle or on a set of double-pointed needles. (You may see instructions telling you to change from a circular needle to a set of double points when the stitches are decreased to the stage where they no longer fit around the circular needle.) Circular knitting has a great many advantages. You cast the stitches onto the circular needle in the usual way, and then join them into a round. You must take care here to ensure that the stitches aren't twisted on the needle, then use the right-hand needle to knit the first stitch off the left-hand needle, pulling the stitches tightly together at the beginning of the round. A marker is placed to indicate the beginning of the round—then round and round you go!

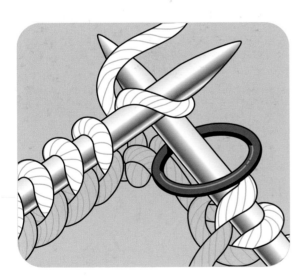

basic bind off

To secure your last row of knitting, you need to bind off. Work the first two stitches on the left-hand needle, then use the point of the left-hand needle to lift the first stitch on the right-hand needle over the second stitch. Knit the next stitch on the left-hand needle, and repeat the procedure. It's a good idea to use a larger needle when binding off, so you don't pull the stitches too tightly. Stitches are usually bound off in the pattern stitch. For example, in k1p1 rib, you would knit and purl the stitches as they present themselves.

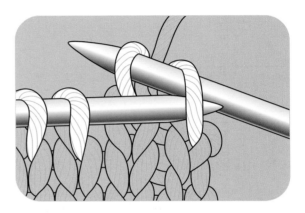

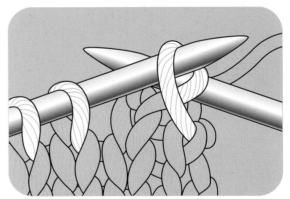

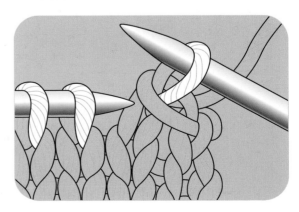

three-needle bind off

Use this technique wherever possible, since it's not only a great time saver, but it creates a less bulky seam with a very neat appearance. It's a particularly useful method of binding off and simultaneously joining shoulder seams. Just as its name suggests, you use three needles. Arrange the two sets of stitches on the needles, with the right sides together, and bind off with a needle one size larger. The bind off is worked in the usual manner, except that you insert the needle into the first stitch on both the needles holding stitches.

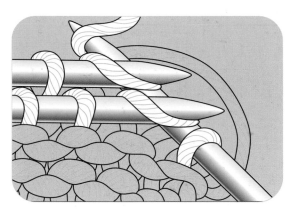

2 Insert the third needle into the next pair of stitches, and knit them together.

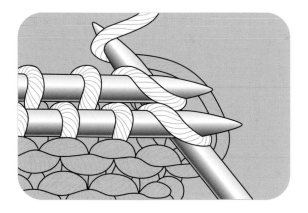

1 Insert the third needle into the first stitch on each needle, and knit them together. You have one stitch on the right-hand needle.

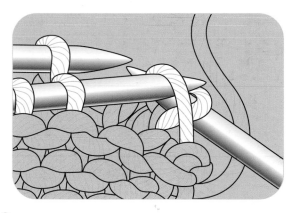

3 Pass the first stitch over the second.

increasing stitches

There are several ways to add a single stitch within your knitting. One of the simplest is to knit into the front and then the back of the same stitch. You can use this technique to make a decorative element within the work, while simultaneously shaping the knitting.

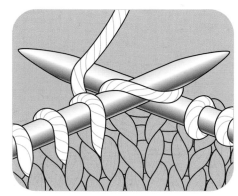

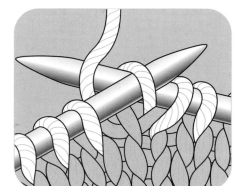

decreasing stitches

As with increasing, many methods exist to reduce the number of stitches on the needle.

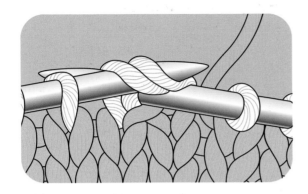

1 Two common decreases are the k2tog, which means knitting two stitches together and which slants to the right,

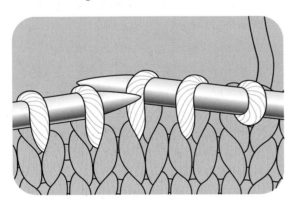

2 The ssk slants to the left and is worked by slipping the first stitch as if to knit, and then slipping the next stitch the same way.

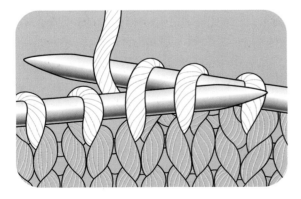

3 Next, knit the two stitches together through the backs of the loops.

picking up stitches

Sweater patterns may call for picking up stitches to place a finished edge on a knitted piece. Sleeve bands on vests, front edge bands on cardigans and jackets, and neckbands are examples. When you're picking up a large number of stitches, circular needles may be necessary because they come in much longer lengths than straight needles.

Beautifully finished bands are not difficult to achieve if you follow a few simple steps. First, divide and mark the edges of the knitting where the stitches will be picked up into equal segments. Count the rows between the markers to ensure even spacing. (Safety pins work well as markers, because they won't fallout of the knitting.) With the right side facing you, carefully separate the edge stitches so that you can see the small space (or hole) between each row of knitting. Push the needle through the hole to the back of the work, then place the yarn around the needle as if to knit, and draw a loop of yarn through with the needle. Continue along the edge in this way, picking up the stitches at a ratio of two stitches for every three rows. (In other words, you'll skip every third space.) When you've picked up all the stitches, continue knitting the bands in the desired pattern stitch.

Remember that the number of stitches you end up with is dependent on the number of rows in the edge you're picking up from. You may end up with a different number of rows than called for in your instructions if you've changed the length of the piece or if your knitting style or yarn choice changed the row gauge.

It's difficult to see whether the stitches have been picked up evenly when they're bunched together on the needle. Unfortunately, some knitters don't check the fit of the garment before completing the finishing. It's very disappointing to

substituting yarns

Ideally, we'd all like to pick out a pattern and have the yarn it specifies readily available, but often this isn't the case. Experienced knitters know that some yarns may be available for a short time only. Even if you are able to find the yarn the pattern specifies, there are reasons you might want to use a different one. Perhaps you're allergic to the wool yarn it calls for, for example, or the cost of the yarn is an important consideration for you, as is the question of garment care. For some knitters, the ability to machine wash an item is crucial, so they want to substitute with a synthetic or machine-washable blend of fibers.

Whatever your reason for substituting one yarn for another, the undertaking is not at all difficult or mysterious, provided you follow this easy process.

- First, study the pattern. What is it that appeals to you? Frequently, color is the first thing we notice. Or, maybe it's the texture, a design detail, or the shape that catches your eye on a certain garment.

- Then, make sure the color, fiber, and texture of your substitution yarn will still achieve the look that attracted you to the design in the first place. You can do that by looking at a couple of factors:

- Study the manufacturer's label. Look at the yardage (meters). This will tell you a great deal. Look at the recommended gauge. If your pattern calls for 5 sts to the inch (2.5 cm), and the ball band says it will knit to an ideal gauge of only 3 sts to the inch (2.5 cm), you can see at once that you might be getting into trouble.

- Examine the texture; feel the "hand" of your proposed substitute yarn. Does the original design have a soft drape? Will your substitute yarn drape as well?

- If you're not sure of your choice, and particularly if the yarn is expensive, buy a ball and test it first. Even if you decide not to use that yarn after all, you can still put it to good use later, and you'll learn more about yarns and their properties. You may be able to find small swatches of yarns you're interested in on display for customers. Handle these, and ask if there may be a tiny scrap of the yarn left over for you to test.

- Finally, do bear in mind that the finished article will not look exactly the same when you substitute a yarn. If you make an informed choice, though, you're likely to be pleased with the results.

find that the neckline fits poorly or that bands don't lie flat, and yet you can easily remedy this problem. Try this method to check the fit. Thread a tapestry needle with a thread in a contrasting color, and take the stitches carefully off the knitting needle. Adjust them evenly on this thread, so you can see how it will look when bound off. If you have too many stitches, your band will be wavy. If there are too few, it will pull in. Count the stitches and decide how many to add or remove. When you're satisfied, place the stitches back on the knitting needle and complete the bands.

blocking

Blocking is the process of smoothing out the knitted pieces to the correct size and shape before you assemble them. The wet blocking method is simple, safe for all yarns, and always gives good results. To block a piece of knitting, first pin it out to the correct shape. Use blocking pins, which are made of stainless steel so they don't rust. Position the pins at regular intervals around the edges of the knitting, then check that the pieces are the correct size by comparing them to the schematic.

better fits

Don't groan if you have to unravel an edge band to make band adjustments. It takes only a few minutes and is well worth it. After all, if you hate the fit, you won't wear the garment, will you?

You'll need to work on a large, flat surface. Blocking boards designed for this purpose are available, or you can work on the floor with a towel under the knitting. Once your pieces are pinned out, spray them lightly with water and leave the knitting to dry. It's amazing how this improves the look of the knitting.

seaming

With a little care, you can create beautiful seams, even if you don't ordinarily spend a lot of time with a sewing needle. In most cases you'll work the seams with the same yarn you use for the knitting, but when the yarn is too textured to use easily, choose a smooth yarn in a matching color. Use a tapestry needle for seaming, and pin the seams together, if necessary, with knitter's pins. These are long and have a large head, so they don't disappear into the knitted fabric. Avoid working with a long length of yarn, as the friction may cause the yarn to break or fray.

mattress stitch

Mattress stitch is an excellent, all-purpose seaming stitch, resulting in an invisible seam. It's always worked with the right side of the work facing you, making it very easy to match stripes. To sew a seam in mattress stitch, first place the two pieces of knitting to be joined on a flat surface. Thread the needle and work upward one stitch in from the edge, passing the needle under the bar between the first and second stitches on one side of the knitting, and then moving to the corresponding stitches on the other side. Pick up two bars and return to the first piece, going into the knitting at the same point you came out, and pick up two bars. Repeat these steps, working from side to side and pulling the seam closed as you go, taking care not to pull so tightly that you cause puckers. You want a flat, neat seam.

When seaming reverse stockinette pieces, use the same method, but take only one bar at a time for better seam control.

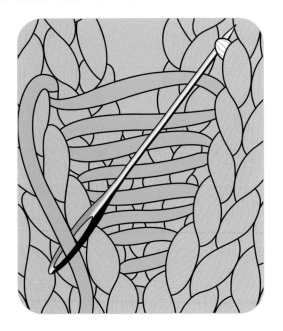

making bobbles

These are very useful embellishments on knitwear. They can be knitted in as the work is progressing or added later. Brightly colored bobbles are a great way to enliven an otherwise plain sweater, while same-colored bobbles lend texture and elegance to knitted pieces. The size of a bobble will vary, depending on the thickness of the yarn and the number of stitches you use.

To knit a bobble:
Cast on one stitch, leaving a length of yarn to secure the bobble with, then k1, p1, k1, p1 into the stitch (5 sts).

Work 4 rows in St st.

Cut the yarn, thread it through a tapestry needle, and draw up tightly through the sts.

Fasten the bobble firmly into position.

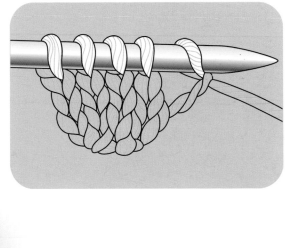

chantilly pink hat

Cathy Carron

Made on large needles with two contrasting colors of yarn, this quick-to-make hat will soon become a wardrobe favorite. The hat stretches for a snug fit.

instructions

crown

Holding 1 strand of each yarn together, CO 12 sts and divide between 3 dpn.

Rnd 1 and all odd rnds: Knit.

Rnd 2: *K1, m1, repeat from * around. (18 sts)

Rnd 4: *K2, m1, repeat from * around. (24 sts)

Rnd 6: *K3, m1, repeat from * around. (30 sts)

Rnd 8: *K3, m1, repeat from * around. (36 sts)

For L Size Only
*K5, m1 4 times, end k12. (40 sts)

NOTE: Switch to circular needle; pm to denote beginning/end of rnd.

turn of crown

Knit 1 rnd.

rise

* K1, p1, repeat from * around.

K1 in stitch below, p1 from * around

Repeat last two rnds until the piece measures 5" (5.5)/13cm (14) from the turn-of-crown.

Knit 1 rnd.

Purl 1 rnd.

BO very loosely.

finishing

Sew in ends and darn together crown hole left at the start.

skill level
Easy

sizes
M (L), 18"(20)/46cm (51)

materials
Paton's *Divine*, 79.5% acrylic/18% mohair/2.5% polyester, 3.5 oz/100g = approx 142yds/129m, 1 ball of Icicle White, 1 ball of Chantilly Rose

Knitting needles in size 11US/8mm dpn or size needed to obtain gauge

Short, circular needle

Stitch marker

Tapestry needle

gauge
8 sts = 4"/10cm

Remember, your gauge must match for your size to match.

fun child's hat

Cathy Carron

This flat-topped design is a great project to showcase one of the new furry novelty yarns. The extra length in the cap area lets you fold up the edges.

instructions

crown

Using size 10 US/6mm dpn, CO 12 sts and divide between 3 dpn.

Rnd 1 and all odd rnds: Knit.

Rnd 2: * K1, m1* - repeat around. [18 sts]

Rnd 4: * K2, m1* – repeat around. [24 sts]

Rnd 6: * K3, m1* – repeat around. [30 sts]

Repeat rnds 1 and 2, each time adding one more k st before each m1 until the rnd is completed. There are 5 (6) sts before the marker. [(42, 48) sts]

Knit 1 rnd.

NOTE: Switch to circular needle; pm to denote beginning/end of rnd.

turn of crown

Purl 3 rnds.

rise

Knit for 6.5" (7.5)/17cm (19) from turn of crown.

BO very loosely.

finishing

Sew in ends and darn together hole left at start.

skill level

Intermediate

sizes

Head circumference = 16" (18)/41cm (46)

materials

Bernat's *Baby Lash*, 70% nylon/30% acrylic, 1.75oz/50g = approx 50yd/47m, 2 balls of pink

Knitting needles in size 10US/6mm dpn or size needed to obtain gauge

Short circular needle

Stitch marker

Tapestry needle

gauge

13 sts /18 rows = 4"/10 cm

Remember, your gauge must match for your size to match.

rainbow scarf

Sally Poole & Catherine Ham

The subtle pattern stitch in this scarf is easy to knit and a great way to showcase enticing yarn. The scarf can be made longer or wider if desired; just purchase extra yarn and join a new ball in the garter stitch rows.

skill level
Easy

finished measurements
Approximately 8.5 x 70"/22cm x 1.8 m

materials
Lion Brand *Moonlight Mohair*, 30% acrylic/25% cotton/10% polyester, 1.75oz/50g = 82yd/75m, 4 balls of Rainbow Falls

Knitting needles in size 10.5US/6.5mm or size to obtain gauge

Tapestry needle

gauge
3 sts = 1"/2.5cm

Remember, your gauge must match for your size to match.

instructions

pattern stitch
Rows 1-3: P1* (yrn, p2tog) repeat from * to last stitch, p1.

Rows 4-19: Knit. (8 garter stitch ridges)

to start
Cast on 26 sts, loosely.

Knit 12 rows. (6 garter stitch ridges)

Work the pattern stitch for approximately 66"/1.67m.

Knit 12 rows. (6 garter stitch ridges)

Bind off, loosely.

finishing
Darn in the yarn ends.

thick & plush mittens

You can brave the weather with a smile on your face and warm hands when you slip on these mittens. Thick chenille yarn makes them soft as a cotton ball and incredibly toasty. The eye-catching variegated boucle cuffs fit snugly to your wrists to keep the cold out while adding a stylish accent.

Lisa Carnahan

skill level

Intermediate

sizes

S (M, L) approx 8" (9, 10)/20cm (23, 25) measured around palm of hand

materials

Lion Brand's *Lion Boucle* super bulky weight, 79% acrylic/20% mohair/1% nylon, 2.5 oz/70g = approx 57yd/52m, 1 skein of Wild Berries

Lion Brand's *Thick & Quick Chenille*, 91% acrylic/9% rayon, approx 100 yd/91m, 1 skein of Periwinkle

Knitting needles in size 11US/8mm, or size needed to obtain gauge

Tapestry needle

gauge

9 sts = 4"/10cm measured over st st using *Chenille*

Remember, your gauge must match for your size to match.

instructions

cuff

With 2 strands of Boucle held together, cast on 16 (18, 20) sts.

Divide onto 3 needles. Join.

Work in k1/p1 rib for 3"/8cm.

Change to 1 strand of Chenille.

Knit 2 rnds, increasing 2 sts evenly spaced on first rnd. [18 (20, 22) sts]

thumb gusset

Rnd 1: M1, place marker, knit to end of rnd.

Rnd 2 and all even rnds: Knit.

Rnd 3: M1, knit to marker, m1, slip marker, knit to end of rnd.

Repeat rnds 2 and 3 until there are 5 (7, 9) sts before the marker.

hand

Knit across 5 (7, 9) gusset sts to marker, and then place them on a holder. Knit to end of rnd. [18 (20, 22) sts]

Work even in st st until the mitten measures 6" (6.5, 7)/15cm (17, 18) from the top of cuff, decreasing 0 (2, 4) sts evenly spaced on last rnd. [18 (18, 18) sts]

top shaping

Rnd 1: *K1, k2tog; rep from * to end of rnd. [12 sts]

Rnd 2: Knit.

Rnd 3: *K2tog; rep from * to end of rnd. [6 sts]

Cut yarn and draw thru remaining sts. Fasten off.

thumb

Place sts from holder onto 3 needles.

Pick up 2 sts along edge of hand above thumb. [7 (9, 11) sts]

Work even in st st on these sts for 2" (2, 2.5)/5cm (5, 6).

Next rnd: K1, *k2tog; rep from * to end of rnd. [4 (5, 6) sts]

Cut yarn and draw through remaining sts. Fasten off.

Weave in ends; repeat for second mitten.

basic essential hat

Cathy Carron

You'll find yourself wondering how you ever did without this hat. Knitted with a mohair and synthetic blend yarn, it offers the best of both worlds: the soft fluffiness of mohair and the easy-care washability of synthetic blends. The simple neutral color allows it to be worn with most anything. Wear it with the brim rolled up or down, as your mood suits you.

instructions

crown
CO 12 sts and divide between 3 dpn.

Rnd 1 and all odd rnds: Knit.

Rnd 2: *K1, m1, repeat from * around. (18 sts)

rnd 4: *K2, m1, repeat from * around. (24 sts)

rnd 6: *K3, m1, repeat from * around. (30 sts)

Repeat rnds 1 and 2, each time adding a k st before each m1 until there 6 (7) sts before the m1 sts. [48 (54) sts]

NOTE: Switch to circular needles and place marker to denote beginning/end of rnd.

Knit until the piece measures 10.5"(11)/27cm (28).

top of crown
BO very loosely.

finishing
Sew in ends on the st st side and pull hole at crown together. Wear hat with rev st st side out and turn brim up.

skill level
Easy

sizes
Head circumference, M: 20-21"/51-53cm, L: 22-23"/56-58cm

materials
Paton's *Divine*, 79.5% acrylic/18% mohair/2.5% polyester, 3.5oz/100g = 142yds/129m, 1 ball of Soft Earth

Double-pointed needles in 10US/6mm or size needed to obtain gauge

Circular needles in 16US/41cm or size needed to obtain gauge

Stitch markers

Tapestry needle

gauge
12 sts = 4"/10cm

Remember, your gauge must match for your size to match.

flirty little bag

Lisa Carnahan

Made from fun novelty fur and nubby chenille yarns, this bright little purse invites attention (and conversation!). The dual handles impart a spunky attitude while being exceptionally soft to hold.

instructions

to start

With 2 strands of Fun Fur held together, loosely CO 20 sts.

Work in garter stitch (knit every row) for 1.5"/4cm.

Change to 1 strand of CiCi and knit 2 rows, decreasing 3 sts evenly spaced across 1st row. (17 sts)

Work in rev st st (purl the RS rows, knit the WS rows) until piece measures 12.5"/32cm.

Change to 2 strands of Fun Fur and knit 1 row increasing 3 sts evenly spaced across row. (20 sts)

Work in garter stitch until piece measures 14"/36cm. BO all sts.

handles (make 2)

With 2 strands of Fun Fur held together, CO 5 sts.

Row 1: Slip 1 st, k4.

Repeat row 1 until piece measures 12"/30cm. Bind off.

finishing

Fold purse in half and sew side seams, then stitch handles to each side of purse.

skill level

Intermediate

finished measurements

7"/18cm wide x 7"/18cm long

materials

Lion Brand's *Fancy Fur*, 55% polyamide/45% polyester, 1.75oz/50g = approx 39yd/35m, 1 ball of Turquoise

Paton's *CiCi*, 68% acrylic/32% nylon, 50g = approx 37yds/33m, 1 skein of Mardi Gras

Knitting needles 10US/6mm or size needed to obtain gauge

Tapestry needle

gauge

10 sts = 4"/10cm in CiCi

Remember, your gauge must match for your size to match.

stripe up the band

Catherine Ham

Festive stripes in your toddler's favorite colors create an energetic cold-weather trio. The sweater is done in symmetrical stripes, while the scarf and hat use fun combinations of thick and thin color.

instructions for sweater

back

Using size 6US/4mm needles and color of choice, cast on 52 (56, 58, 62, 66) sts and work in k1p1 rib for 1.5" (2, 2, 2, 2)/4cm (5, 5, 5, 5).

Next row: Increase 6 sts evenly spaced across the row. [58 (62, 64, 68, 72) sts]

Change to size 8US/5mm needles and work stripe pattern in st st until the piece measures 7.5" (8.5, 9, 10.5, 12)/19cm (22, 23, 27, 30) from the beginning. Place markers for the underarm.

Continue working the back until the piece measures 13" (14.5, 15.5, 17.5, 19.5)/33cm (37, 39, 44, 50).

BO 19 (19, 19, 20, 22) shoulder sts, work 20 (24, 26, 28, 28) sts and place them on a holder for back neck, BO 19 (19, 19, 20, 22) shoulder sts.

skill level

Intermediate

sizes

2 (4, 6, 8, 10) years

finished measurements

Chest: 26" (27, 29, 30, 32)/66cm (69, 74, 76, 81)

Length: 13" (14.5, 15.5, 17.5, 19.5)/33cm (37, 39, 44, 50)

materials

Lion Brand's *Wool-Ease* worsted weight, 80% acrylic/20%wool, 3oz/85g = approx 197yd/180m, 1 ball each of 6 colors

Knitting needles in size 6 and 8US/4 and 5mm or size needed to obtain gauge

Short circular knitting needle or set of four double-pointed needles, in size 10.5US/7mm or size needed to obtain gauge

Stitch marker

Tapestry needle

gauge

18sts/24 rows = 4"/10cm

Remember, your gauge must match for your size to match.

NOTE: The sweater is worked in stripes of 6 rows each. The sleeves are striped in the same sequence as the body. All ribbings are worked in one color. You may follow the sequence of stripes used here, or arrange the stripes as desired.

front

Work for back until the piece measures 10.5" (12, 13, 14.5, 16.5)/27cm (30, 33, 37, 42) from the beginning.

Begin Neck Shaping
Work 24 (25, 25, 27, 29) sts. Put the remaining 34 (37, 39, 41, 43) sts on a holder.

Turn and work one row.

Keeping stripe pattern, dec 1 st at neck edge every other row 5 (6, 6, 7, 7) times. Continue in pattern until work measures the same as the back.

BO 19 (19, 19, 20, 22) shoulder sts.

Rejoin yarn to sts on the holder, work 10 (12, 14, 14,14) sts and leave on a holder for front neck. Working on these remaining 24 (25, 25, 27, 29) sts, complete the neck shaping to match the first side.

sleeves

Using size 6US/4mm needles and color of choice, cast on 28 (30, 32, 32, 34) sts and work in K1p1 rib for 1.5" (2, 2, 2, 2)/4cm (5, 5, 5, 5).

Next row: Increase 2 (2, 2, 4, 4) sts evenly across the row. [30 (32, 34, 36, 38) sts]

Change to size 8US/5mm needles and work in stripe pattern.

Begin Sleeve Shaping

Increase 1 st on each side every 3rd (4th, 4th, 4th, 4th,) row 10 (11, 12, 14, 15) times. [50 (54, 58, 64, 68) sts]

Continue working until the sleeve measures 7.5" (10, 11, 12.5, 14)/19cm (25, 28, 32, 36).

BO the stitches.

finishing

Block all the pieces.

Join shoulder seams.

neckband

With the circular needle or double-pointed needles, and color of choice, pick up and knit approx 54 (62, 66, 68, 70) sts around the neck edge, including the sts left on holders. Work 1"/2.5cm in rib.

BO loosely in rib.

Pin sleeves into place between the markers and sew the seams.

Sew the side and sleeve seams, matching the stripes carefully.

Darn in the yarn ends.

skill level
Easy

sizes
2 (4, 6, 8, 10) years

finished measurements
Approx 8 x 72"(20cm x 1.8m)

materials
Lion Brand's *Wool-Ease* worsted weight, 80% acrylic/20%wool, 3oz/85g = approx 197yd/180m, leftovers from sweater

Knitting needles in size 6 and 8US/4 and 5mm or size needed to obtain gauge

Short circular knitting needle or set of four double-pointed needles, in size

10.5US/7mm or size needed to obtain gauge

Stitch marker

Tapestry needle

gauge
18sts/24 rows = 4"/10cm

Remember, your gauge must match for your size to match.

NOTE: The scarf is worked in random stripes.

instructions for scarf

to start
With any color yarn and size 8US/5mm needles, cast on 40 sts.

Work stripes in st st in colors of choice until the scarf measures approx 72"/183cm.

BO loosely.

NOTE: The scarf is designed to roll inwards

finishing
Darn in the yarn ends.

instructions for rolled-edge hat

to start

Using a color of choice and size 6US/4mm needles, cast on 80 (88, 96) sts and work 1"/2.5cm in st st.

Change to larger needles and stripe pattern of choice. Work until the hat measures 6" (7, 8)/15cm (18, 20) from the beginning.

Next row: *K2tog, repeat from * to the end of the row. [40 (44, 48) sts]

Repeat this row once more. [20 (22, 24) sts]

Cut yarn, thread through tapestry needle, draw up the remaining stitches tightly and fasten off securely.

finishing

Sew up the center back seam, reversing the seam on the rolled edge.

Darn in the ends.

skill level

Easy

sizes

S (M, L)

materials

Lion Brand's *Wool-Ease* worsted weight, 80% acrylic/20%wool, 3oz/85g = approx 197yd/180m, left-overs from sweater

Knitting needles in size 6 and 8US/4 and 5mm or size needed to obtain gauge

Short circular knitting needle or set of four double-pointed needles, in size 10.5US/7mm or size needed to obtain gauge

Stitch marker

Tapestry needle

gauge

18sts/24 rows = 4"/10cm

Remember, your gauge must match for your size to match.

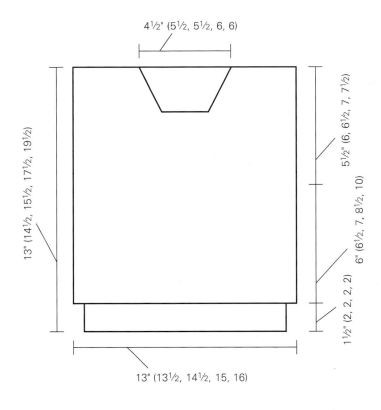

4½" (5½, 5½, 6, 6)

13" (14½, 15½, 17½, 19½)

5½" (6, 6½, 7, 7½)

6" (6½, 7, 8½, 10)

1½" (2, 2, 2, 2)

13" (13½, 14½, 15, 16)

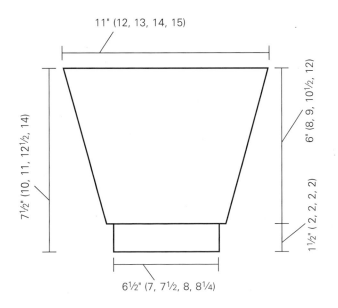

11" (12, 13, 14, 15)

7½" (10, 11, 12½, 14)

6" (8, 9, 10½, 12)

1½" (2, 2, 2, 2)

6½" (7, 7½, 8, 8¼)

ribbon yarn shawl

This lovely yarn drapes beautifully, so the shawl can be worn as a rectangle, or folded into a triangle and worn any number of ways. What an elegant accessory piece!

Rhonda Black

skill level
Easy

finished size
Approx 26x76"/66x193cm, excluding fringe

materials
Lion Brand's *Trellis* bulky weight, 100% nylon, 1.75oz/50g = approx 115yd/105m, 8 balls in

Champagne

Patons' Brilliant, 69% acrylic/19% nylon/12% poly-ester, 1.75 oz/50g = 166yd/152m, 1 ball each of Gold Glow and Crystal Cream

24"/61cm circular knitting needle in size 19US/15mm or size needed to obtain gauge

Size K crochet hook

Tapestry needle

gauge
9 sts = approx 4"/10cm

Remember, your gauge must match for your size to match.

instructions

to start

(NOTE: 5 balls of Trellis are used to knit the shawl. The remaining three balls are used in the fringe.)

Using Trellis, cast on 60 sts and work in garter st (knit every row) until you have just enough yarn left in the 5th ball to bind off all the stitches.

Darn in the yarn ends.

edging

Holding the two colors of Brilliant together as one yarn, work single crochet all around the edges of the shawl.

TIP: Join in a new ball of yarn at the beginning of a row.

fringe

The fringing on this shawl is 11"/28cm long. Wrap Trellis around a piece of cardboard cut to the desired fringe length and cut to the strands at one end.

Starting at any point on the crocheted edge of the shawl, fold two strands of the Trellis in half, insert the crochet hook into the front of one single crochet stitch, pull the Trellis through and tighten to secure the loop.

Continue adding the fringe in this way to the single crochets all around the shawl.

Cut the remaining Brilliant into the same length as the Trellis and add randomly around the shawl to add even more sparkle to the fringe.

novelty yarn scarf

This dazzling scarf will quickly become a favorite accessory when you discover how it transforms a simple shirt, sweater, or dress into a striking fashion statement. Featured in the scarf are mohair, ladder, and ribbon yarns in a kaleidoscope of color. The open pattern allows you to appreciate the beauty of each individual yarn.

Stacey Budge

skill level

Intermediate

finished measurements

5 x 54"/13cm x 1.37m before tassels

materials

Lion Brand's *Trellis* bulky weight, 100% nylon, 1.75oz/50g = approx 115yd/105m, 1 ball in Rainbow

Lion Brand's *Moonlight Mohair*, bulky weight, 57% acrylic/28% mohair/9% cotton/6% metallic polyester, 1.75oz/50g = approx

82yd/75m, 1 ball of Rainbow Falls

Lion Brand's *Incredible*, 100% Nylon, 1.75 oz/50g = approx. 110yd/100m, 1 skein of Rainbow

Knitting needles in size 11US/8mm or size needed to obtain gauge

Tapestry needle

gauge

16 sts = 4"/10cm

Remember, your gauge must match for your size to match.

instructions

to start

NOTE: No need to cut the yarn at the end of a row; just pick up the yarn waiting for you at the end of the row you just knitted. Alternate using Rainbow, Rainbow Falls, and Incredible Rainbow for each row.

Cast on 20 sts.

Rows 1-7: Knit all sts.

Row 8: K1, *yo3, k1, repeat from * to the end of the row.

Row 9: K1, *drop the next three sts (all the YOs), k1, repeat from * to end.

Repeat rows 1-9 until scarf measures 54"/137cm.

Bind off loosely.

finishing

Cut several 15"/38cm lengths of each yarn type for tassels. Securely attach 2 strands of each yarn for each tassel. Sew in ends.

bead & wire cuff

Cathy Carron

This trendy bracelet showcases the beauty of knit stitches. A variety of looks can be created by varying the wire color and the type of beads.

instructions

knitting with beads

It's easier than it might look. Before you begin, first string all the beads you will be using on to the wire with which you will be knitting. When it comes time to knit a bead, just bring a bead close up to where you make the stitch. While making the stitch, push the bead through the hole at the same time. If you are knitting a stitch where a bead was placed in the previous row, knit through the back loop of that stitch unless instructed otherwise so the bead will pop forward on the knitted "cloth."

knitting with wire

See page 86 for basic knitting with wire instructions.

to start

CO 42 sts.

Divide the 42 sts evenly by knitting onto 3 dpn.

Knit2 rnds.

*Knit2, K1 with a bead, repeat from * around.

Knit1 rnd.

*Knit1, K1 with a bead , repeat from * around.

Knit1 rnd.

*Knit1 with a bead, k2, repeat from * around.

Knit3 rnds.

BO and weave wire ends into the bracelet.

attaching another spool

This pattern uses two spools of wire, so at some point another spool will have to be attached. Change spools as you would yarns—just let the ends hang 3 to 5"/8 to 13cm, then go back later and tie them off.

skill level
Easy

finished measurements
Wrist 7-8"/18-20cm

materials
2 spools of 26-gauge copper wire in color of your choice

Glass beads

Knitting needles 9 US/5.5mm dpn or size needed to obtain gauge

Tapestry needle

Kitchen shears

gauge
Approx 5.5 sts = 4"/10cm

Remember, your gauge must match for your size to match.

shimmering fuchsia hat

This cheery hat showcases an array of pinks and magentas to produce an overall pleasing fuchsia glow. To obtain the same effect, knit this project holding two strands of yarn together using a mohair yarn and a novelty nub yarn. Shiny filaments in the novelty yarn gleam when the light catches them.

Cathy Carron

instructions

crown
Holding one strand each of Bling Bling and Divine together, CO 12 sts and divide between 3 dpn.

Rnd 1 and all odd rnds: knit.

Rnd 2: *K1, m1, repeat from * around. (18 sts)

Rnd 4: *K2, m1, repeat from * around. (24 sts)

Rnd 6: *K3, m1, repeat from * around. (30 sts)

Round 8: *K4, m1, repeat from * around. (36 sts)

For L Size Only
Round 10: *K5, m1, repeat from * around. (42 sts)

NOTE: Switch to circular needle and place marker to denote beginning/end of rnd.

turn of crown
Purl 3 rnds even.

rise
Knit 1 rnd.

Purl 1 rnd.

Repeat last two rnds until the piece measures 4.5" (5)/11cm (13) from the turn of the crown.

Purl 2 rnds.

BO very loosely.

finishing
Sew in ends and sew together hole left at crown at start.

skill level
Easy

sizes
M: 20-21"/51-53cm head circumference, (L: 22-23"/56-58cm)

materials
Bernat's *Bling Bling*, 100% nylon, 1.75 oz/50g = approx 90yds/82m, 1 ball in Cabaret Crimson

Paton's *Divine*, 79.5% acrylic/18% mohair/2.5% polyester, 3.5oz/100g = approx 142yds/129m, 1 ball in Richest Rose

Double-pointed needles in size 11US/8mm or size needed to obtain gauge

Circular needle in size 16US/41cm or size needed to obtain gauge

Stitch marker

Tapestry needle

gauge
8 sts = 4"/10cm

Remember, your gauge must match for your size to match.

unisex sweater

Sally Poole &
Catherine Ham

Casual and comfy in softly faded colors, this sweater looks great with your favorite denims or cords. The simple shape is stylized with crisp side vents and a tab neckline.

instructions

back

With smaller needles, cast on 86 (90, 95, 99, 104) sts and work 1.5"/4cm in garter st.

Change to larger needles and keeping 4 sts at each side in garter st for the vents, work in st st for a further 3"/8cm.

Next row, RS facing, k 4, increase 1 st, k to last 4 sts, increase 1 st, k to end. [88 (92, 97, 101, 106) sts]

Continue working in st st until the work measures 18.5" (19, 19, 19.5, 19.5)/47cm (48, 48, 50, 50) from the beginning.

Armhole Shaping

Bind off 7 (7, 8, 8, 9) sts at beginning of next 2 rows.

Dec 1 st each side, every other row 6 (7, 8, 8, 9) times.

Continue until piece measures 27" (27.5, 28, 28.5, 29)/69cm (70, 71, 72, 74). [62 (64, 65, 69, 70) sts]

skill level
Intermediate

sizes:
XS (S, M, L, XL)

finished measurements
Chest: 39" (41, 43, 45, 47)/99cm (104, 109, 114, 119)

Length: 27" (27.5, 28, 28.5, 29)/69cm (70, 71, 73, 74)

materials
Bernat's *Denimstyle*, 70% acrylic/30% soft cotton, 3.5oz/100g = approx 196yd/179m, 6 (7, 7, 7, 8) balls of Faded Khaki

3 buttons

Knitting needles in sizes 6 and 8US/4 and 5mm or size needed to obtain gauge

24"/61cm circular needle in size 6US/4mm or size needed to obtain gauge

Stitch holders

Tapestry needle

gauge
18sts/24 rows = 4"/10cm in st st.

Remember, your gauge must match for your size to match.

Shape Shoulders

BO 5 (5, 5, 6, 6) sts beginning of next 2 rows.

BO 5 (6, 5, 6, 6) sts beginning of next 2 rows.

BO 6 (6, 6, 6, 6) sts at beginning of next 2 rows.

Leave remaining 30 (30, 33, 33, 34) back neck sts on a holder.

front

Work as for back until the work measures 21" (22, 22, 22.5, 23)/53cm (56, 56, 57, 58) from the beginning.

Begin Placket

Work 27 (28, 29, 31, 31) sts and place on holder for the left front, bind off center 8 (8, 7, 7, 8) sts and work to end.

Right Front

Continue working on these 27 (28, 29, 31, 31) sts until piece measures 26" (26.5, 27, 27.5, 28)/66cm (67, 69, 70, 71).

Begin Neck Shaping

With RS facing, k 5 (5, 6, 6, 6) sts, leave these sts on a holder for the neckband and work to end.

BO 2 sts at neck edge every row 2 times.

K 2 tog at neck edge 2 (3, 3, 3, 3) times.

Work until piece measures 27" (27.5, 28, 28.5, 29)/69cm (70, 71, 72, 74) from the beginning.

Shape Shoulder

Work shoulder shaping to correspond with back.

Left Front: with RS facing, rejoin yarn and complete to match left front, reversing all shapings.

sleeves

With smaller needles, cast on 38 (40, 44, 44, 46) sts and work 1.5"/4cm in garter st.

Change to larger needles and work in st st.

Begin Sleeve Shaping

Increase one st on each side every 4th row 15 (12, 15, 13, 16) times, then every 6th row 4 (6, 4, 6, 4) times. 76 (76, 82, 82, 86) sts on the needle.

Work until sleeve measures 17" (17.5, 17.5, 17.5, 18)/43cm (44, 44, 44, 46) from the beginning.

Cap Shaping

Bind off 7 (7, 8, 8, 9) sts on each side.

Dec 1 st each side, every other row 6 (7, 8, 8, 9) times.

Dec 1 st each side every row 13 (12, 12, 12, 12) times.

All sizes: BO 3 sts at the beginning of the next 4 rows.

Bind off rem 12 (12, 14, 14, 14) sts.

neckband

Join shoulder seams.

With circular needle and RS facing, pick up and k 5 (5, 6, 6, 6) front neck sts from the holder, 13 (12, 13, 12, 13) side neck sts, 30 (30, 33, 33, 34) back neck sts from holder, 13 (12, 13, 12, 13) side neck sts, and 5 (5, 6, 6, 6) front neck sts from the holder. [66 (64, 71, 69, 72) sts]

Working back and forth, work 1"/2.5cm in garter st and bind off loosely.

Placket Finishing

With RS facing, starting at neck edge of placket opening, pick up 28 (27, 30, 29, 32) sts evenly along left placket edge. Work in garter stitch for 1.5"/4cm. Bind off. Mark the position of the buttons, spacing them evenly.

Work overlap in the same way, working buttonholes to correspond with the button positions.

To work a buttonhole: BO 2 sts. On the next row, cast on 2 sts over the previously BO sts. Sew the overlap neatly to the bound-off edge of the garment piece, and stitch the underlap to the same edge on the inside.

finishing

Join side seams, leaving the vents open.

Join sleeve seams.

Pin sleeve into armhole and seam in place.

Sew on the buttons.

Darn in all loose ends neatly.

yarn alternative

If you like the weight and warmth of a wool-blend yarn, consider substituting Lion Brand's Wool-Ease worsted weight yarn (80% acrylic/20% wool, 3oz/85g = approx 197yd/180m). The gauge is 16 sts/24 rows = 4"/10cm and the sweater will take the same number of same number of balls as indicated above.

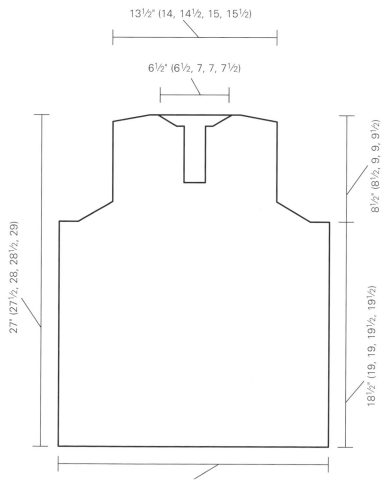

13½" (14, 14½, 15, 15½)

6½" (6½, 7, 7, 7½)

8½" (8½, 9, 9, 9½)

27" (27½, 28, 28½, 29)

18½" (19, 19, 19½, 19½)

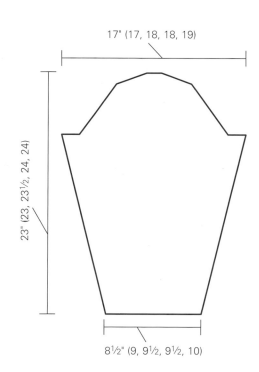

17" (17, 18, 18, 19)

23" (23, 23½, 24, 24)

8½" (9, 9½, 9½, 10)

fold-down collared sweater

Catherine Ham

This tempting sweater is quick to knit and easy to wear with the collar buttoned high or casually open. The textured yarn adds drama and is available in a selection of luscious colors. What are you waiting for?

instructions

back

With smaller needles, cast on 45 (49, 49, 53, 55) sts and work 2.5"/6cm in k1p1 rib for all sizes.

Next row: Increase 6 (5, 7, 6, 7) sts evenly across the row. [51 (54, 56, 59, 62) sts]

Change to larger needles and work in rev St st until the piece measures 14.5" (15, 15, 15.5, 15.5)/37cm (38, 38, 39, 39) from the beginning.

Armhole Shaping
BO 4 (4, 4, 5, 5) sts at the beginning of the next 2 rows.

Dec 1 st each side, every other row 3 (4, 4, 4, 4) times. [37 (38, 40, 41, 44) sts]

Continue working until the piece measures 23" (23.5, 24, 24.5, 25)/58cm (60, 61, 62, 64).

Shaping Shoulder and Back Neck
RS facing, BO 4 (4, 4, 4, 4) sts at beginning of next row, work 6 (7, 7, 8, 8).

skill level
Intermediate

sizes
XS (SM, M, L, XL)

finished measurements
Chest: 37" (39, 41, 43, 45)/94cm (99, 104, 109, 114)

Length: 24.5" (25, 25, 26, 26.5)/62cm (64, 64, 66, 67)

materials
Bernat's *Galaxy*, 77% acrylic/8% polyester/7.5% mohair/7.5% alpaca, 1.75oz/50g = approx 60yd/55m, 10 (11, 12, 14, 15) balls of Mars

24"/61cm circular knitting needles in sizes 9 and

10.5US/5.5 and 6.5mm or size needed to obtain gauge

2 buttons

Smooth yarn or embroidery floss to sew seams

Tapestry needle

NOTE: You may choose to fasten the collar with a brooch or pin, in which case the buttonhole instructions can be ignored

Sweater is worked in Rev St st

gauge
11sts/18 rows = 4"/10cm

Remember, your gauge must match for your size to match.

Join in a second ball of yarn, work the next 17 (16, 18, 17, 20) sts and leave on a holder for back neck, work to the end of the row. BO 4 (4, 4, 4, 4)

sts at beginning of the next row (WS).

Working both sides at the same time, dec 1 st at each neck edge. BO 3 (4, 4, 4, 4) sts at each shoulder edge at the beginning of next row. Work one row. Bind off the rem 3 (3, 3, 4, 4) sts at each shoulder edge. Fasten off.

front

Work as for back, including all shaping until the piece measures 22" (22.5, 23, 24, 24)/56cm (57, 58, 61, 61).

Begin Neck Shaping

Work 13 (14, 14, 15, 15) sts, join in a second ball of yarn, work the center 11 (10, 12, 11, 14) sts and leave on a holder for front neck, work to the end of the row.

Working both sides at the same time, dec 1 st at each neck edge every other row 4 times for all sizes. [9 (10, 10, 11, 11) sts]

Continue working until piece measures 23 (23.5, 24, 24.5, 25)/58cm (60, 61, 62, 64) from the beginning.

Shape Shoulders

Work shoulder shaping as for the back.

sleeves

With smaller needles, cast on 21 (23, 23, 23, 25) sts and work 2.5"/6cm in rib.

Next row: Increase 3 sts evenly across the row. [24 (26, 26, 26, 28) sts]

Change to larger needles and work in Rev st st.

Sleeve Shaping

Inc 1 stitch on each side every 4th row 4 (1, 4, 3, 3) times and then every 6th row 8 (9, 8, 9, 9) times. There will be 48 (48, 50, 50, 52) sts on the needle.

Shape Sleeve Cap

BO 4 (4, 4, 5, 5) sts at each side.

Dec 1 st at each side, every other row, 3 (4, 4, 4, 4) times.

Dec 1 st at each side, every row, 7 (7, 8, 6, 7) times.

Dec 1 st at each side, every 2nd row, 2 (1, 1, 2, 2) times.

All sizes: BO 2 sts at beginning of the next 4 rows.

BO rem 8 sts.

collar

Join Shoulder Seams

With smaller circular needle, RS facing, starting 1"/2.5cm below left shoulder seam, pick up and knit approx 66 (66, 70, 70, 72) sts around the neck, including the stitches left on holders.

When you have picked up the stitches around the neck and returned to the starting point, pick up 5 sts carefully underneath those previously picked up, for the underlap.

Turn the work and continue in ribbing, working back and forth in rows. (Place a marker to remind you to turn, as it's easy to knit these 4 underlap sts into a continuous row until you have a few more rows worked). Work in ribbing until the collar measures 4"/10cm. Make a buttonhole on the overlap by working 4 sts, CO the next 2 sts and work to the end of the row. and BO loosely in rib.

Next row: work to the BO sts, cast on 2 sts and finish the row. Change to the larger circular needle and continue in ribbing until the collar measures 7"/18cm. Make another buttonhole. Work 1"/2.5cm further and BO loosely in rib.

NOTE: If necessary use a larger size needle to BO.

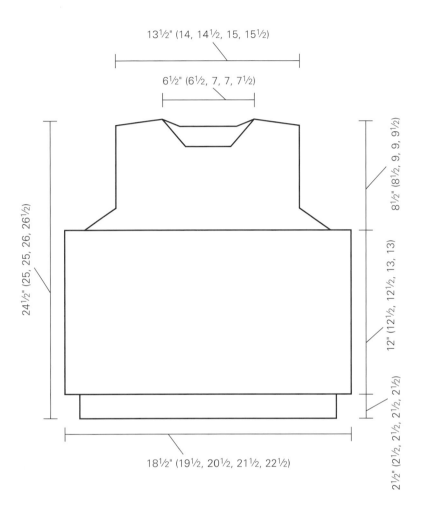

13½" (14, 14½, 15, 15½)

6½" (6½, 7, 7, 7½)

8½" (8½, 9, 9, 9½)

24½" (25, 25, 26, 26½)

12" (12½, 12½, 13, 13)

2½" (2½, 2½, 2½, 2½)

18½" (19½, 20½, 21½, 22½)

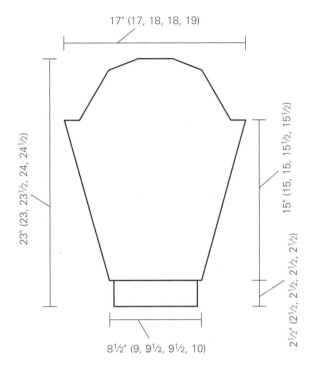

17" (17, 18, 18, 19)

23" (23, 23½, 24, 24½)

15" (15, 15, 15½, 15½)

2½" (2½, 2½, 2½, 2½)

8½" (9, 9½, 9½, 10)

finishing

Sew side and sleeve seams.

Pin sleeves into armhole and seam.

Darn loose ends in neatly.

Sew on buttons to correspond to buttonholes.

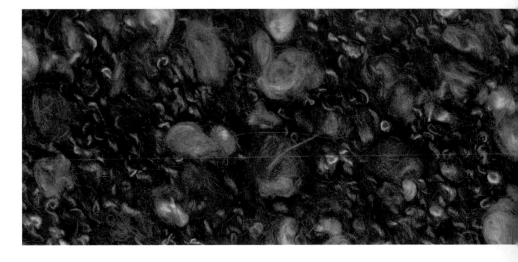

knit clutch purse

Novelty yarns make wonderful accessories, and this easy clutch purse is no exception. A simple stripe pattern on the flap adds a designer touch.

Lisa Carnahan

instructions

flap

Using Swan, cast on 15 sts and knit 3 rows.

Knit rows 4, 5, 6, and 7 with Dove.

Knit rows 8, 9, 10, and 11 with Swan.

Repeat rows 4-11 three more times.

Knit 4 rows with Dove.

Knit 3 rows with Swan.

Bind off.

body

With Swan, pick up 35 sts along side edge of flap.

Work in garter stitch (knit every row) for 5"/13cm. Place markers on each end of this row.

Work in garter stitch for an additional 5"/13cm.

With Dove, knit 3 rows. Bind off.

finishing

Fold bag in half at marked row. Sew side seams.

Fold flap over.

skill level

Easy

finished measurements

7 x 5"/18 x 13cm

materials

Bernat's *Boa*, 100% polyester, 1.75 oz/50g = 71yd/65m, 1 skein of Swan, 1 skein of Dove

Knitting needles in size 8 US/5mm or size needed to obtain gauge

Tapestry needle

gauge

5 sts = 1"/2.5cm in garter st.

Remember, your gauge must match for your size to match.

child's stuffed toy & matching hat

Catherine Ham

Remember when you were growing up how you and that special doll or stuffed animal were inseparable? You toted it everywhere! When you present this multicolored toy (lovingly named "Frazzle") and matching tasseled hat to a special child, step back and watch the same type of friendship blossom. As an added plus, the set knits up quick and easy, and is a great way to use yarn scraps.

instructions for toy

body

Using Wool-Ease, cast on 57 sts and work 2 rows in st st.

Decrease 1 st at each side on next and every following 3rd row until one st remains.

Cut yarn and fasten off.

Repeat all steps to make a second body piece.

legs

Using colors of choice, cast on 10 stitches and work stripes in stocking stitch until work measures approx 8"/20cm.

Cut yarn.

With yarn of choice for the feet, work one row.

In the next row increase one stitch in every stitch on the needles. (20 sts)

skill level

Easy

finished measurements

Approx 12 x 14"/30 x 35cm

materials

Lion Brand's *Wool-Ease* worsted weight, 80% acrylic/20% wool, 3oz/85g = approx 197yd/180m, 1 ball of color of choice

Small amounts of worsted weight yarn in colors of choice*

Knitting needles in Size 8 US/5mm or size to obtain gauge

Buttons

Stuffing

Tapestry needle

*Frazzle's legs and curly locks can be made in oddments of yarn of any weight; adjust knitting needle sizes accordingly.

gauge

18 stitches and 24 rows = 4"/10cm

Remember, your gauge must match for your size to match.

SAFETY NOTE! If Frazzle will be used by child under 3, embroider the features and do not use buttons.

Continue working in stocking stitch until the foot measures 2"/5cm, then knit 2 sts tog ALL across the row. (10 sts)

Cut yarn, leaving a tail of 2 or 3"/5-8cm.

Thread a tapestry needle, thread through the sts, taking them off the needle, and draw up the sts tightly. Fasten off.

Repeat all steps to make second leg.

hair

Using yarns of choice, cast on 30 stitches and cast them off again.

NOTE: You can vary the types of yarn and the number of stitches as you please. Repeat to make as many curly locks as desired.

finishing

Sew the body pieces together, leaving an opening to insert stuffing. Stuff lightly and close opening.

Sew the foot seams and stuff lightly. Sew a few stitches across the top of the feet to hold the stuffing in place.

The legs are not stuffed. The leg edges will roll inward naturally, but you may stitch the leg seam if you prefer.

Sew the legs to the body.

Sew on buttons for the eyes and nose, or embroider them on.

Attach Frazzle's curly locks as desired.

skill level
Easy

sizes
Small (medium, large)
16" (18, 20)/41cm (46, 51)

materials
Lion Brand's *Wool-Ease* worsted weight, 80% acrylic/20%wool, 3oz/85g = approx 197yd/180m, approx 1.75oz/50g total needed for all sizes

Knitting needles in size 6 and 8US/4 and 5mm or size needed to obtain gauge.

*If you prefer to knit in the round, short circular needles use in sizes 6 and 8US/4 and 5mm and a set of double-pointed needles in size 8US/5mm

Tapestry needle

NOTE: Curly locks (top-knot) can be made from any weight of yarn.

gauge
18 sts/24 rows = 4"/10cm measured over st st using *Wool-Ease*

Remember, your gauge must match for your size to match.

instructions for hat

to start
Using color of choice and size 6US/4mm needles, cast on 72 (82, 92) sts and work 1"/2.5cm in st st. *NOTE: If the hat will be knit in the round, cast on 70 (80, 90) sts and work circularly; change to the double-pointed needles when necessary.

Change to size 8US/5mm needles and continue in st st, changing colors as desired until the work measures 4" (4.5, 5)/10cm (11, 13) from the beginning.

shape the crown

Row 1: K1,*k5 (6, 7), k2tog, repeat from * to the last st, knit1.

Row 2 and every even row: Purl.

Row 3: K1,*k4 (5, 6), k2tog, repeat from * to the last st, k1.

Row 5: K1,*k3 (4, 5), k2tog, repeat from * to the last st, k1.

Continue decreasing 10 stitches this way on every knit row until there are 22 sts remaining. Purl one row. Next row, RS facing, knit 2 stitches tog all across the row. Eleven sts remain. Cut the yarn, leaving a tail. Thread this through a tapestry needle and draw up the stitches tightly. Fasten off securely.

finishing

Sew up the center back seam, reversing the seam on the rolled edge.

Make curly locks as directed for Frazzle toy and attach securely at the top of the hat. Darn in the yarn ends.

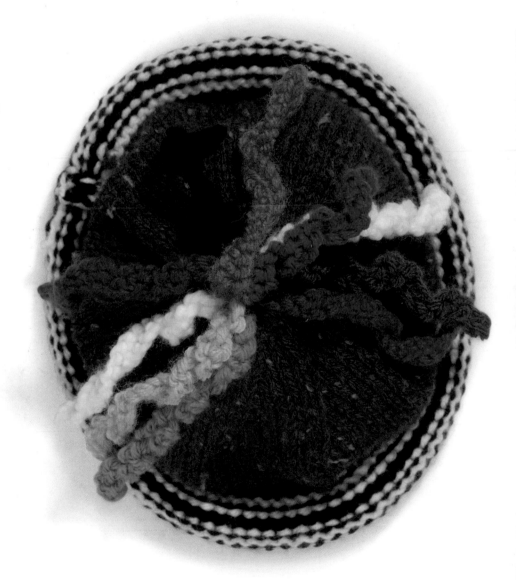

peppermint tutu scarf

Terri Geck

The wonderful blend of fibers in this new novelty yarn creates a festive, confetti-like look that's fun to knit with and even more fun to wear. Alternate bands of your favorite colors to maximize the effect.

instructions

to start

Row 1: With Pear Green, CO 1 st.

Row 2: Knit in front and back of st with 1 increase made. (2 sts)

Row 3: In front, increase in first sts, k1. (3 sts)

Row 4: K 2, increase in next st. (4 sts)

Row 5: Increase in first st, k across. (5 sts)

Row 6: Knit across to last st, increase in last st. (6 sts)

Rows 7-20: Repeat Rows 5 and 6 seven more times. (20 sts)

Row 21: With Pear Green, knit across to last st, join White, knit 1 st.

Row 22: With White, k 2 with Pear Green in back, twist Pear Green and White together, knit across with Pear Green.

Keeping continuity of pattern, move next color over one st on each row and twisting the two colors tog as you change, joining next color on last st of every 20th row from previous color change. Follow striping pattern as follows: Pear Green, White, Raspberry, White, ending with a Raspberry stripe.

Bind off last stripe. Keeping continuity of pattern, BO2 sts at the beginning of the 11th row, then every other row until no sts remain.

Weave in ends.

skill level

Intermediate

size

5 x 66"/13 x 168cm

materials

Moda Dea's *Tutu*, 43% nylon, 22% cotton, 22% acrylic, and 13% rayon, 1.76oz/50g = approx 92yd/84m, 1 ball of White, 1 ball of Pear Green, 1 ball of Raspberry

Knitting needles in size 10.5US/6.5mm or size needed to obtain gauge

Yarn needle

Tapestry needle

gauge

16 sts and 20 rows = 4"/10cm

Remember, your gauge must match for your size to match.

scarf with mitten pockets

Catherine Ham

This playful kitten scarf is more than just another pretty face. The bright cats decorate pockets that can be used to hold mittens or cold hands. Kitten faces are only one embellishment possibility; if your young scarf wearer would prefer dinosaurs, puppies, fish, or bunnies, just get out your scrap box and set your imagination free.

instructions

to make the scarf
Cast on 15 sts and work in garter st for approx 56"/142cm.

Bind off.

ears (make 4)
Using the yarn and needles of choice, cast on 2 sts. Knit one row. Working in garter st, increase one st at the beginning of each row until there are 16 sts on the needle. Bind off.

skill level
Easy

finished measurements
Approx 4 x 48"/10 x 122cm

materials
Scarf

Lion Brand's *Homespun*, bulky weight, 98% acrylic/2% polyester, 6oz/170g = approx 185yd/167m, 1 skein Candy Apple

Knitting needles in size 10US/6mm or size needed to obtain gauge

Tapestry needle

Several yards of worsted-weight yarn

Needles of appropriate size for the yarn used for ears

Small amount of yarn suitable for the whiskers (ribbon or cord may also be used)

Buttons (if desired)

gauge
14 garter sts/20 rows = 4"/10cm

Remember, your gauge must match for your size to match.

finishing
Fold up 4"/10cm at each end of the scarf to form the mitten pockets and sew in place.

Attach the ears to the pocket tops as shown.

Sew on buttons for eyes and nose.

NOTE: If the scarf is for a very young child, embroider these features or use felt appliqués instead of using buttons.

Attach whiskers securely.

Darn in any loose ends.

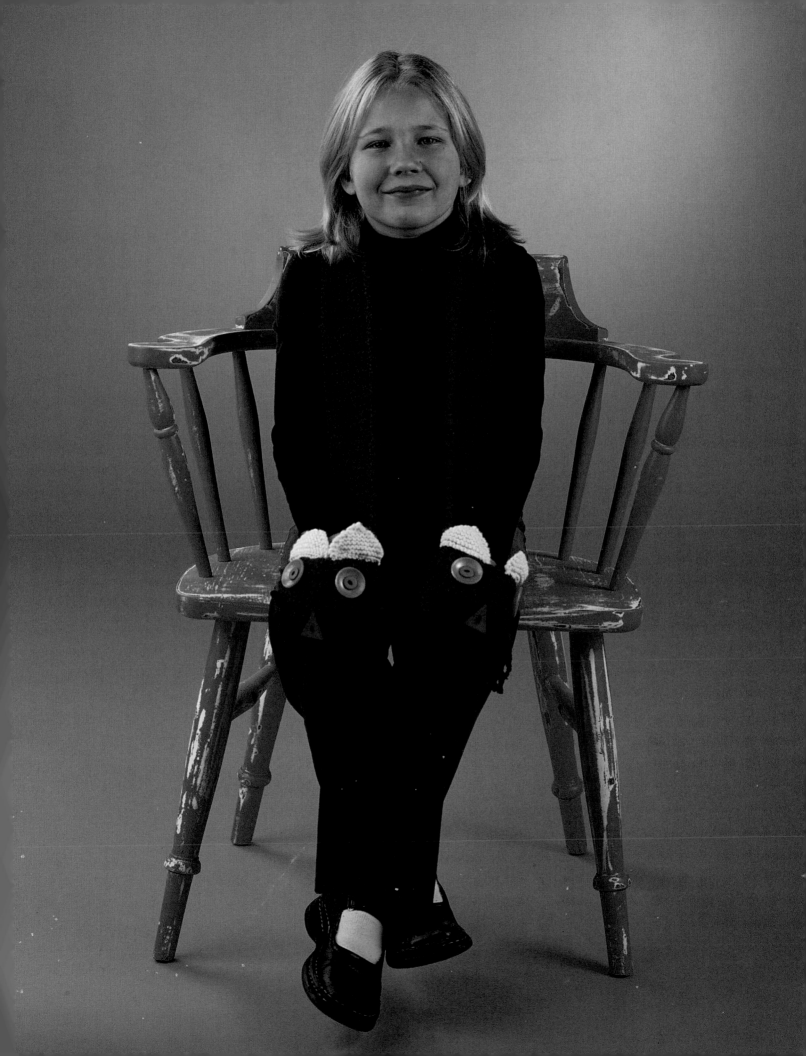

checkerboard vest

This clever vest features a multi-colored checkerboard border that's easy to knit and fun to wear.

Catherine Ham

instructions

to start

Using Dark Red and smaller needle, cast on 132 (136, 144, 152, 160) sts and knit 4 rows. (2 garter stitch ridges)

Join Sunset Red and knit 2 rows. (1 garter st ridge)

Join in Purple Vista and knit 2 rows (1 garter st ridge).

Next row (RS): With Dark Rose, k1, *yfwd k2tog, repeat from * to the last stitch, k1.

Knit 3 rows. (2 garter st ridges)

Next 4 rows: RS facing and working in st st: *k2 in red, k2 in purple, repeat from * to end of row.

RS: With Dark Rose knit 2 rows. (1 garter st ridge)

Next 4 rows: Beginning with Purple Vista, work the color pattern as before in st st. Cut the contrast yarns and continue in Dark Rose only.

Next 2 rows: With Dark Rose, knit.

Next row (RS): K1, *yfwd k2tog, repeat from * to the last stitch, k1.

Knit 3 rows. (2 garter st ridges)

Continue working in st st until the vest measures 14.5" (14.5, 15, 15, 15.5)/38cm (38, 38, 38, 39) from the cast on edge.

Divide for fronts and back.

right front

RS: Knit 29 (31, 33, 34, 34) sts for the right front and place the remaining sts on a holder. Purl one row.

Begin Neck Shaping
RS facing: decrease 1 st at neck edge every 2nd row 2 (1, 0, 1, 0) times, then every 4th row 10 (11, 12, 12, 13) times. [17 (19, 21, 21, 21) sts]

Continue working until the piece measures 23.5" (24, 24.5,

25, 26)/60cm (61, 62, 64, 66). Bind off the shoulder sts.

Replace the sts on the needle, join the yarn, BO 8 (6, 6, 8, 12) sts for the underarm, knit 58 (62, 66, 68, 68) sts for the back and leave these on a holder, BO 8 (6, 6, 8, 12) sts for the underarm, knit 29 (31, 33, 34, 34) sts for the left front.

left front

Working the decreases at the neck edge, complete to match the right front.

back

Replace the sts on the needle, join the yarn and continue working in st st until the piece measures 23" (23.5, 24, 24.5, 25.5)/58cm (60, 61, 62, 65) from the beginning.

RS facing: Knit 18 (20, 22, 22, 22) place center 22 (22, 22, 24, 24) sts on a holder for the back neck, join a second

skill level

Intermediate

sizes

To fit bust 32" (34, 36, 38, 40)/81cm (86, 91, 97, 102)

finished measurements

Bust: 35" (37, 39, 41, 43)/89cm (94, 99, 104, 112)
Length: 23.5" (24, 24.5, 25, 26)/60cm (61, 62, 64, 66)

materials

Bernat's *Soft Boucle*, 98% acrylic/2% polyester, 5oz/140g = approx 255yd/232m, 2 (3,3,3,4) balls of Dark Rose

Lion Brand's *Color Waves* bulky weight, 73% acrylic/27% polyester, 3oz/85g = approx 125yd/118m, 1 ball each of Sunset Red and Purple Vista

24"/61cm and 16"/41cm circular knitting needles in size 8 and 10US/5 and 6mm or sizes needed to obtain gauge

Tapestry needle

5 buttons

gauge

15 sts/22 rows = 4"/10cm measured over st st

NOTE: The vest is knitted in one piece to the underarm, then the work is divided and the back and fronts are worked separately.

ball of yarn, knit 18 (20, 22, 22, 22).

On next row, decrease 1 st at each neck edge.

Continue working each shoulder until piece measures 23.5" (24, 24.5, 25.5, 26)/60cm (61, 62, 65, 66).

Bind off 17 (19, 21, 21, 21) sts across each shoulder.

finishing

Join the Shoulders.

Armhole Edging

RS facing: With shorter circular needle and Dark Rose, pick up approx 74 (77, 79, 83, 89) sts around armhole edge. Work in k1p1 rib for 1"/2.5cm. Bind off loosely in rib.

Front Band

Mark the position for the buttons on the left front, placing the first button .5"/1cm below the first neck decrease, and the last button .5"/1cm above the bottom cast on edge. Space the others evenly in between.

RS facing: With smaller circular needle and Dark Rose, beginning at lower right front edge, pick up and knit 66 (66, 68, 68, 70) sts to first neck decrease, 38 (40, 41, 43, 46) sts along right front neck edge, 30 (30, 30, 32, 32) sts along the back of the neck, including the sts on the holder, 38 (40, 41, 43, 46) along left front neck edge and 66 (66, 68, 68, 70) sts down left front edge. [238 (242, 248, 254, 264) sts]

Work .5"/1cm in k1p1 rib.

Buttonhole Row

Work buttonholes opposite the button markers on the right side. (To make a buttonhole: yfwd, k2tog.)

Continue in rib until the front band measures 1"/2.5cm. Bind off loosely in rib.

Sew on the buttons. Darn in loose ends neatly.

Shape the vest on a flat and spray lightly with water to block. Allow to dry.

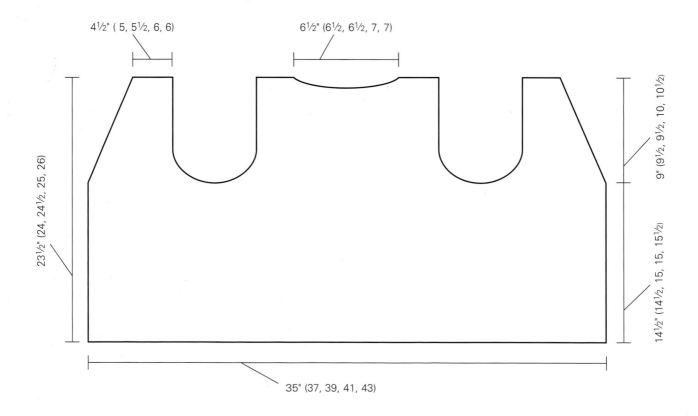

4½" (5, 5½, 6, 6)

6½" (6½, 6½, 7, 7)

9" (9½, 9½, 10, 10½)

23½" (24, 24½, 25, 26)

14½" (14½, 15, 15, 15½)

35" (37, 39, 41, 43)

two can play

Catherine Ham

Two kinds of yarn and wonderful colors combine to make this energetic kids' sweater. Your action-packed youngster will love it, and it's so quick to knit that you will, too.

skill level
Easy

sizes
4 (6, 8, 10, 12) years

finished measurements
Chest: 27" (29, 30, 32, 34)/69cm (74, 76, 81, 86)

Length: 14.5" (15.5, 17.5, 19.5, 21)/37cm (39, 44, 50, 53)

materials
Lion Brand's *Lion Boucle* super bulky weight, 79% acrylic/20% mohair/1% nylon, 2.5 oz/70g = approx 57yd/52m, 3 (4,5,6,7) balls of Hard Candies

Lion Brand's *Wool-Ease* worsted weight, 80%acrylic/20%wool, 3oz/85g = approx 197yd/180m, 1 (1, 1, 1, 2) balls of Navy

Knitting needles in size 6, 10.5, and 11US/5, 7, and 8mm or size needed to obtain gauge

Short circular knitting needle, or set of four double-pointed needles, in size 10.5US/7mm, or size needed to obtain gauge

Stitch holders

Tapestry needle

gauge
Lion Boucle Gauge: 10 sts/14 rows = 4"/10cm

Wool-Ease Gauge: 18sts/24 rows = 4"/10cm

Remember, your gauge must match for your size to match.

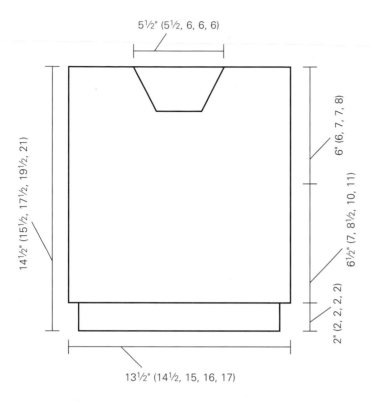

5½" (5½, 6, 6, 6)

14½" (15½, 17½, 19½, 21)

6" (6, 7, 7, 8)

6½" (7, 8½, 10, 11)

2" (2, 2, 2, 2)

13½" (14½, 15, 16, 17)

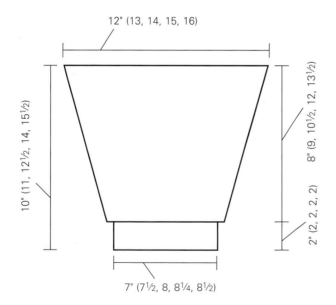

12" (13, 14, 15, 16)

10" (11, 12½, 14, 15½)

8" (9, 10½, 12, 13½)

2" (2, 2, 2, 2)

7" (7½, 8, 8¼, 8½)

instructions

back of body

Using Boucle and smaller needles, cast on 32 (32, 34, 36, 38) sts and work 2"/5cm in k1, p1 rib.

Increase 2 (4, 4, 4, 4) sts evenly across the row. [34 (36, 38, 40, 42) sts]

Change to larger needles and work in st st until the piece measures 8.5" (9, 10.5, 12, 13)/22cm (23, 27, 30, 33) from the beginning.

Place markers for the underarm. Continue working until the back measures 14.5" (15.5, 17.5, 19.5, 21)/37cm (39, 44, 50, 53).

BO 10 (11, 11, 12, 13) shoulder sts, work the next 14 (14, 16, 16, 16) sts and leave on a holder for the back neck, BO 10 (11, 11, 12, 13) shoulder sts.

front of body

Work as directed for the back until the piece measures 12" (13, 14.5, 16.5, 18)/30cm (33, 37, 42, 46) from the beginning.

Begin Neck Shaping

Work to center 6 (8, 10, 10, 10) sts, attach another ball of yarn, knit the center 6 (8, 10, 10, 10) sts and leave them on a holder for the front neck. Complete the row.

Working both sides at the same time, dec 1 st at each neck edge every other row 4 (3, 3, 3, 3) times. [10 (11, 11, 12, 13) sts]

Continue working until the piece measures 14.5" (15.5, 17.5, 19.5, 21)/37cm (39, 44, 50, 53) from the beginning.

BO shoulder stitches.

pattern stitch for sleeves

Row 1: Knit.

Row 2: Purl.

Row 3: Knit.

Row 4: Purl.

Rows 5-10: Knit.

Using Wool-Ease and size 6US/4mm needles, cast on 30 (32, 32, 34, 34) sts and work 2"/5cm in rib.

Increase 2 (2, 4, 4, 4) sts evenly across the row. [32 (34, 36, 38, 38) sts]

Change to larger needles and work in the pattern stitch.

Sleeve Shaping

Increase 1 st on each side every 4th row 11 (12, 14, 15, 17) times. [54 (58, 64, 68, 72) sts]

Continue working until the sleeve measures 10" (11, 12.5, 14, 15.5)/25cm (28, 32, 36, 39) from the beginning.

BO the sts.

neckband

Join the shoulder seams.

With the circular needle or set of double pointed needles, using Boucle, pick up and knit approx 36 (40, 44, 44, 44) sts around the neck edge, including the sts left on holders. Work 1"/2.5cm in k1, p1 rib.

BO sts loosely in rib.

finishing

Pin sleeves into place between the markers and sew the seams.

Sew the side and sleeve seams.

Darn in yarn ends.

mirror image afghan

This afghan is the perfect project for both beginning knitters and for those who like to knit on the go. The pattern is created with squares alternately knit with two yarns, then pieced together to create an optical illusion.

Fatema, Khadija, and Hajera Habibur-Rahman

instructions

NOTES: There are a total of 100 blocks joined together. Seed stitch borders are worked separately and sewn to the edges.

When alternating colors, carry previous color up to next row on knit side and resume with color indicated on chart so you do not need to cut strands or weave in so many ends when changing colors.

special abbreviations

Inc 1: Knit in front, then in back of the stitch (makes 2 stitches from 1 stitch).

Skp: Slip one stitch, knit one stitch, passed slipped stitch over knit stitch (decreases 1 stitch).

K2tog: Knit 2 stitches together (decreases 1 stitch).

K3tog: Knit 3 stitches together (decreases 2 stitches).

pattern stitch

Seed Stitch (on an odd number of stitches)

Row 1 (RS): *K1, p1; rep from * across.

Rep row 1 for seed st.

to start

With Tundra, CO 3 sts.

Row 1 (RS): Inc 1, knit across to last stitch, Inc 1.

Row 2 and every even row: Purl.

Repeat rows 1 and 2 until 9 sts are on needle.

Next Row: Purl.

Rows 7-12: With Silver, repeat rows 1 and 2 three times.

Rows 13-18: With Tundra, repeat rows 1 and 2 three times.

Row 19: Skp, knit across to last 2 sts, k2tog. (19 sts)

Row 20: Purl.

skill level
Easy

finished measurements
Afghan: 50x53"/1.27x1.35m, blocked, with seed stitch border made from 4.5"/11cm squares

materials
Lion Brand's *Moonlight Mohair*, bulky weight, 35% mohair/30% acrylic/25% cotton/10% polyester metallic, 1.75oz/50g = approx 82yd/75m, 6 balls of Tundra, 6 balls of Glacier Bay

Patons' *Brilliant*, 69% acrylic/19% nylon/12% polyester, 1.75 oz/50g = 166yd/152m, 7 balls of White Twinkle

Knitting needles size 10US/6mm or size needed to obtain gauge

Tapestry needle

Cardboard, 5"/13cm wide, for making tassels

gauge
14 sts/18 rows = 4"/10cm in st st using mohair

18 sts/24 rows = 4"/10cm in st st using glitter

Remember, your gauge must match for your size to match.

Repeat Rows 19 and 20 twice more.

Rows 25-30: With Silver, repeat rows 19-20 three times.

Rows 31-34: With Tundra, repeat rows 19-20 twice.

Row 35: Skp, k1, k2tog.

Row 36: Purl.

Row 37: K3tog.

Bind Off.

Square A
Make 50.

Work Mirror Square Pattern in Tundra and Silver.

Square B
Make 50.

Work Mirror Square Pattern replacing Tundra with Glacier.

joining squares
With Tundra or Glacier, seam squares together according to the placement diagram. Make sure that squares are turned according to the placement diagram.

seed stitch border 1 (make 2)
With Tundra, CO 9 sts. Work in st st for 2"/5cm, change to color C, beg working seed st pattern until border measures 48"/1.2m from beginning. Change to Glacier, work in st st for 2"/5cm. Bind Off.

seed stitch border 2 (make 2)
With C, CO 9 sts. Work in seed st pattern until border measures 49"/1.25m. Bind off.

joining borders
Attach Border 1 to the top and bottom of the afghan, then attach Border 2 to both sides of the afghan, including both edges of previously attached Border 1.

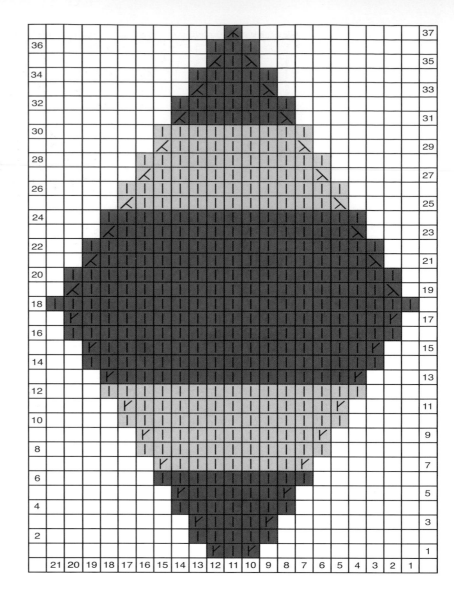

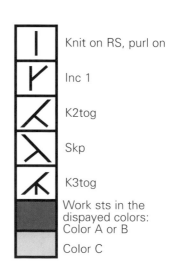

	Knit on RS, purl on
	Inc 1
	K2tog
	Skp
	K3tog
	Work sts in the dispayed colors: Color A or B
	Color C

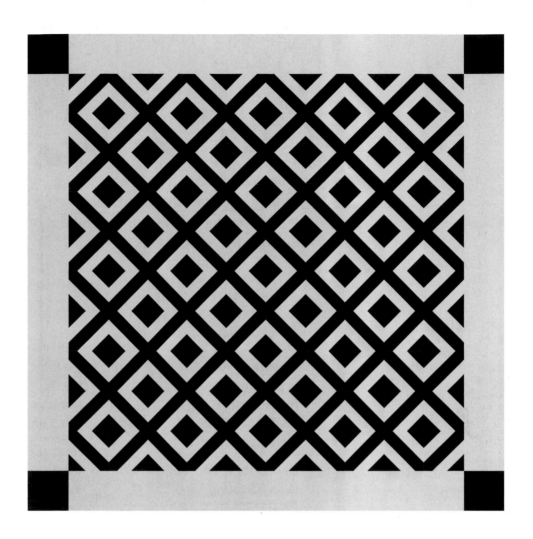

finishing

Block afghan and cable borders lightly.

tassels (make 4)

Using Silver, make tassels by wrapping yarn ten times around cardboard. Cut a 10"/25cm yarn strand. Pull from cardboard. Wrap around head of tassel and secure by knotting at side. Using a tapestry needle, pull strand through the middle of the tassel's head. Attach to corner of afghan. Repeat for other three corners. Trim tassels.

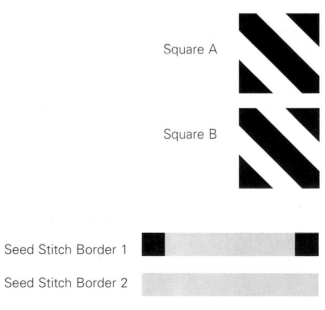

Square A

Square B

Seed Stitch Border 1

Seed Stitch Border 2

child's cardigan jacket

Catherine Ham

This classic jacket for a special young lady is knit in one piece to the underarm. The simple (and easy!) stitch pattern adds interest to the knitted fabric, while the novelty fur edgings create a fun, dressy look.

instructions

pattern stitch

Row 1: Knit.

Row 2: Purl.

Row 3: *K1,p1* to last stitch, k1.

Row 4: Purl.

body

Using Fancy Fur cast on 121 (129, 137, 145, 153) stitches and knit 4 rows.

Change to Wool-Ease and work in pattern stitch until piece measures 8.5" (9, 10.5, 12, 13)/22cm (23, 27, 31, 33) from the beginning.

Divide for Fronts and Back

With RS facing, work 25 (27, 29, 31, 32) sts for the right front, bind off 10 (10, 10, 10, 12) sts for underarm, work the next 51 (55, 59, 63, 65) sts for the back, bind off the next 10 (10, 10, 10, 12) sts for underarm and work to end of row (left front).

Next row (WS): Work across the 25 (27, 29, 31, 32) sts of the left front and place the remaining sts on a holder.

skill level

sizes

2 (4, 6, 8, 10) years

finished measurements

Chest: 27" (28, 30, 32, 34)/69cm (71, 76, 81, 86)

Length: 15" (16, 18, 20, 22)/38cm (41, 46, 51, 56)

materials

Lion Brand's *Wool-Ease*, worsted weight, 80% acrylic/20% wool, 3oz/85g = approx 197yd/180m, 2 (3, 3, 4, 4) balls of Colonial Blue

Lion Brand's *Fancy Fur*, 55% polyamide/45% polyester, 1.75oz/50g = approx 39yd/35m, 2 (2, 2, 3) balls of Brilliant Blue

Knitting needles in size 8 US/5mm or size needed to obtain gauge

Stitch holders

Tapestry needle

NOTE: Since the jacket is worked in one piece to the underarm, a circular needle accommodates the stitches more easily, allowing the work to be divided as the back and fronts are worked separately.

gauge

18 sts and 24 rows = 4"/10cm measured over st st using *Wool-Ease*

Remember, your gauge must match for your size to match.

Left Front

Shape Armhole

RS facing, decrease 1 st at the armhole edge every other row 4 (4, 4, 5, 5) times.

Continue working in pattern stitch until the piece measures 12" (13, 14.5, 16.5, 18)/31cm (33, 37, 42) from the beginning, ending with a RS row.

Begin Neck Shaping

At neck edge, work 8 (8, 7, 7, 7) sts, place these on a holder and work to the end of the row. Decrease 1 st every other row at neck edge 4 (5, 7, 7, 7) times.

Continue working in pattern until piece measures 13.5" (14.5, 16.5, 18.5, 20)/34cm (37, 42, 47) from the beginning. [9 (10, 11, 12, 13) sts]

Shape Shoulder

RS facing, BO 3 (3, 3, 4, 4) sts at the beginning of the next row (armhole edge).

Work one row.

BO 3 (3, 4, 4, 4) sts at the beginning of the next row.

Work one row.

BO 3 (4, 4, 4, 5) sts at the beginning of the next row.

Cut yarn and fasten off.

Right Front

Replace sts from the holder onto the needle, join in yarn at underarm (WS of work will be facing) and work to match the left front, reversing all shaping.

Back

With WS of work facing, join yarn at underarm and shape the armhole at each side as worked for the fronts. Continue working in pattern stitch until the back measures 13.5" (14.5, 16.5, 18.5, 20))/34cm (37, 42, 47, 46) from the beginning.

Shape the shoulders as given for the fronts.

Place the remaining 25 (27, 29, 29, 29) back neck stitches on a holder.

sleeves

Using Fancy Fur cast on 33 (35, 37, 39, 39) sts and knit 4 rows.

Change to Wool Ease and work in pattern stitch.

Begin Sleeve Shaping

Increase one stitch on each side every 4th row 3 (3, 3, 2, 7) times, and then every 6th row 4 (5, 6, 8, 6) times until there are 47 (51, 55, 59, 65) sts on the needle.

Continue working until the sleeve measures 10" (11, 12.5, 14, 15.5)/25cm (28, 32, 36, 40) from the beginning.

Shape Sleeve Cap

Bind off 5 (5, 5, 5, 6) sts on each side.

Dec 1 st on each side every other row 4 (4, 4, 5, 5) times.

Dec 1 st on each side every row 2 (3, 5, 5, 6) times.

Bind off 1 (2, 2, 2, 2) sts at the beg of next 4 rows.

Bind off remaining 21 (19, 19, 21, 23) sts.

finishing

Block the pieces.

Join shoulder seams together.

Neck Finishing

With RS facing and using Wool-Ease, pick up and knit 8 (8, 7, 7, 7) sts from holder on right front, 11 (13, 15, 15, 15) side neck sts, 25 (27, 29, 29, 29) back neck sts from the holder, 11 (13, 15, 15, 15) sts from left side neck, and 8 (8, 7, 7, 7) sts from holder on left front. [63 (69, 73, 73, 73) sts]

Change to Fancy Fur and work in garter stitch (knit all rows) for 1"/2.5cm. BO sts off loosely.

Sew sleeve seams.

Pin sleeve into armhole and seam in place.

Front Bands
Right front edging

With RS facing and using Wool-Ease, pick up and knit 56 (58, 64, 72, 78) sts evenly along right front edge. Change to Fancy Fur and work 1"/25cm in garter stitch.

BO all sts.

Work **left front edging** as for right front.

Apply closures as desired. Darn in yarn ends.

optional closures

There are many ways this jacket can be fastened. The model shown here fastens with snaps carefully sewn into the fur bands. A pretty pin, cords, or ribbons are another option. If buttons are used, select some with shanks so they don't get lost in the fur trim. Mark the position of the buttons on the left front band and make buttonholes to correspond on the right front band.

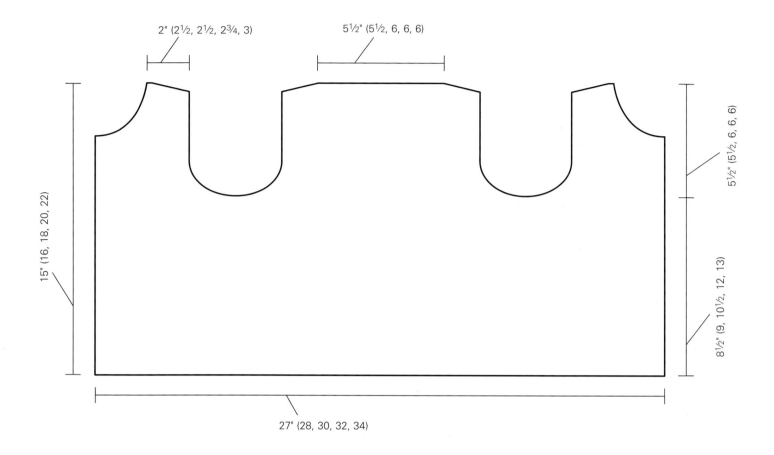

2" (2½, 2½, 2¾, 3)

5½" (5½, 6, 6, 6)

15" (16, 18, 20, 22)

27" (28, 30, 32, 34)

5½" (5½, 6, 6, 6)

8½" (9, 10½, 12, 13)

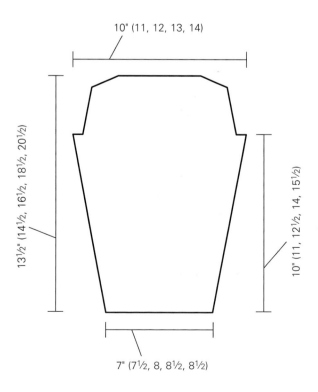

10" (11, 12, 13, 14)

13½" (14½, 16½, 18½, 20½)

10" (11, 12½, 14, 15½)

7" (7½, 8, 8½, 8½)

child's summer top

This perky little top for your favorite little miss is a hot winner. With so many colors to choose from, shouldn't you make more than one?

Catherine Ham

instructions

back

Using Lime, cast on 75 (79, 81, 85, 91) sts and work 6 rows in st st.

Cut Lime yarn and join in Purple. Work two rows in st st.

Begin Pattern Stitch

Row 1 (RS): K2 (4, 5, 7, 3), *sl1purlwise, k6; repeat from * to last 3 (5, 6, 8, 4) sts, sl1 purlwise, k2 (4, 5, 7, 3).

Row2: Purl.

Continue in pattern until the work measures 7" (7.5, 8.5, 9, 10.5)/ 18cm (19, 22, 23, 27) from the beginning.

Armhole Shaping

BO 7 (6, 6, 6, 6) sts at beginning of next 2 rows.

Dec 1 (1, 1, 1, 1) st each side, every other row, 6 (6, 6, 5, 6) times. [49 (55, 57, 63, 67) sts]

Continue in pattern until work measures 11" (12, 13.5, 14.5, 16.5)/28cm (30, 34, 37, 42) from the beginning.

Shape Shoulders and Back Neck

RS facing, BO 4 (5, 4, 5, 5) sts at beginning of next row.

At beginning of next row, BO 4 (5, 4, 5, 5) sts, work 8 (9, 8, 11, 11) sts, join in a second ball of yarn, work the center next 25 (27, 31, 31, 35), leave these sts on a holder and complete the row.

At beginning of next row, BO 4 (4, 4, 5, 5) sts and dec 1 st at each neck edge.

BO 4 (4, 4, 5, 5) sts at beginning of next row. BO 3 (4, 5, 5, 5) sts at beginning of next 2 rows. End off.

front

Work as for back, including all shaping, until work measures 9.5" (10, 12, 12.5, 14)/24cm (25, 30, 32, 36) from the beginning.

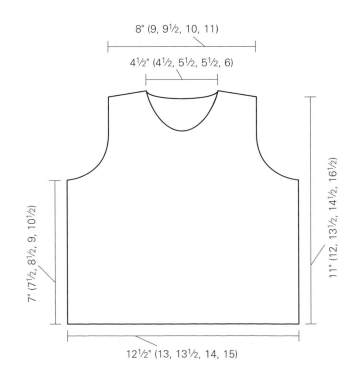

8" (9, 9½, 10, 11)

4½" (4½, 5½, 5½, 6)

7" (7½, 8½, 9, 10½)

11" (12, 13½, 14½, 16½)

12½" (13, 13½, 14, 15)

Neck Shaping

RS facing, work 20 (23, 23, 26, 27) sts.

Join in a second ball of yarn, work center 9 (9, 11, 11, 13) sts, leave these sts on a holder and work the rem 20 (23, 23, 26, 27) sts. Working both sides at the same time, BO 2 (2, 2, 2, 2) sts at neck edge 2 (2, 2, 2, 3) times.

Dec 1 st at each neck edge, every other row 5 (6, 7, 7, 6) times.

Continue working until the piece measures same as back to the start of the shoulder shaping.

Shape Shoulders

Work shoulder shaping as for back.

finishing

Join shoulders.

Neck Edging

RS facing, using the circular needle and Purple yarn, pick up and knit approx 84 (90, 92, 96, 104) sts around the neck, including the sts on the holders.

Change to Lime yarn and work 6 rnds in rev st st. BO loosely.

Armhole Edgings

RS facing, with smaller needles and Purple yarn, pick up and knit approx 62 (65, 72, 78, 84) sts evenly around the armhole edge. Change to Lime yarn and work 6 rows in rev st st. BO loosely.

Sew up side seams.

Darn in the yarn ends.

skill level

Intermediate

sizes

2 (4, 6, 8, 10) years

finished measurements

Chest: 25" (26, 27, 28, 30)/64cm (66, 69, 71, 76)

Length: 11" (12, 13.5, 14.5, 16.5)/28cm (30, 34, 37, 42)

materials

Lion Brand's *Micro-spun* sport weight, 100% micro-fiber acrylic, 2.5 oz/70g = approx 68yd/154m, 2 (2, 3, 3, 3) balls of Purple, 1 ball of Lime

Knitting needles in size 3 and 4US/3.25 and 3.5mm or size needed to obtain gauge.

16"/40.5 cm circular needle in size 4US/3.5mm

Stitch holders

Tapestry needle

gauge

24 sts/32 rows = 4"/10cm

Remember, your gauge must match for your size to match.

bead and wire necklace

Cathy Carron

If you can knit with yarn, you can knit with beads and wire, which opens up a new world of colorful opportunities. The basic techniques are the same, although you may notice a decrease in your knitting speed.

instructions

knitting with wire
When knitting with wire, remember everything you know about knitting with yarn except the tactile feel. Wire feels different—it's not as pliable—but it's enough so that you can make a stitch.

Working with wire goes more slowly than working with yarn, so take your time and enjoy the sculpting process of wire knitting.

casting on with wire
The best method is to make a slip knot and then knit a stitch into the slipknot placing the new stitch on the left hand needle. Repeat this process until you achieve the desired number of stitches.

making i-cord
I-cord is a technique for making knitted cord. It is knitting in-the-round with a small number of stitches. If you haven't made I-cord before, you might want to try doing so with yarn first to get the idea of what you are doing.

It goes like this: Cast 3 sts onto a dpn. With another dpn, knit the 3 sts and then move the 3 sts from the left hand side of the right needle to the right end of the right hand dpn and knit them again—keep repeating this until you achieve the desired length.

to start
First string all the beads you will be using onto the wire with which you will be knitting.

CO 3 sts.

Knit 4 I-cord rows.

Knit1 with a bead, but don't push the bead through the loop as you would normally when knitting beads, K2.

Repeat the last 5 rows until all the beads are used or until you have made the necklace as long as you want.

BO and weave the wire ends into the opposite end of the strand. Fasten off the ends making the necklace.

skill level
Easy

finished measurement
30"/76cm circle

materials
Spool of 28-gauge beading wire

Crystal beads

Knitting needles: 4US/3.5 mm metal dpn

Tapestry needle

Scissors

gauge
Gauge is not critical in this project.

leg warmers

Stacey Budge

instructions

leg warmers (make 2)
Using dpn, cast on 54 sts. K27, place marker, k27, place marker. Work in st st for 1"/2.5cm. Work in 3x3 rib for 3"/7.5 cm.

Changing to st st, knit for 15"/38cm, increase 1 st before each marker every 30 (10) rows, 3 (9) times, switching to circular needle when you can.

Work in 3x3 rib for 3"/7.5cm. Work in st st for 1"/2.5cm. Bind off loosely. Repeat for second leg warmer.

finishing
Sew in ends.

yarn alternative
Many projects made with lightweight yarns, such as Sassy Stripes, can also be made in a heavier weight yarn as long as you take the time to get the right gauge. Lion Brand's Wool-Ease worsted weight yarn (80% acrylic/20% wool, 3oz/85g = approx 197yd/180m) was used in the swatch below.

Since Wool-Ease is a larger yarn, start by working with a size 4 needle to make a gauge swatch. Increase the needle sizes if needed until you match the gauge. You will need 3 balls of a main color and a ball each for stripes; if you don't want stripes, you'll need 4 balls.

tips
Cut the yarn for each stripe before you begin to knit to keep your yarns from tangling. Using cut lengths also makes the transition between colors more even by controlling the tension on that slipped stitch as you tie the two ends together.

If you make horizontal stripes while knitting in the round, you get a jog where the colors change. The easiest way to handle this problem is to slip the first stitch of the new color on the 2nd round of the new color.

skill level
Easy

sizes
S/M (M/L)

finished measurements
28"/71cm long

11"/28cm circumference at ankle, 12" (14.5)/30cm (37) at top

materials
Moda Dea's Sassy Stripes, 100% acrylic, 1.76oz/ 50g = approx 152yd/140m, 4 balls

Knitting needles in size 5US/3.75mm or size to obtain gauge and short circular needle

Stitch markers

Row counter

Tapestry needle

gauge
20 sts = 4"/10cm

Remember, your gauge must match for your size to match.

doggie sweater & collar

Marilyn Hasting

This practical and elegant dog sweater keeps your best friend warm. The design features a removable collar that can be worn with or without the sweater. Make several with your novelty yarn scraps, then mix and match for stylish fun!

instructions for sweater

stitches
Seed rib stitch: K1, p1 on right side, purl on wrong side

neck and shoulders
Loosely CO 70 sts (drawn in by ribbing to 12"/30cm), k1, p1 ribbing around for 5"/13cm, being careful not to twist sts as you start the rnds. For a good fit, continue ribbing on the front/chest with about a third of the stitches, (here 5"/13cm) using an odd number for a purl st at each end to set off the ribbing.

Increase rapidly by adding 4 sts EVERY rnd, by knitting in the front and back of 4 sts, one on each side of the front ribbing and 2 centered on the back about 2"/5cm apart. Increase for 5 rnds (20 sts).

leg slits and beyond
NOTE: You need to join a new ball of yarn to knit the chest between the leg slits and again

skill level

Advanced

size

To fit small dog; adapt pattern as directed for larger dogs

measurements

12"/30cm circumference for neck

17"/43cm circumference for shoulders

4"/10cm chest width (between front leg slits)

11"/28cm back length

See notes at end for fitting larger dogs

materials

Lion Brand's *Wool-Ease*, worsted weight, 80% acrylic/20% wool, 3oz/85g = approx 197yd/180m, Wheat. One ball for a small dog, more for larger dogs.

Knitting needle 8US/5mm short circular needle, or size to obtain gauge

Stitch markers

Tapestry needle

gauge

18 sts = 4"/10cm in st st

to knit both sides of the chest after it is split.

About 2"/5cm below neck ribbing, 4"/10cm apart (=17sts), start each slit by increasing one stitch at top of each slit so there will be a purl stitch on the

each edge of each slit (purl stitches recede and only the 2nd, knit, stitch shows). Knit the center stitches in rows in ribbing for about 1"/2.5cm, then split those stitches (just like you did for the leg slits, increasing

so a purl stitch is on each outside edge). Continue each side separately in ribbing for another 1"/2.5cm while decreasing 1 st every other row inside the 1st k st on the edge (so the knit stitch on the edge gradually crosses over the stitches of the ribbing).

Work the back the same 2"/5cm as the front with p1, k1, p1 on each edge and st st between. When both sides of both slits are the same length continue across them, purling together the purl stitches on both sides of the slits to maintain the rib pattern.

Continue knitting and decreasing inside each edge, until the back is 9"/23 cm long. Keep decreasing but switch to seed rib for the last 1"/2.5 cm to keep the sweater from curling, and bind off all stitches as knit stitches to continue the line of knit stitches across the bottom back edge.

finishing
Weave in ends, block if needed.

other sizes
The necessary measurements are:

(1) neck/head circumference

(2) length from neck to top of front legs (for slit placement)

(3) shoulder circumference at top of front leg slits

(4) chest width between leg slits

(5) length of back.

CO an even number of stitches for (1), and rib for as long as you want the collar.

In the length of (2) you need to increase enough stitches to reach the circumference of (3).

Split the body for legs the distance of (4) apart, the length of the split depending on the size of the dog and how cooperative he is in getting dressed.

Decrease each edge at the rate that will reach the width you want across the lower back for the desired back length.

materials
Short length of leftover *Wool-Ease* from dog sweater

Bernat's *Boa*, 100% polyester, 1.75oz/50g = approx 71yd/65m, 1 ball Doo Doo Bird

Knitting needles size 8US/5mm dpn

instructions for fancy collar

Use 50 sts for small dog and 70 sts for proud owner. CO loosely with a smooth yarn such as Wool-Ease; continue around with fancy yarn for the depth you want, and BO loosely with smooth yarn. Tip: It's easier to CO and BO with a smooth yarn; they provide the edge with a bit more body and don't show in the finished collar. Wear the more furry purl side out.

mini music tote

Stacey Budge

This stylish little pouch is perfect for the person on the go keeping their ipod or cell phone snugly at their fingertips for quick and easy access. The colorful contrasting fringe adds a touch of whimsy for free spirits. This project can easily be adapted to accommodate a pair of glasses or small wallet.

instructions

stitch
Icord: Using dpn, *k4, slide sts to the other end of the needle, bring yarn around the back, repeat from * around

to start
Holding together one strand of the Microspun and one strand of Fun Fur cast on 24 sts. Work 1"/2.5cm in garter stitch. Cut the Fun Fur and pick up a second strand of Microspun. Holding both ends together,

work in 2x2 rib for 4"/10cm. Use 3-needle bind off to seam the bottom edge. Pick up 4 sts on the inside of the bag. Work icord for 45"/114cm. Thread end through the four loops to fasten off. Repeat for the other strap.

finishing
Cut several 12"/30cm lengths of Fun Fur for tassels. Attach securely to the ends of the icord straps, then sew in ends.

skill level
Easy

finished measurements
About 2 x 5"/5 x 13cm plus 45"/1.14m ties

materials
Lion Brand's *Microspun*, sport weight, 100% microfiber acrylic, 2.5oz/70g = approx 168yds/154m, 1 ball of color of choice

Lion Brand's *Fun Fur*, 100% polyester, 1.5oz/40g = approx 57yds/52m, 1 ball of color of choice

Knitting needles is size 4US/3.5mm double-pointed needles or size needed to obtain gauge

Stitch marker

Tapestry needle

gauge
20 sts/28 rows= 4"/10cm

Remember, your gauge must match for your size to match.

all-season shell

Terri Geck

All the warm colors of fall are represented in this wonderfully plush knit shell, but it's perfect to wear any time of the year alone or under a blazer. The nubby-textured yarn is very forgiving, making this a perfect project for beginners.

skill level
Easy

sizes
S (M, L)

finished measurements
32" (34, 36)/81cm(86, 91)

materials
Moda Dea's *Cache*, 75% wool/22% acrylic/3% polyester, 1.76oz/50g = approx 72 yd/66m, 4 (4,5) balls of Tootsie

Knitting needles in size 15US/10mm, or size needed to obtain gauge

Knitting needles in size 15 US/10mm 24"/61cm circular or size needed to obtain gauge

Tapestry needle

gauge
10 sts/17 rows = 4"/10cm using seed st using *Cache*

Remember, your gauge must match for your size to match.

instructions

pattern stitch
Seed stitch: Worked over uneven number of sts). K1, *p1, k1; repeat from * around. Repeat this row for pattern.

to start
Cast on 67 (71, 75) sts. Place marker; join in circle.

Rnds 1-6: K1, *P1, K1; rep from * around.

Next Rnd: Inc 1 st in first st, work seed st over next 31 (33, 35) sts, inc 1 st in next st. Place marker, inc 1 st in next st, seed st to end of round, increasing 1 st in last st. [71 (75, 79)] sts

Work even in seed stitch for 6 rnds.

Inc. Rnd: Inc 1 st in first st, work to 1 st before marker, inc 1 st in each of next 2 sts, work to end, inc 1 st in last st. Rep this inc rnd every 7th rnd twice more. [83 (87, 91)] sts.

Work even until approx 10" (10.25, 10.5)/25cm (26, 27) from beginning.

Armhole Shaping
(RS): K2tog, work seed st to 3 sts before marker, k1, k2tog, turn.

(WS): K2, p2tog, work to last 4 sts, p2tog, k2. Continue with k2 selvage sts each side, dec 1 st each side every other row 3 times more. [34 (36, 40) sts]

Work even until armhole measures 6.5" (7, 7.25)/17cm (18, 18). Place sts on a holder.

front

Rejoin yarn to sts for front and work as for back until armhole measures 4.5" (5, 5.5)/11cm (13, 14).

Neck Shaping (RS)

Work 9 (10, 12) sts, place center 15 sts on a holder for neck, join 2nd ball of yarn and work to end. Working both sides at once, dec 1 st each side of neck every other row 4 times. [5 (6, 8) sts each side] Place sts on a holder.

finishing

Weave tog 5 (6, 8) shoulder sts from holders.

Neckband

Pick up and k 50 sts evenly around neck edge, including sts from holders. Join and work in seed st for 6 rnds. Bind off loosely. Weave in ends.

fun and functional socks

Socks are often a mental roadblock for new knitters, but once you've worked your way through your first pair, you'll be knt- ting your way through dozens of fanciful variations. Add stripes, work heels and toes in contrasting colors, or create contrasting cuffs in novelty yarns.

Marilyn Hastings

skill level

Advanced

size

Custom fit (see below)

materials

Lion Brand's *Wool-Ease*, worsted weight, 80% acrylic/20% wool, 3oz/85g = approx 197yd/180m, 1 to 2 balls*

Knitting needles: one set of dpn in size 7US/4.5mm or size appropriate for your yarn.

1yd/.9m contrasting yarn to hold place of heel until you are ready to knit.

Tapestry needle

*NOTE: One ball will usually make a pair of socks, depending on foot size and leg length you use. To be safe, start with 2 balls (the second ball can be in a second color); you can use the 2nd ball for another pair if 1 ball is enough, or to make contrasting parts if you need more than 1 ball.

gauge

5 sts = 4"/10cm

NOTE: Tighter, more dense, gauge may help your socks wear longer.

instructions

to start

Measure around the ball of your foot and/or your ankle; they will be about the same. (For a specific example, we will use 8"/20cm.) Multiply by your gauge. (8" x 5 sts/1"=40 sts)

Adjust this number slightly to fit the pattern stitch you will use. Remember that knitting is resilient and usually doesn't have to be exact. For basic socks, this pattern uses a k1, p1 ribbing, so you will need an even number for circular knitting. For a well-fitting sock, the ribbing can be continued down the top of the foot. To center that ribbing on the top of the foot, half of the number of stitches should be an odd number. (Use 42 sts, an even number since half of 42 is 21, an odd number.)

CO loosely, using a method that stretches and recovers well. (Cast 42 sts onto dpn.)

Join into a circle, being careful that the stitches are not twisted.

K1, p1 rib for the length of the sock top.

Continue ribbing on the top of the foot on about one-fourth of the stitches, with a purl stitch at each side, while the other three-fourths of the stitches change to st st. (Rib 11 sts, st st on 31 sts.)

After about .5"/1cm, knit the strand of contrasting yarn across the st sts; this is where the heel will be knit later. Knit over that contrasting/place-holding yarn with your sock yarn, and continue knitting the tube for the foot in ribbing and st st as established.

About 2"/5cm before the end of the foot, begin decreasing for the toe. Arrange stitches on the needles so the ribbing is centered on one needle; split the st sts between the other 2 needles.

Now continue in st st only and decrease 4 sts every other round. Do the 4 decreases in 1 st in from the division between the top and bottom of the toe. Use ssk at the beginning and k2tog at the end of each side of the top and bottom of the toe.

When you have decreased for about 2"/5cm, weave the remaining sts together. (Weave last 6 sts of the top to last 6 sts of the bottom.)

Carefully remove the contrasting yarn while putting the sts from both sides back on the dpn. Make the heel the same way you made the toe, with the stitches from each side of the removed contrasting yarn, i.e., decrease 4 sts every other round, one stitch in from the sides of the heel. Weave the last 1-1.5"/3-5cm of stitches together.

finishing

With tapestry needle weave in ends and, if necessary, draw together holes that may remain at the beginning of heel.

NOTE: You might want to make the heel before the toe on your first sock, so you can try it on to decide where to start decreasing the toe. You can use the first sock to measure where to start the toe.

variations

* Make your heels and toes in contrasting colors or choose a variegated yarn for stripes.

* Make a short cuff, and stripe it all.

* Create a contrasting lace top, made after a little ribbing at the top of the sock (see far right sock in project photo). This Shetland lace stitch is done on a multiple of 10 sts, so 40 sts were used. The lace pattern is: *k1, yo, k3, (sl1, k2tog, psso), k3, yo, repeat from * around. Knit 1 rnd. Repeat these 2 rnds and center lace panels on front, back, and sides. Change color for the foot, and use contrasting yarn to hold the heel stitches about .5"/1cm after the end of lace. The stitch count wasn't right here to center ribbing on the top of the foot, so the whole foot is worked in st st.

skill level

Intermediate

sizes

34" (36, 38, 40, 42, 44, 46, 48)/86cm (91, 97, 102, 107, 112, 117, 122)

finished measurements

Chest: 41" (43, 45, 47, 49, 52, 53, 55)/104cm (109, 114, 119, 124, 132, 135, 140)

Length: 24" (24.5, 25, 26, 26.5, 27, 27.5, 28)/61cm (62, 64, 66, 67, 69, 70, 71)

materials
for one sweater

Lion Brand's *Wool-Ease Thick and Quick* worsted weight, 80% acrylic/20% wool, 3oz/85g = approx 197yd/180m, 6 (6, 7, 7, 8, 8, 9, 9) balls of Wheat*

Lion Brand's *Wool-Ease Thick and Quick* worsted weight, 80% acrylic/20% wool, 3oz/85g = approx 197yd/180m, 1 (1, 1, 1, 1, 1, 2, 2) balls of Wood*

Knitting needles in size 11 and 13US/8 and 9mm or size needed to obtain gauge.

24"/61cm circular needle in size 11US/8mm

Tapestry needles

gauge

9 sts/16 rows = 4"/10cm

Remember, your gauge must match for your size to match.

*NOTE: Instructions are written for the sweater using Wheat as the main color; for the second version, reverse the yarn amounts for each color.

stripe a match

These fun his and hers sweaters are designed for casual comfort and warmth in reverse stockinette stitch. The body areas of the sweaters are knit from side seam to side seam, with the color patterns reversed in the sweaters.

Catherine Ham

instructions

back

Using MC, and the larger needle, cast on 28 (28, 28, 30, 30, 30, 30, 30) sts and work 1"/2.5 in rev st st for all sizes.

Shape Right Armhole

At the beginning of the next row, WS facing, cast on 22 (22, 23, 24, 25, 25, 26, 27) sts for the armhole. Turn and knit the cast on sts and to the end of the row. [50 (50, 51, 54, 55, 55, 56, 57) sts]

Work in rev st st until the shoulder measures 9.25" (9.25, 10.25, 10.75, 11.25, 11.75, 12.25, 12.75)/ 23cm (23, 26, 27, 29, 30, 31, 32) from the armhole edge (this is the center back).

Join in Wood and work in stripe pattern of 2 rows Wood, 2 rows Wheat, until a further 9.25" (9.75, 10.25, 10.75, 11.25, 11.75, 12.25, 12.5) have been worked.

Shape Left Armhole

WS: At beginning of the next row bind off 22 (22, 23, 24, 25, 25, 26, 27) sts and knit to the end of the row.

Work another 1"/2.5cm for all sizes, continuing stripes.

BO the remaining 28 (28, 28, 30, 30, 30, 30, 30) sts.

front

TIP: Read through the instructions before beginning. This will make it clear how the v-neckline is shaped.

Using Wheat work as given for the back until the shoulder measures 6" (6, 6, 7, 7, 8, 8, 8)/15cm (15, 15, 18, 18, 20, 20, 20) from the armhole edge.

Right Front V-neck Shaping

WS: At neck edge, BO 3 (3, 3, 3, 4, 4, 3, 3) sts, knit to the end of the row.

RS: Purl to last 3 sts before neck edge, purl 2 sts tog, purl 1.

WS: At neck edge, BO 3 (3, 3, 4, 4, 4, 3, 3) sts, knit to the end of the row.

RS: Purl to last 3 sts before neck edge, purl 2 sts tog, purl 1.

WS: At neck edge, BO 3 (3, 3, 4, 4, 4, 3, 4) sts, knit to the end of the row.

RS: Purl to last 3 sts before neck edge, purl 2 sts tog, purl 1.

WS: At neck edge, BO 4 (4, 4, 4, 4, 4, 4, 4) sts, knit to the end of the row.

RS: Purl to last 3 sts before neck edge, purl 2 sts tog, purl 1.

WS: At neck edge, BO 4 (4, 4, 4, 5, 5, 4, 4) sts, knit to the end of the row.

RS: Purl to last 3 sts before neck edge, purl 2 sts tog, purl 1.

WS: At neck edge, size 48/122 only, BO 4 sts.

Center Front Neck

Join in Wood and work in stripe pattern as given for the back, and at the same time.

Left Front V-neck Shaping

Reverse the neck shaping by casting on the required number of sts on the WS rows and increasing 1 stitch on the RS rows until the V-neck shaping is complete. Continue working to match the right front shoulder.

Shape left armhole

Work as given for the back.

sleeves (make 2)

Using smaller needles and MC, cast on 18 (18, 18, 18, 22, 22, 22, 22) and work 2"/5cm in k2 p2 rib for all sizes.

Next row: Increase 2 (2, 4, 4, 2, 2, 4, 4) sts evenly across the row.

[20 (20, 22, 22, 24, 24, 26, 26) sts]

Change to larger needles and work in rev st st.

Sleeve Shaping

Increase 1 st on each side every 2nd row 1 (1, 1, 2, 2, 2, 2, 3) times, then every 4th row 11 times. [44 (44, 46, 48, 50, 50, 52, 54) sts]

Work straight until sleeve measures 18" (18, 18, 19, 19, 19, 20, 20)/46cm (46, 46, 48, 48, 48, 51, 51) from the beginning. BO.

finishing

Block all pieces lightly.

Bottom Band

Using the circular needle, RS facing, pick up and knit approx 56 (60, 64, 66, 68, 68, 72, 72) sts evenly across the bottom of the front.

Work in k2 p2 rib for 2"/5cm. BO loosely in rib.

Repeat for the back.

Neckband

Seam shoulders.

RS facing, using the circular needle, start at the center front V, pick up and knit approx 61 (63, 65, 67, 69, 71, 73, 75) sts evenly around the neck. Work k2 p2 rib back and forth in rows for 1"/2.5cm. BO loosely in rib. Overlap the neckband edges to the right or the left as appropriate and stitch in place neatly.

Join side seams.

Sew up the sleeve seams, leaving 1"/2.5cm open at the top. Pin sleeves into armhole, with open ends of sleeve seams placed to the 1"/2.5cm horizontal edge of armhole. Stitch armhole seam.

Neatly darn loose ends.

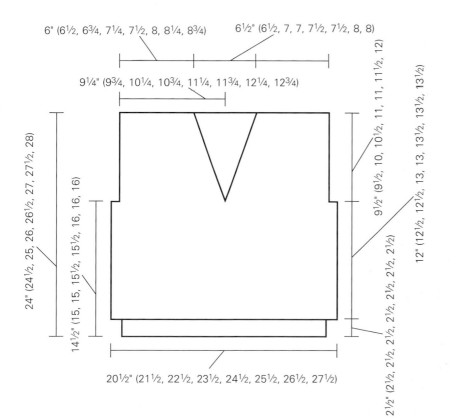

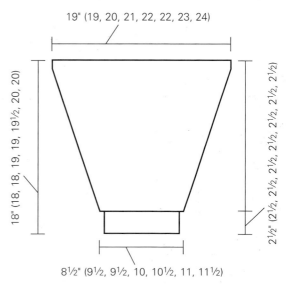

stepping stones afghan

Thick and chunky chenille yarns knit in a slip stitch pattern creates this striking pattern that's easy to master and quick to knit.

Fatema, Khadija and Hajera
Habibur-Rahman

instructions

PATTERN NOTE: When working from chart, work the stitches in the displayed color

special abbreviations

Stockinette stitch (st st): *Knit one row, purl next row; repeat from * until desired length

Sl 1 wyif: Slip 1 st as to purl with yarn in front

Sl 1 wyib: Slip 1 st as to purl with yarn in back

stitches

Stepping Stone Stitch (Chart A, multiple of 4)

to start

Rows 1 and 3 (RS): With Ruby Print, k2, *sl 1 wyib, k3; rep from * to last 2 sts, sl 1 wyib, k1.

Rows 2 and 4: With Ruby Print, k1, *sl 1 wyif, p1, k2; rep from * to last 3 sts, sl 1 wyif, p1, k1.

Rows 5 and 7: With Khaki, k1, *sl 1 wyib, k3; rep from * to last 3 sts, sl 1 wyib, k2.

Rows 6 and 8: With Khaki, k1, *p1, sl 1 wyif, k2; rep from * to last 3 sts, p1, sl 1 wyif, k1.

Rep rows 1-8 for pat.

afghan

With Khaki, cast on 80 stitches. Work st st until the afghan measures 8"/20cm. Work rows 1-8 of the pattern st nine times (sse chart on following page), then repeat rows 1-4 once more. Change to Khaki, work st st for 7"/18cm. Work rows 1-8 nine times, then repeat rows 1-4 once more. Change to Khaki, work st st for 8"/20.3 cm. Bind off.

finishing

Weave the ends in.

fringe

Make 42 in Ruby Print.

skill level

Intermediate

finished measurements

Approx 37 x 57"/.94 x 2.4m

materials

Lion Brand's *Chenille Thick and Quick*, super bulky weight, 91% acrylic/9% rayon, approx 100yd/91.4m, 5 balls of Khaki, 4 balls of Ruby Print

Lion Brand's *Chenille Thick and Quick*, super bulky weight, 91% acrylic/9% rayon, approx 75yd/68.5m, 4 balls of Ruby Print

Knitting needles in size 11US/8mm or size needed to obtain gauge

Tapestry needle

Large crochet hook

Cardboard strip, 5"/13cm wide, for making the fringe

gauge

8 sts/16 rows = 4"/10cm in st st

Remember, your gauge must match for your size to match.

Using Ruby Print, make each fringe group by wrapping yarn 4 times around cardboard. Cut yarn along one edge of the cardboard.

Fold the yarn in half. Insert crochet hook from wrong side to the right side of the afghan, and slip the loop of yarn onto the crochet hook. Draw the loop through the afghan and slip the ends of the yarn through the loop. Pull the ends to tighten.

Attach 21 fringe groups evenly along end side of the afghan and 21 groups evenly on the opposite edge. Trim fringe.

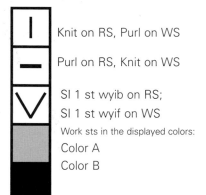

Knit on RS, Purl on WS

Purl on RS, Knit on WS

Sl 1 st wyib on RS;
Sl 1 st wyif on WS
Work sts in the displayed colors:
Color A
Color B

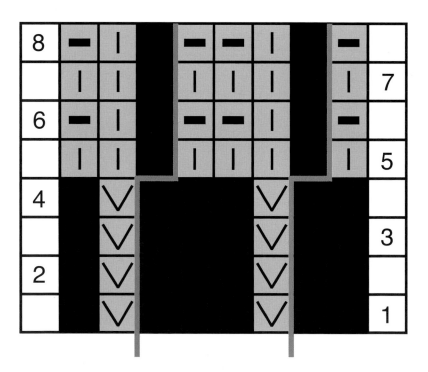

moonlight capelet

Quick to knit, easy to wear, this sweetly simple capelet will add sparkle to any outfit. The simple stitch pattern at the top and bottom is easy to knit and adds a classic touch.

Catherine Ham

instructions

to start

Starting from the bottom, cast on 154 (162, 170) sts loosely and work 1"/2.5cm in st st for the self-edging (This will roll).

Next row WS facing: Knit.

RS facing: K1, *yo, k2tog, repeat from * to the last stitch, k1.

Next row: (WS) knit.

Continue working in st st until the piece measures 5" (6, 7)/13cm (15, 18) from the cast on edge.

Begin Shaping

1st decrease row: RS facing: *k3, k2tog, repeat from * to last 4 (2, 0) sts, knit to end. [124 (130, 136) sts]

All sizes: Work a further 5"/13cm in st st.

2nd decrease row: RS facing: *k2, k2tog, repeat from * to last 0 (2, 0) sts, knit to end. [93 (98, 102) sts]

All sizes: Continue working in st st as before for a further 5"/13cm.

3rd decrease row: RS facing: *k1, k2tog, repeat from * to last 0 (2, 0)sts, knit to end. [62 (66, 68)sts]

All sizes, next row: Purl.

Next two rows: Knit.

RS facing: K1 *yo, k2tog, repeat from * to the last stitch, k1.

Knit 5 more rows and BO all sts loosely.

skill level

Intermediate

sizes

S (M, L)

finished measurements

Length: 15" (16, 17)/38cm (41, 43)

Circumference at neck: 22" (23, 24)/56cm (58, 61)

Circumference of bottom edge: 52" (55, 58)/132cm (140, 147)

materials

Lion Brand's *Moonlight Mohair*, bulky weight, 57% acrylic/28% mohair/9% cotton/6% metallic polyester, 1.75oz/50g = approx 82yd/75m, 4 (5) balls of color of choice

24"/61cm circular knitting needle in size 10.5US/6.5mm or size needed to obtain gauge

3 or 5 buttons, as desired

Tapestry needle

NOTE: The capelet may be fastened with a pin if you prefer; if you choose that option, ignore the instructions for buttons/buttonholes.

gauge

12 sts / 18 rows = 4"/10cm in st st.

Remember, your gauge must match for your size to match.

finishing

Button Band

With RS facing, pick up and knit approx 45 (48, 51) sts along left front of capelet.

NOTE: Do not pick up any stitches below the eyelet edging on the bottom of the capelet in order to allow the self-edging to roll.

Work .5"/1cm in garter stitch and BO loosely.

Starting .5"/1cm below the neck edge, place markers for three or five buttons as you prefer, evenly spaced.

Buttonhole Band

With RS facing, pick up and knit 45 (48, 51) sts along right front of capelet.

Work .5"/1cm in garter stitch and make buttonholes to correspond with the button placement.

NOTE: Buttons with shanks work best. To make a buttonhole: (yo, k2tog). BO all sts when the band measures 1"/2.5cm.

Sew on buttons and darn in yarn ends.

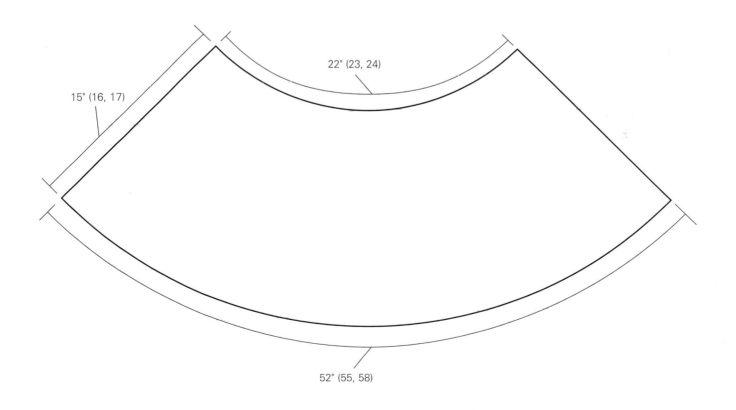

15" (16, 17)

22" (23, 24)

52" (55, 58)

crochet

Welcome to the crochet chapter! Whether you're new to the craft or an expert with hook and yarn, you'll find dozens of projects to make for yourself and as gifts.

Although knitting has received a lot of media attention lately, several studies show crocheters outnumber knitters by at least two to one, and crochet is one of the hottest trends in ready-to-wear clothing. The precise reasons for this popularity difference remain a mystery, but certainly the ease of mastering crochet stitches and the dazzling way they showcase novelty yarns are contributing factors. Crocheted garments are also extremely versatile, looking great in both formal and casual styles.

As you review the projects in this chapter, remember that yarns can be substituted as long as you take care to match the gauge. Yarn colors are included in the patterns, but can be changed to suit your fancy or availability.

Enjoy!

crochet basics

tools & supplies

books

Hooks come in a variety of sizes and materials, and most are so inexpensive you can easily afford to experiment to find your favorties.

The size of the hook is determined by the diameter of its shaft, so the size and shape of the actual hook can vary from company to company. The smallest hook currently available is U.S. size 16 which is .6mm and used for crocheting fine thread. The largest is a plastic jumbo hook in size S which is almost 3⁄4 inch (2cm) thick. Choose jumbo hooks when you're crocheting with several yarns held together as one.

stitch markers

Stitch markers vary from plain, plastic loops to sterling silver wire with semiprecious gemstones. In a pinch, however, you can use anything that marks a place in your crochetwork that you can later remove, such as a contrasting colored yarn or a safety pin. When purchasing stitch markers, look for open ends and avoid ring stitch markers, which are only for sliding between stitches on knitting needles.

tapestry needles

Tapestry needles are large, blunt needles with eyes lage enough to thread with yarn. They're available in several sizes and materials. Choose a size that you can easily thread with your yarn.

yarn!!!

Many of today's yarns are nothing short of incredible. Arranged on store shelves, they form an inviting array of texture and color just waiting to be explored. The hardest part is choosing which yarns you'll use!

beginner yarns

The easiest yarn for beginners is a basic acrylic or wool with an even, springy texture throughout. Choosing pale colors will help you be able to doublecheck the accuracy of your stitches, as errors can be more clearly detected in a single, light to medium color yarn.

crochet hook sizes

Use the following table as a guide for the hook sizes used in this book. Keep in mind that sizes may vary slightly from company to company between letter name and metric size. Begin your project with whichever size hook gives you the intended gauge.

U.S.	METRIC	U.K.
K-10.5	6.5	2
J-10	6	4
I-9	5.5	5
H-8	5	6
G-6	4	7
F-5	3.75	8
E-4	3.5	9
D-3	3.25	10

specialty yarns

Once you have mastered a few basic crochet stitches, you can use almost any yarn. Specialty yarns can pose their own challenges, however, so note the tips below.

Try to crochet loosely with chenille or yarns with slubs (thick bumps in the yarn). Working this way, you'll be able to slide the hook easily into all the stitches.

Many specialty yarns lack the springy quality of wool and acrylic yarns, making them more difficult to handle. If you love a specialty yarn but have trouble crocheting with it, try holding a thin strand of wool or acrylic yarn together with your specialty yarn as you crochet. You'll find that you can manipulate the stitches much easier. Choosing a contrasting or theme-colored yarn is also a great way to add your own color sense and customize your own creation.

yarn sizes

The chart below lists commonly used terms to describe yarn thickness, as well as a general idea of which hook size to use with which yarn. Holding two or more strands of a thin yarn together as one will give you the same result as crocheting with thicker yarn. The texture of the yarn will also make a difference in the gauge of your work. Don't forget to make a swatch and measure to find your gauge. This will help determine the accurate hook size.

yarn types & textures

There is an amazing variety of yarn textures on the market today. Many things can affect a yarn's texture. The following glossary lists of some of these factors.

Bouclé. A bumpy-textured yarn made by plying two or more strands of yarn together so that they create little loops along the yarn's surface.

Chenille. A soft, fuzzy-textured yarn made by plying strands of thread together with many small strands caught perpendicular to the yarn so that they tuft out.

Mercerized. Cotton thread treated with sodium hydroxide which pre-shrinks it, gives it a shiny finish, and allows it to absorb dye colors better.

Mohair. An airy, hairy yarn from the Angora goat. Blends that resemble mohair are called mohair-type yarn.

Ply. The number of strands twisted together to make the finished yarn or thread.

Slub. A thick bump along the yarn made by spinning the yarn more loosely at that point and/or having more fiber at that point. Originally this was not desirable in spinning because it showed the spinner lacked control over the materials. Now it's a design element in many yarns.

Space-dyed. A variegated yarn that has had different colors of dye poured along spaces of the hank of yarn.

Spot-dyed. A variegated yarn that has been treated with spots of dye throughout the skein of yarn.

Variegated. A yarn dyed different colors so that it changes from one color to the next along the length of yarn. This can be done by hand or machine. Machine dying results in a regular repeat of the color pattern while hand dying produces a more random effect.

yarn weights & hook sizes

WEIGHT	DESCRIPTION	HOOK SIZES
Lace	Thread or very thin yarn	16–1 or B
Fingering	Thin sock yarn, about 1/16 inch (1.6mm) thick	B–D
Sport	Traditionally used for baby items and thicker socks	E–G
DK	Between sport weight and worsted weight, relatively new in the U.S., though common in the UK	G–H
Worsted	About 1/8 inch (3 mm) thick, there is also a light (towards DK) and heavy (towards Bulky) version. This is the most famiiar yarn size and probably the size yarn of most crochet projects made in the U.S. in the last 50 years.	H–I
Bulky	A thick, yarn quick to crochet	I–K
Super Bulky	A very thick yarn, 1/4 inch (6 mm) or more in diameter	K and larger

terminology

Many of the basic terms and phrases used in crochet instructions are unique. They regularly appear in abbreviated form. For your convenience, a table of abbreviations appears in this chapter.

Brackets [ ] or parentheses ( ). Used to enclose a sequence of stitches meant to be repeated. You'll be instructed how many times to repeat the sequence following the closing punctuation.

Chain space. To create a space by making a chain between stitches. To stitch in a chain space, pass the hook under the the chain, in the space, and complete the stitch.

Fasten off. To pass through the last loop of yarn.

Foundation. The beginning chain of your project.

Place marker. To slide a stitch marker into the two loops of the top chain of the stitch just completed.

Post. The vertical part of the stitch, more evident in double and triple crochet stitches.

Round. Working around a piece, either a tube or a circle, continuously. You can spiral or join chain up and continue.

Row. A horizontal line of stitches in which a level is completed and there is a step up to the next level.

Shell. A group of stitches formed in the same stitch or space.

Step up. To chain one or more stitches at the end of a row in order to position the yarn and hook at the level of the next row. For single crochet you chain one, for half double crochet you chain two, for double crochet you chain three. This is also called the turning chain. In crochet directions, it is sometimes listed at the end of a row and sometimes at the beginning of the row.

Tail. The loose end of the yarn.

Turning chain. Another name for step up.

Weave in end. With a tapestry needle, stitch the yarn tail into the crochetwork for about 2 inches (5cm) so it's hidden. Stitch back and forth, locking the yarn in place so it won't loosen. Clip the tail close to the crochetwork.

Work even. To continue in a pattern stitch with no increase or decrease until the piece measures the indicated size, or for the number of rows or stitches indicated.

Yarn over. To wrap the yarn around the hook from back to front.

gauge

One of the most common phrases in knitting and crochet books is, "take time to check the gauge." Why is that said so much, and what does it mean? Even though the directions for making each crochet stitch are specific, every person is an individual and has her own slightly different way of holding the yarn and the hook and making the stitches. Because of this, even though two people use the same tools and materials, they may make their stitches a different size. Project instructions are based on a specific stitch size. This doesn't matter too much for a scarf, but for something like a vest, if you don't match the gauge given, your finished piece will end up too small or too large. To check your gauge, make a sample with the materials listed, at least 4 inches (10 cm) square, then measure the stitches and rows to see if they're the same as the gauge listed. If they're too big, you'll need to make another sample using a smaller hook size. Use a larger hook if your stitches are too small. This does take extra time, but it's the only way you'll end up with the finished project you're expecting.

abbreviations

beg	begin/beginning
bpdc	back post double crochet
ch	chain (s)
ch sp	chain space
dc	double crochet
fpdc	front post double crochet
fphtr	front post half triple crochet
hdc	half double crochet
hk	hook
htr	half triple crochet
rep	repeat
rnd	round (s)
sp	space
sc	single crochet
sk	skip
sl st	slip stitch
st	stitch
sts	stitches
tr	triple crochet
yo	yarn over

basic stitches

holding the yarn & hook

To make even stitches, you'll need to be able to control the tension of the yarn and hold your project as you work. A good way to control the tension is to wrap the yarn around the little finger of your left hand, then pass it behind and over your index finger. This way the yarn isn't too tight or loose as you wrap the hook and pull through loops for each stitch. Use your thumb and other fingers on your left hand to hold the work as you make your stitches.

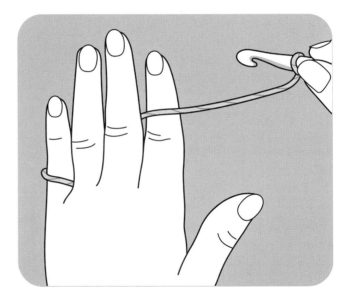

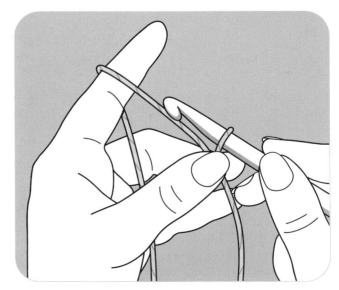

making a slip knot

A slip knot is the first step in almost all crochet projects.

To make a slip knot:

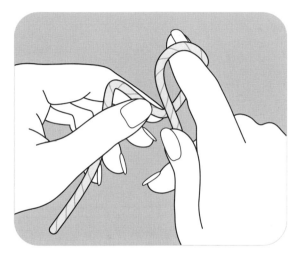

1 Hold the tail of the yarn in your right hand and loop the yarn over itself with the skein-end in your left hand.

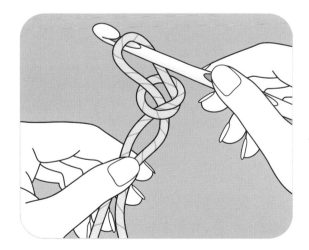

2 With your left hand, push a second loop up through the bottom of the first loop.

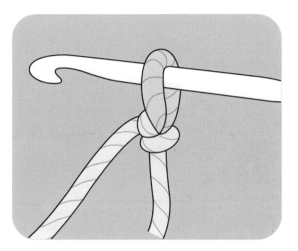

3 Put your hook through the new loop. Tighten the knot by pulling on both ends of the yarn, then pull on the skein end of the yarn to make the slip knot tighten up to the hook.

equivalent terms

Crochet terminology is different in America than in European countries. All of the instructions in this book are written using American standards. The following table shows the equivalent European terms.

U.S. Terms	Equivalent Terms
slip stitch (sl st)	single crochet
single crochet (sc)	double crochet
half double crochet (hdc)	half treble crochet
double crochet (dc)	treble crochet
triple crochet (tr)	double treble

making a chain (ch)

Almost every project in this book begins by making a chain of stitches as a foundation for your crochetwork. To make a chain, first make a slip knot. With the hook through the slip knot, wrap the yarn around the hook (yo), and pull it through the slip knot (loop). Repeat this step to make the number of chains indicated in the instructions.

turning chains

The turning chain is sometimes used as one of the stitches for the row and sometimes it's just to get you to the right level to begin the next row. When the turning chain is used as a stitch on the row, you don't crochet in the first stitch at the beginning of the row (the turning chain takes up this space) and you do crochet in the top chain of the turning chain at the end of the next row.

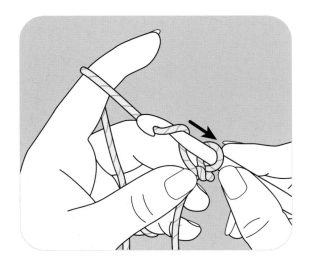

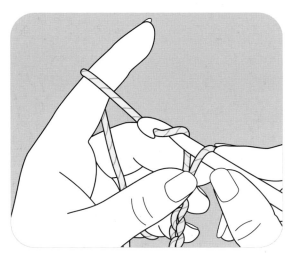

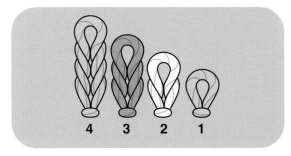

slip stitch (sl st)

Push the hook through the second chain from the hook (1 chain and 1 loop on hook). Wrap the yarn around the hook (yo), and pull through both stitches on the hook (1 loop on hook).

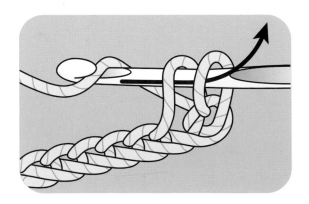

single crochet (sc)

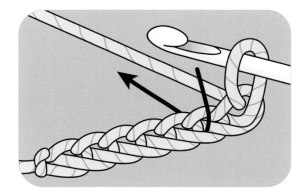

1 Push the hook through the second chain from the hook (1 chain and 1 loop on hook).

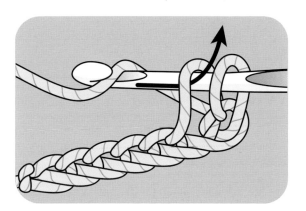

2 Wrap the yarn around the hook (yo), and pull through the chain (2 loops on hook). Wrap the yarn around the hook again, and pull through both loops on the hook (1 loop on hook).

half double crochet (hdc)

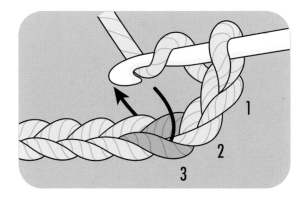

1 Wrap the yarn around the hook, then push the hook through the third chain from the hook (1 chain and 2 loops on hook).

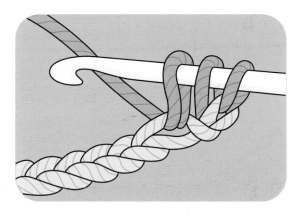

2 Wrap the yarn around the hook (yo), and pull through the chain (3 loops on hook).

3 Wrap the yarn around the hook (yo), and pull through all the loops on the hook (1 loop on hook).

double crochet (dc)

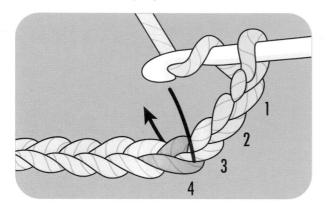

1 Wrap the yarn around the hook, insert the hook through the fourth chain from the hook (1 chain and 2 loops on hook).

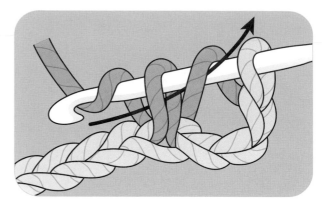

3 Wrap the yarn around the hook (yo), and pull through 2 loops on the hook (2 loops on hook).

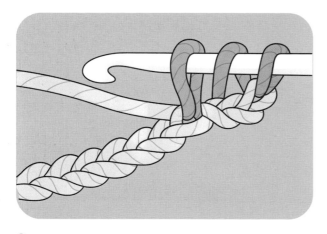

2 Wrap the yarn around the hook (yo), and pull through the chain (3 loops on hook).

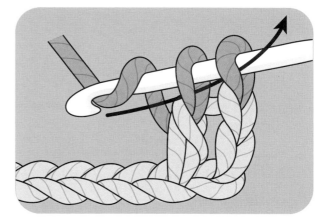

4 Wrap the yarn around the hook (yo), and pull through the last 2 loops on the hook (1 loop on hook).

loosen up, beginners!

Many beginning crocheters pull their stitches very tight, creating uneven, unsightly crochet. Remember that pulling your stitches too tight makes it difficult to complete each stitch because the loops close so tightly they can't slide easily off the hook, which in turn makes it difficult to slide the hook into these tightly formed stitches when you start working in the the next row.

half triple crochet (htr)

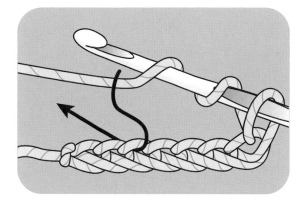

1 Wrap the yarn around the hook (yo) twice, and push the hook through the fifth chain from the hook (1 chain and 3 loops on hook).

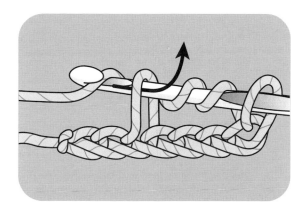

2 Wrap the yarn around the hook (yo), and pull through the chain (4 loops on hook).

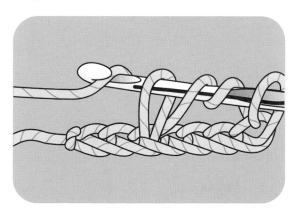

3 Wrap the yarn around the hook (yo), and pull through all the loops on the hook (1 loop on hook).

changing colors

When crocheting with more than one color, it helps to understand what's happening to the stitches as they're made. If you change colors for a single crochet stitch, your new color will slant to the left at the top. The last yarn over (yo) you pull through the last two loops on the hook actually sits between the stitch just made and the next stitch, causing the slant. The next row of stitches passes through this yarn over, breaking up the color pattern and making it look awkward. Because of this, most times you will need to change to the new yarn color for the last yarn over of the stitch before the stitch with the new color. Doing so will give your colorwork a much smoother appearance.

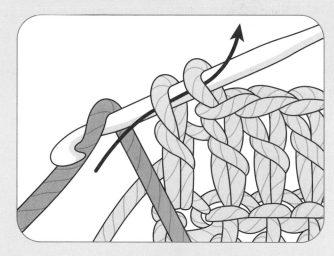

triple crochet (tr)

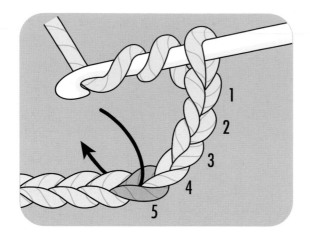

1 Wrap the yarn around the hook (yo) twice, and push the hook through the fifth chain from the hook (1 chain and 3 loops on hook).

2 Wrap the yarn around the hook (yo), and pull through the chain (4 loops on hook).

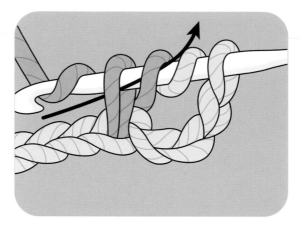

3 Wrap the yarn around the hook (yo), and pull through 2 loops on the hook (3 loops on hook).

4 Wrap the yarn around the hook (yo), and pull through 2 loops on the hook (2 loops on hook).

5 Wrap the yarn around the hook (yo), and pull through 2 loops on the hook (1 loop on hook).

crocheting into rows of stitches

The preceding instructions show you how to begin a row of crochetwork from the foundation chain. To crochet into the following rows of stitches, push the hook under through both sides of the top loop on the edge of the fabric, then complete the stitch as usual.

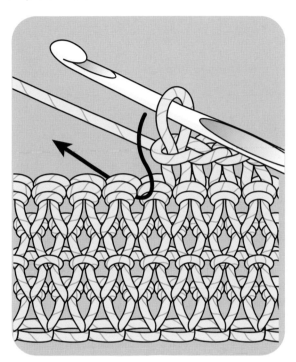

joining into a ring

When beginning a circular project, you'll make a chain and join it into a ring with a slip stitch (sl st). To do this, insert the hook into the first chain you made, yarn over (yo), and pull through the chain and the loop on the hook. Pull your work tightly. Your first row or round may be made by inserting the hook into the ring, rather than into the chains of the ring, to make each stitch.

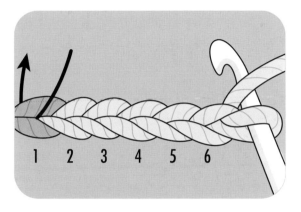

joining at the end of a round

At the end of each round on a circular (not spiralled) project, you'll need to complete the round by joining the first and last stitch together with a slip stitch. To do this you'll make a slip stitch in the last chain of the step up chain.

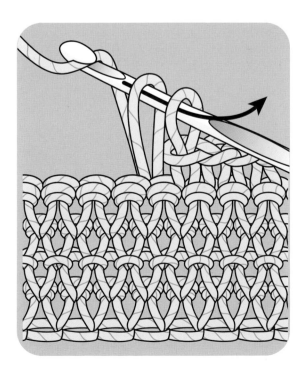

variations

single crochet into the back half of the stitch

The top surface of each stitch is made of a chain. The back half of the stitch is the single strand of the loop which is farthest away from the side you're working. Push the hook into that strand only, then complete the stitch.

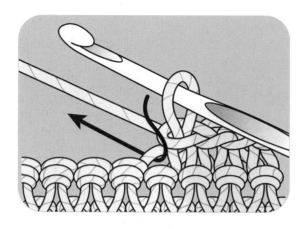

making a shell

Make the indicated number of stitches in the same place, such as 4 double crochet in 1 stitch, or 4 double crochet in 1 chain space. How many stitches are in one place, and how big the space is (1 stitch or a chain space of 3 stitches) will determine how much the shell fans out or stays as a square block of stitches.

threading a needle

To easily thread a tapestry needle with thick, fuzzy yarn, fold the yarn over the needle, then slide the yarn off the needle, and pinch the fold tightly. Next, push the eye of the needle between your pinched fingers, sliding it onto the folded yarn, and pull the yarn through

crocheting backwards

Single crocheting backwards around the edge of a project creates a textured, undulating finished edge. To crochet backwards, insert the hook into the stitch to the right of the beginning of the yarn. Wrap the yarn around the hook and pull through the stitch on the hook. Now, wrap the yarn around the hook and pull through both loops on the hook. Be sure to make very loose stitches so they don't pull on the edges of the piece, causing it to pucker.

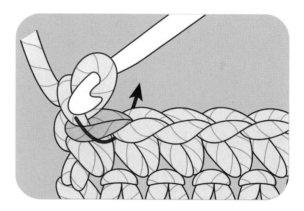

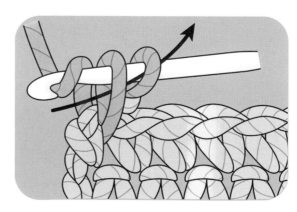

advanced stitches

front post double crochet (fpdc)

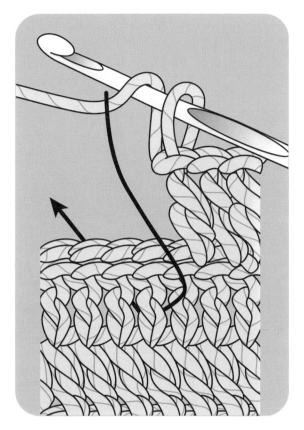

1 Wrap the yarn around the hook, and push the hook behind the post of the stitch in the row below. Complete as in steps 2–4 for double crochet (dc).

back post double crochet (bpdc)

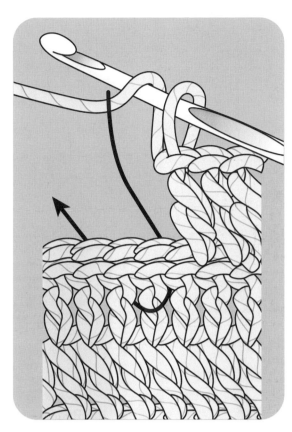

1 Wrap the yarn around the hook. Entering from the back side of the fabric, push the hook around the post of the stitch in the row below. Complete as in steps 2–4 for double crochet (dc).

quality counts

Even, uniform stitches are the mark of well-done crochet. To achieve them, choose crochet hooks that are the same width all the way to the hook, rather than those that taper down and then widen out just before the hook.

front post half triple crochet (fphtr)
1 Wrap the yarn around the hook (yo) twice. Push the hook behind the post of the stitch in the row below.

2 Complete as in steps 2 and 3 for half triple crochet (htr).

fun fur wristlet purse

Marty Miller

Where fashion is concerned, special occasions call for special accessories. Crocheted in show-stopping red eyelash yarn, this small pouch purse defines style while holding all your essentials. The drawstring handle makes this a perfect purse for dangling from a wrist.

instructions

stitches

Chain st (ch)

Single crochet (sc)

Double crochet (dc)

Slip stitch (sl st)

to start

With one strand each of A and B held tog as one, ch 2.

Rnd 1: 6 sc in second ch from hook (6 sc), do not join, work in a spiral marking end of each rnd and moving marker up as work progresses.

Rnd 2: 2 sc in each sc around (12 sc).

Rnd 3: *2 sc in next sc, sc in next sc, repeat from * around (18 sc).

Rnd 4: *2 sc in next sc, sc in each of next 2 sc, repeat from * around (24 sc).

Rnd 5: *2 sc in next sc, sc in each of next 3 sc, repeat from * around (30 sc).

Rnd 6: *2 sc in next sc, sc in each of next 4 sc, repeat from * around (36 sc).

Rnds 7-20: Sc in each sc around (36 sc). At the end of Rnd 20, sl st in next sc to join.

Rnd 21: Ch 5, skip first sc, skip next 2 sc, * dc in next sc, ch 2, skip 2, repeat from * around, sl st in 3rd ch of beg ch-5 (12 ch-2 spaces).

Rnd 22: Ch 3, 2 dc in next ch-2 space, 3 dc in each ch-2 space around, sl st in 3rd ch of beg ch-3 (36 sts).

Rnd 23: Ch 1, sc in each dc around (36 sc), sl st in first sc to join. Fasten off.

drawstring handles (make 2)

With A, ch 100.

Sl st in 2nd ch from hook, sl st in each ch across. Fasten off.

finishing

Tie the ends of each Drawstring in a knot and cut the yarn leaving a 1"/2.5cm tail. Weave the ties over then under the sts in rnd 22, so that the ends of the ties are on opposite sides. Tie the two ends on each side together with an overhand knot.

roomy carryall

Go ahead—trek a country lane or beat the pavement of the urban jungle; this spacious backpack won't disappoint. The thick wool yarn in dirt-defying earth tones not only crochets up fast, but is quite durable—a must for any dependable knapsack. Snug up the nifty drawstring to secure your cargo, fasten the chunky toggle button, and let the journey begin!

Carrie McWhithey

instructions

stitches

Single crochet (sc)

Single crochet increase (sc inc)

Decrease (dc)

to start

Starting with spice, ch 4, join with sl st.

Spiral around, mark beginning of round. Distribute increases evenly around.

Rnd 1: Sc 8 in ring.

Rnd 2: Sc 12. (4 sc and 4 sc inc)

Rnd 3: Sc 15. (9 sc and 3 sc inc)

Rnd 4: Sc 19. (11 sc and 4 sc inc)

Rnd 5: Sc 24. (14 sc and 5 sc inc)

Rnd 6: Sc 29. (19 sc and 5 sc inc)

Rnd 7: Sc 34. (24 sc and 5 sc inc)

Rnd 8: Sc 40. (28 sc and 6 sc inc)

Rnd 9: Sc 46. (34 sc and 6 sc inc)

Rnd 10: Sc 50. (42 sc and 4 sc inc)

Rnd 11: Sc 54. (46 sc and 4 sc inc)

Rnd 12: Sc 60. (48 sc and 6 sc inc)

Rnd 13: Sc 67. (53 and 7 sc inc)

Rnds 14-17: Sc 67.

Rnd 18: Drop spice in front, pick up wheat, sc 67.

Rnd 19: Drop wheat, pick up charcoal, sc 67.

Rnd 20-21: Drop charcoal, pick up spice, sc 67.

skill level

Intermediate

finished size

32"/81cm circumference; 14"/36cm deep

materials

Lion Brand's *Wool-Ease Thick & Quick*, 80% acrylic, 20% wool, 6oz/170g = 106 yd/97m per ball, 3 balls Spice and 1 ball Charcoal

Lion Brand's *Wool-Ease Thick & Quick*, 6oz/170g, 106 yd/97m per ball, 86% acrylic, 10% wool, 4% rayon

Stitch marker

1"/2.5cm glass bead or charm

Rnds 22-23: Sc 67 with charcoal.

Rnd 24: Sc 67 with spice.

Repeat rnds 18-24.

For 9 rnds, sc 67 with spice.

For 3 rnds, sc 67 with charcoal. For 1 rnd, sc 67 with spice.

For 1 rnd, (sc 5, ch 1, skip 1), repeat around.

Last row, sc around. Do not fasten off.

elephant flap

Row 1: Continue with spice, and sc 9, turn.

Row 2: Ch 3, dc 18, turn.

Row 3: Ch 3, dc 18, turn.

Row 4: (Do not chain), skip first stitch and dc 15, skip 1, dc in last stitch, turn.

Row 5: Skip 1, dc 13, skip 1, dc in last stitch, turn.

Row 6: Skip 1, dc 11, skip 1, dc in last stitch, turn.

Row 7: Skip 1, dc 9, skip 1, dc in last stitch, turn.

Row 8: Skip 1, dc 7, skip 1, dc in last stitch, turn.

Row 9: Skip 1, dc 5, skip 1, dc in last stitch, turn.

Row 10: Skip 1, dc 3, skip 1, dc in last stitch, turn.

Rows 11-13: ch 3, dc 3.

Row 14: Ch 3, join with sl st in last stitch to form loop for fastener.

Cut, fasten off, and tie ends, then turn bag inside out.

left strap

Hold bag upright, back facing you. Insert hook, through (into, under, and back out) second stitch to the left of center just above top gray row, sc one, and repeat four more sc across to the left. Turn.Ch 4, dc 4, turn, for 16 rows.

Turn bag upside down. Insert hook into last stitch of strap, making sure the strap isn't twisted.

Insert hook through second spice row past the bottom wheat row, two stitches from center. Sc one, turn bag, insert hook through next stitch in bag, as well as through next stitch in strap and sc one.

Repeat for remaining stitches of strap. Sc once more into bag alone, ch 1, cut, pull through and tie inside bag.

right strap

Repeat instructions for left strap starting in 7th st to the right of center in the spice row just above the gray row.At the end of strap, insert hook through last stitch in strap and through 7th stitch to the right of center in spice row just under last wheat row, sc across, and finish same as left strap.

tie

Using charcoal, ch 115. Cut and fasten off.

finishing

Insert one end of tie through front hole in second row from the top (where you ch 1 and skipped 1), leaving the end coming through front hole, and bring chain through each hole around.

Sew the glass charm on bag where it can come through the loop at the end of the elephant's trunk to secure the pack closed.

three-in-one-poncho

This poncho is crocheted in two identical pieces, then crocheted together at the top, leaving a center neck opening. The rib pattern allows it to be worn in three distinct ways: widthwise so the neckline forms a boat neck, lengthwise so the neckline forms a v-neck, and on the diagonal so the neckline is asymmetrical.

Marty Miller

instructions

stitches

chain st (ch)

double crochet (dc)

front post double crochet (fpdc): Insert hook from front to back to front again around the post of next st, yo, draw yarn through, (yo, draw yarn through 2 loops on hook) twice

half double crochet (hdc)

Make sure you crochet loosely and have an approximate gauge.

rectangle (make 2)

Ch 72.

Row 1 (RS): Dc in 4th ch from hook, dc in each ch across, turn (70 sts).

Row 2: Ch 2, fpdc around the post of each st across to last st, hdc in space bet last 2 sts, turn (70 sts).

Rows 3-35: Rep Row 2. Fasten off.

skill level

Intermediate

finished measurements

One size fits most adults

Each Rectangle = 20 x 38"/51 x 97cm

materials

Lion Brand's *Homespun*, 98% acrylic/2% polyester, 6oz/170g = approx 185yd/169m, 6 balls Antique

Crochet hook size N-15 US/10mm or size needed to obtain gauge

Yarn needle

gauge

7.5 sts and 7 rows in pattern = 4"/10cm. (Because of the stretchiness of the fabric, gauge is not too important with this poncho.

finishing

Joining

With WS of 2 Rectangles facing, matching sts all around, working through double thickness, with long edges on top, join yarn in top right-hand corner, ch 1, sc in each of first 29 sts. Fasten off. Skip next 12 sts for neck opening. Working through double thickness, join yarn in next st, ch 1, sc in each of next 29 remaining sts. Fasten off.

Neck Trim

With RS of Poncho facing, join yarn in one shoulder seam on neck edge, ch 1, sc in each st around, sl st in first sc to join (24 sc). Fasten off. Weave in ends.

moonlight pillow

Use this fun pillow covering to add an instant pop of color and texture to any room. As an accent pillow, it is equally at home on a leather couch as it is on a chenille bedspread. The generous mohair loops exude a playful and relaxed attitude.

Marty Miller

skill level
Intermediate

finished measurements
12 x 12"/30 x 30cm

materials
Lion Brand Yarn's *Moonlight Mohair*, 30% acrylic/25% cotton/10% polyester, 1.75oz/50g = 82yd/75m, 6 balls Glacier Bay

Crochet hook size K10.5 US/6.5mm or size needed to obtain gauge

Contrasting yarn for markers

Tapestry needle

12"/30cm square pillow form

gauge
10 sts and 14 rows in pattern = 4"/10cm

Remember, your gauge must match for the size to match.

instructions

stitches
chain st (ch)

loop st: Worked with WS facing, loops appear on the RS. Loop size is determined by how loosely you wrap yarn once around index finger.

Wrap yarn twice around left index finger behind current row, insert hook in next st, catch both strands of the wrapped yarn with the hook and draw through the stitch, yo, draw yarn through 3 loops on hook (loop st made).

single crochet (sc)

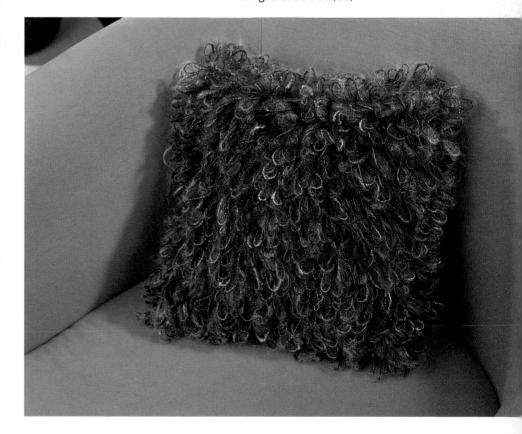

front

Starting at bottom, ch 31.

Row 1 (RS): Sc in 2nd ch from hook, sc in each ch across, turn (30 sc).

Row 2: Ch1, loop st in each sc across, turn (30 loop sts).

Row 3: Ch1, sc in each loop st across, turn (30 sc).

Row 4-39: Rep Rows 2-3 (23 times).

Row 40: Rep Row 2.

back

Back is made in 2 pieces that will overlap, leaving an opening to insert pillow form. Top Half will overlap Bottom Half.

Top Half

Starting at bottom, work same as Front through Row 30. Fasten off.

Bottom Half

Starting at bottom, work same as Front through Row 14. Place a marker at each end of Row 10.

Rows 15-20: Ch 1, sc in each st across, turn (30 sc). Fasten off at end of Row 20.

finishing

Place Top Half of Back over Bottom Half, with RS facing up, and bottom edge of Top Half aligned with markers in Row 10 of Bottom Half. Pin pieces together along side edges. With yarn needle and yarn, sew Top and Bottom Halves together across sides.

With WS of Front and Back facing, matching sts, working through double thickness, join yarn in any corner st, ch 1, *2 loop st in corner st, loop st in each st across to next corner; rep from * around, sl st in first loop st to join.

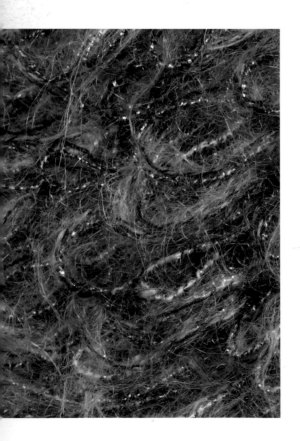

i'm a little tea pot

Cynthia Preston

This whimsical hat will look darling atop of its lucky recipient. The cotton yarn is cozy and durable so it will last through many hours of outdoor play. If desired, add more flowers or change their color to reflect your youngster's favorite.

instructions

stitches

chain st (ch)

half double crochet (hdc)

picot: ch 2, sl st in last sc made

single crochet (sc)

single crochet decrease (sc2tog)

top

Starting at center top, leaving a 4"/10cm tail, wrap A twice around index and middle fingers of left hand for center ring, slide off fingers.

Rnd 1 (RS): Ch 1, work 10 sc in ring, sl st in first sc to join (10 sc). Pull on tail to tighten center ring.

Rnd 2: Ch 1, working in back loops of sts, *sc2tog in next 2 sts; rep from * around, sl st in first sc to join (5 sc). Stuff beg tail into center of Button for filling.

Rnd 3: Ch 1, working in front loops of sts, 2 sc in each sc around, complete last sc with B, drop A to WS, do not join, work in a spiral, place a marker in first st of rnd, move marker up as work progresses (10 sc).

Rnd 4: Working in both loops of sts, *2 sc in next sc, sc in next sc, rep from * around (15 sc).

Rnd 5: Sc in each sc around (15 sc).

Rnd 6: *2 sc in next sc, sc in each of next 2 sc, rep from * around (20 sc).

Rnd 7: Sc in each sc around (20 sc).

Rnd 8: *2 sc in next sc, sc in each of next 4 sc, rep from * around (24 sc).

Rnd 9: Sc in each sc around (24 sc).

Rnd 10: *2 sc in next sc, sc in each of next 5 sc, rep from * around, complete last sc with B, drop A to wrong side (28 sc).

NOTE: There's no need to cut the white yarn, just pick it up again at the end of the round.

skill level

Advanced

finished size

Child's size S (L)

Hat circumference: 19 (22)"/48 (56)cm

materials

Lily's *Sugar 'n Cream*, 100% cotton yarn, 2.5oz/71g = 120yd/109m, 1 ball each of White (A), Yellow (B), Red (C), and Dark Pine (D) or any worsted-weight yarn

Crochet hook size F-5 US/3.75mm or size needed to obtain gauge

Yarn needle

Contrasting yarn for markers

gauge

15 sts = 4"/10cm

Remember, your gauge must match for the size to match.

Rnd 11: With B, working in back loops of sts, *2 sc in next sc, sc in each of next 3 sc; rep from * around, complete last st with A from rnd below, drop B to WS (35 sc).

Rnd 12: With A, working in both loops of sts, sc in each sc around (35 sc).

Rnd 13: *2 sc in next sc, sc in each of next 4 sc, rep from * around (42 sc).

Rnd 14: Sc in each sc around, complete last sc with B from 2 rnds below, drop A to WS (42 sc). Fasten off A.

Rnd 15: With B, *2 sc in next sc, sc in next sc; rep from * around (63 sc).

Size Small Only

Rnds 16-27: Sc in each sc around, complete last sc with A, drop B to WS (63 sc).

Rnd 28: With A, sc in each sc around, complete last sc with B, drop A to WS (63 sc).

Rnd 29: With B, sc in each sc around, complete last sc with A, drop B to WS (63 sc). Fasten off B.

Rnds 30-31: With A, sc in each sc around (63 sc).

Rnd 32: Sl st loosely in each sc around, sl st in next sl st to join. Fasten off A.

Size Large Only

Rnd 16: Sc in each sc around (63 sc).

Rnd 17: *2 sc in next sc, sc in each of next 8 sc, rep from * around (70 sc).

Rnds 18-30: Sc in each sc around, complete last sc with A, drop B to WS (70 sc).

Rnd 31: With A, sc in each sc around, complete last sc with B, drop A to WS (63 sc).

Rnd 32: With B, sc in each sc around, complete last sc with A, drop B to WS (63 sc). Fasten off B.

Rnds 33-34: With A, sc in each sc around (63 sc).

Rnd 35: Sl st loosely in each sc around, sl st in next sl st to join. Fasten off A.

teapot spout (both sizes)

Starting at end of Spout, with B, ch 9 and join into a ring with 1 sl st in first ch.

Rnd 1: Ch 1, sc in top loop of each ch around, sl st in first sc to join, place marker (9 sc).

Rnds 2-4: Ch 1, sc in each sc around (9 sc).

Rnd 5: Ch 1, 2 sc in each of first 2 sc, sc in each of next 5 sc, 2 sc in each of last 2 sc (13 sc).

Rnd 6: Ch 1, sc in each sc around (13 sc).

Rnd 7: Ch 1, 2 sc in each of first 2 sc, sc in each of next 9 sc, 2 sc in each of last 2 sc (17

sc). Fasten off leaving a 12"/30cm sewing length.

sew on spout

With end of round (where marker was) at bottom, align top of last rnd of Spout with Rnd 16 (17) of Teapot. With yarn needle and sewing length, sew last rnd of Spout to Teapot.

handle

Starting at top end, with B, leaving a 12"/30cm sewing length, ch 6.

Row 1: Sc in 2nd ch from hook, sc in each ch across, turn (5 sc).

Rows 2-14 (2-15): ch 1, sc in each sc across, turn (5 sc).

Row 15 (16): Ch 1, sc in first sc, 2 sc in each of next 3 sc, sc in last sc, turn (8 sc).

Row 16 (17): Ch 1, sc in each sc across, turn (8 sc).

Row 17 (18): Ch 1, sc in each of first 5 sc, 2 sc in each of next 2 sc, sc in each of last 5 sc, turn (10 sc). Fasten off, leaving a 12"/30cm sewing length to sew the handle into the tube.

sew on handle

Align top edge of Handle with Rnd 16 (17) of Teapot on opposite side from Spout. With yarn needle and sewing length, sew Handle in place.

large rose

With B, ch 4 and join into a ring with 1 sl st in first ch.

Rnd 1 (RS): Ch 1, work 10 sc in ring, sl st in first sc to join (10 sc). Fasten off B.

Rnd 2: With RS facing, join C in any sc in Rnd 1, ch 3, (2 dc, ch 3, sl st) in same sc, skip next sc, *(sl st, ch 3, 2 dc, ch 3, sl st) in next sc; rep from * around, sl st in first sl st to join (5 petals made). Fasten off leaving a 12"/30cm sewing length.

baby rose

With C, ch 4 and join into a ring with 1 sl st in first ch.

Rnd 1: Ch 1, *sc in ring, ch 2, sl st in last sc made for picot; rep from * 4 times (5 picots made). Fasten off leaving a 12"/30cm sewing length.

leaf (make 2 for small hat; 3 for large hat)

With D, ch 6, sl st in 2nd ch from hook, sc in next ch, hdc in next ch, sc in next ch, sl st in last ch. Fasten off leaving a 12"/30cm sewing length.

assembly

With yarn needle and sewing lengths, sew Roses and Leaves onto Teapot as pictured. Weave in ends.

faux velvet baby afghan, hat, & booties

Nanette Seale

Finally—A fabulous novelty yarn for babies! The tightly tufted chenille used to create these projects feels like velvet, and the pastel color palette is perfect for baby afghans, booties, hats, and jackets.

instructions for afghan

stitches

chain st (ch)

single crochet (sc)

half double crochet (hdc)

slip stitch (sl st)

to start

Ch 72 with D.

Row 1: Sc in 2nd ch from hook, sc in each ch across, turn (71 sc).

Row 2: Ch 1, sc in each st across, turn (71 sc). Fasten off D, join E.

Row 3: With E, ch 1, 2 hdc in first st, skip next st, *2 hdc in next st, skip next st; rep from * across, ending with hdc in last st, turn (71 hdc).

Row 4: Rep Row 3. Fasten off E, join B.

Rows 5-53: Rep Row 3 working in the following color sequence: *2 rows B; 2 rows F; 2 rows C; 5 rows A; 2 rows D; 2 rows E; rep from * twice; then work 2 rows B; 2 rows F

Rows 54-55: With F, ch 1, sc in each st across, turn (71 sc). Fasten off.

border

Rnd 1: With RS facing, join B in any corner st, ch 1, sc evenly around, working 3 sc in each corner, sl st in first sc to join. Fasten off. Weave in ends.

skill level

Intermediate

finished size

Fits 6-12 months; hat circumference = 17 1/2"/44cm

materials

Lion Brand's *Velvetspun*, 100% polyester, 3oz/85g = 54yd/44m, 1 skein each of White (A), Bluebell (B), Pastel Yellow (C), Carnation (D), Lavender (E), and Pastel Green (F)

Crochet hook size K-10.5US/6.5mm

1 yd/.9m double-faced satin or grosgrain ribbon in matching color (.5"/13mm wide)

Contrasting yarn for markers

Yarn needle

gauge

8 sts and 8 rows sc = 4"/10cm

Remember, your gauge must match for the size to match.

stitches

chain st (ch)

single crochet (sc)

to start

Starting at center top, wrap A twice around index finger of left hand for center ring, slide off finger.

Rnd 1: Ch 1, 6 sc in loop, do not join, work in a spiral, place a marker in first st of rnd, move marker up as work progresses (6 sc). Pull on tail to tighten center ring.

Rnd 2: 2 sc in each st around (12 sc)

Rnd 3: *2 sc in next sc, sc in next sc; rep * around (18 sc)

Rnd 4: *2 sc in next sc, sc in each of next 2 sc; rep * around, complete last sc with D (24 sc). Fasten off A.

Rnd 5: With D, *2 sc in next sc, sc in next 3 sts; rep * around, sl st in next sc to join (30 sc). Fasten off D, join E.

Rnd 6: With E, ch 1, sc in each sc around, sl st in first sc to join (30 sc). Fasten off E, join B.

Rnds 7-14: Rep Row 6, working in the following color sequence: 1 row B; 1 row F; 1 row C; 2 rows A; 1 row F; 1 row C; 1 row B.

curlique (make 1 each with b and f)

Leaving a sewing length, ch 11, 3 sc in 2nd ch from the hook, 3 sc in each ch across (30 sc). Fasten off, leaving a sewing length. With sewing lengths, tie both Curliques to center top of Hat.

skill level

Intermediate

finished measurements

4.5"/11cm long, 4.5"/11cm high from sole to edge of cuff

instructions for booties (make 2)

Starting at center bottom, with A, ch 5.

Rnd 1: 3 sc in 2nd ch from hook, sc in each of next 2 ch, 3 sc in last ch, working on oppo-

site side of foundation ch, sc in each of next next 2 ch, sl st in first sc to join (10 sc).

Rnd 2: Ch 1, 2 sc in each of the first 3 sc, sc in next 2 sc, 2 sc in each of the next 3 sc, sc in last 2 sc, sl st in first sc to join (16 sc).

Rnd 3: Ch 1, *2 sc in next sc, sc in next sc; rep from * twice, sc in each st around, sl st in first sc to join (19 sc).

Rnd 4: Working in back loops of sts, ch 1, sc in each sc around, sl st in first sc to join (19 sc).

Rnd 5: Working in both loops of sts, ch 1, sc in each sc around, sl st in first sc to join (19 sc).

Rnd 6: Ch 1, [sc2tog in next 2 sts] 3 times, sc in each st around, sl st in first sc to join (16 sc). Fasten off A, join D.

Rnd 7: With D, ch 1, [sc2tog in next 2 sts] twice, sc in each of next 10 sc, sc2tog in last 2 sts, sl st in first sc to join (13 sc). Fasten off D, join E.

Rnd 8: With E, ch 1, sc in each st around, sl st in first sc to join (13 sc).

Rnds 9-11: Rep Rnd 8, working in the following color sequence: 1 rnd B; 1 rnd F; 1 rnd C.

finishing

Starting and ending at front of Bootie, weave a 15"/38cm length of ribbon through the sts in Rnd 8. Tie in a bow. Trim ends of ribbon to desired length.

denim bucket bag

Marty Miller

Don't let the festive look of the eyelash yarn fool you—this is one sturdy bag. The first few rounds are crocheted with a smaller hook so the stitches are tight, eliminating the need for lining and resulting in self-supporting sides with minimal slouching. So load it up, this bag can take it!

skill level

Intermediate

finished size

Approx 21"/53cm around and 8.5"/22cm deep

materials

Lily's *Sugar 'n Cream*, 100% worsted weight cotton , 2.5oz/71g = 120yd/109m, 3 balls of Cornflower Blue (A) or any worsted weight yarn

Lion Brand's *Fun Fur*, 100% polyester, 1.75oz/50g = 64yd/59m, 1 ball of Indigo (B)

Crochet hook sizes H-8 US/5mm and I-9 US/5.5mm or sizes needed to obtain gauge

Yarn needle

Contrasting yarn for markers

gauge

With H-8 hook and one strand each of A and B held together as one, 10 rnds = 4"/10cm

Remember, your gauge must match for the size to match.

instructions

stitches

chain st (ch)

single crochet (sc)

bag

With H-8 hook and one strand each of A and B held together as one, ch 2.

Rnd 1 (RS): 6 sc in 2nd ch from hook, do not join, work in a spiral, place a marker in first st, move marker up as work progresses (6 sc).

Rnd 2: 2 sc in each sc around (12 sc).

Rnd 3: *2 sc in next sc, sc in next sc; rep from * around (18 sc).**Rnd 4:** *2 sc in next sc, sc in each of next 2 sc, rep from * around (24 sc).

Rnd 5: *2 sc in next sc, sc in each of next 3 sc, rep from * around (30 sc).

Rnd 6: *2 sc in next sc, sc in each of next 4 sc, rep from * around (36 sc).

Rnds 7-15: Continue working in established pattern, increasing 6 sc evenly spaced in each rnd (90 sc at end of Rnd 15).

Rnds 16-20: Sc in each sc around (90 sc).

Rnd 21: With I-9 hook, *sc2tog in next 2 sts, sc in each of next 13 sc; rep from * around (84 sc).

Rnd 22-24: Sc in each sc around (84 sc).

Rnd 25: *Sc2tog in next 2 sts, sc in each of next 12 sc; rep from * around (78 sc).

Rnds 26-28: Sc in each sc around (78 sc).

Rnd 29: *Sc2tog in next 2 sts, sc in each of next 11 sc; rep from * around (72 sc).

149

Rnds 30-42: Sc in each sc around (72 sc). At end of last row, sl st in next sc to join. Fasten off.

handle

With I-9 and one strand each of A and B held together as one, ch 6.

Row 1 Sc in 2nd ch from hook (5 sc).

Row 2: Ch 1, sc in each sc across (5 sc).

Rep Row 2 until Handle measures 28"/71cm from beg (approximately 100 rows) or desired length. Fasten off.

finishing

Place one end of Handle along top edge of Bag, on RS, with end of Handle covering joining at end of last rnd.

With H-8 hook and 1 strand each of A and B held together as one, working through double thickness, join yarn in first st of Handle and corresponding st on Bag, ch 1, matching sts, sc in same st, sc in each of next 4 sts. Fasten off. Without twisting Handle, join other end of Handle to 5 corresponding sts on opposite side of Bag. Weave in ends.

NOTE: You will be working from the right side (outside) of the bag. Because of the nature of the fur yarn, the inside of the bag will be furrier than the outside. If you prefer the furrier look, turn the bag inside out before attaching the handles.

chenille hat & scarf set

If cool weather sneaks up on you or if you need a quick gift,
whip up this snug hat and scarf set. The thick chenille makes
this fashion pair incredibly soft and warm, while the novelty
yarn trim adds a touch of whimsy. This project will yield quick
results and admiring compliments.

Carrie McWithey

skill level

Intermediate

finished measurements

Fits most adults

Hat circumference = 22"/56cm; Length from center top to brim = 10"/25cm

Scarf = 5 x 76"/13 x 193cm

materials

Lion Brand's *Chenille Thick & Quick*, 91% acrylic/9% rayon, 100yd/90m, 3 skeins of Periwinkle (A)

Lion Brand's *Fancy Fur*, 55% polymide/45% polyester, 2 balls of Stained Glass (B)

Crochet hook size J-10/6mm or size needed to obtain gauge

Tapestry needle

gauge

8 sts and 4 rows dc = 4"/10cm

Remember, your gauge must match for the size to match.

instructions for hat

stitches

chain st (ch)

double crochet (dc)

single crochet (sc)

single crochet decrease (sc2tog)

slip stitch (sl st)

NOTE: Hat worked on WS and will be turned inside out to be worn. Carry all colors on outside of work.

to start

Starting at center top, with A, ch 4 and close into a ring with 1 sl st in first ch.

Rnd 1 (WS): Work 10 sc in ring, do not join, work in a spiral, place a marker in first st, move marker up as work progresses (10 sc).

Rnd 2: 2 dc in each sc around (20 dc).

Rnd 3: *Dc in next dc, 2 dc in next dc; rep from * around (30 dc).

Rnd 4: *Dc in each of next 3 dc, 2 dc in next dc; rep from * 6 times, dc in each of next 2 dc (37 dc).

Rnd 5: *Dc in each of next 6 dc, 2 dc in next dc; rep from * 6 times, dc in each of next 2 dc (42 dc).

Rnd 6-9: Dc in each dc around (42 dc).

Rnd 10: Sc in each dc around (42 sc).

Rnd 11: Join one strand of B, working with 1 strand each of A and B held tog as one, *sc in each of next 8 sc, sc2tog in next 2 sts; rep from * 3 times, sc in last 2 sc (38 sc). Fasten off A.

Rnd 12: With B, sc in each sc around, sl st in next sc to join. Fasten off B. Weave in ends. Turn inside out to wear.

instructions for scarf

stitches
chain st (ch)

double crochet (dc)

single crochet (sc)

single crochet decrease (sc2tog)

slip stitch (sl st)

to start
With A, ch 12, turn.

Row 1: Dc in 4th ch from hook, dc in each of next 7 ch, turn (8 dc).

Rows 2-80: Ch 3, dc in each dc across (8 dc). Fasten off, leaving a 4"/10cm tail.

side border
Leaving a 4"/10cm tail, join B in corner dc in last row of Scarf, working across long edge of Scarf, ch 1, sc around the post of row-end st, sc in base of st; rep from * across to corner st (160 sc). Fasten off, leaving a 4"/10cm tail.

Rep Side Border on other long edge of Scarf.

fringe
Cut 4 8"/20cm lengths of B. Using 2 strands for each Fringe, single knot one Fringe in each corner of Scarf, working sewing lengths into Fringe.

Cut 18 8"/20cm lengths of A. Using one strand for each Fringe, single knot one Fringe into each st across each short edge of Scarf. Trim Fringe even as desired.

versatile wrap/overskirt

Wear this soft, open stitch wrap as a capelet or, if you're a fashion maven, tied around your waist as an overskirt. This design is perfect for showcasing your favorite novelty yarn.

Carrie McWithey

instructions

stitches
Stitch (V-st): 1 dc, ch 1, 1dc) in same space as first dc).

to start
With (A), ch 95, cut and fasten off.

Row 1: Skip 25 from end of the chain, work 45 dc, ch 4, turn.

Row 2: (Skip 2, V-st, ch 1), repeat for 14 V-sts, then ch 1, dc in last st.

Row 3: Turn, ch 3, V-st (before first V-st of last row) then ch 1, and V-st between each V-st for 15 V-sts, ch 1, dc in last st.

Row 4: Turn, ch 3, (V-st, ch1) between previous V-sts, dc in last st. (16 V-sts)

Row 5: Turn, ch 3, (V-st, ch1) between previous V-sts, dc in last st. (17 V-sts)

Row 6: Turn, ch 3, dc 55 (3 dc in each V-st, 4 dc between V-sts spread evenly across).

Row 7: Turn, ch 3, dc 57. (55 dc and 2 dc inc)

Row 8: Turn, ch 3, dc 59. (57 dc and 2 dc inc)

Row 9: Turn, ch 4 (skip 1, dc 1, ch 2), repeat across.

Row 10: Turn, ch 1, sc 1 in each dc, 2 sc in ch-2 sp across. Cut and fasten off.

border
Using (B), sc along chain from the end, along side, bottom, other side, and other chain.

finishing
Cut, fasten off, and tie together the strands of the 2 yarns leaving 2"/5cm of yarn at end of chain on each side.

skill level
Intermediate

finished measurements
8"/20cm deep

24"/61cm around top

materials
Patons' *Divine*, 79.5% acrylic/18% mohair/2.5% polyester, 3.5oz/100g = 142yds/129m, 1 ball of Night Sky (A)

Patons' *Cha Cha*, 100% nylon, 1.75oz/50g = 77yds/69m, 1 ball Black (B)

Size J-10 US/6mm crochet hook or size needed to obtain gauge

gauge
6 dc = 4"/10cm

NOTE: Wrap is worked from the top.

Remember, your gauge must match for the size to match.

ribbon yarn purse

Marty Miller

Whether you're on a walking tour of Europe or just running errands on the weekend, this stylish bag will hold all your things with room to spare. The multi-colored ribbon yarn ensures you'll find no shortage of outfits to pair it with. You can easily adjust the strap length to suit your style; over the shoulder or add a few inches and wear it bandolier-style. The purse is crocheted on the bias and edged with a picot stitch.

skill level

Intermediate

finished size

Purse = 9"/23cm wide x 16"/41cm tall on one side; 8"/20cm on the other side

Handle = 26"/66cm long

materials

Lion Brand's *Incredible*, 100% Nylon, 1.75 oz/50 g = 110yd/100m, 5 skeins of Copper Penny

Crochet Hook size K-10.5/6.5mm or size needed to obtain gauge

Yarn needle

gauge

15 sts and 12 rows sc = 4"/10cm

Remember, your gauge must match for the size to match.

instructions

stitches

chain st (ch)

picot: ch 3, sc in 3rd ch from hook

single crochet (sc)

single crochet decrease (sc2tog)

front/back(make 2)

Starting at one bottom corner of Purse, ch 2.

Row 1 (RS): Sc in 2nd ch from hook, turn. (1 sc.

Row 2: Ch 1, 3 sc in next sc, turn. (3 sc)

Row 3: 2 sc in first sc, sc in next sc, 2 sc in last sc, turn. (5 sc)

Rows 4-8: Ch 1, 2 sc in first sc, sc in each sc across to last sc, 2 sc in last sc, turn. (15 sc at end of Row 8)

Row 9: Ch 1, sc in each sc across, turn. (15 sc)

Row 10: Ch 1, 2 sc in first sc, sc in each sc across to last sc, 2 sc in last sc, turn. (17 sc)

Row 11: Ch 1, sc in each sc across, turn. (17 sc)

Rows 12-29: Rep Rows 10-11 nine times. (35 sc at end of Row 29)

Row 30: Ch 1, 2 sc in first sc, sc in each sc across to last 2 sc, sc2tog in last 2 sc, turn. (35 sc)

Row 31: Ch 1, sc in each sc across, turn. (35 sc.

Rows 32-53: Rep Rows 30-31 eleven times. (35 sc at end of Row 53)

Row 54: Ch 1, sc2tog in first 2 sc, sc in each sc across, turn. (34 sc)

Row 55: Ch 1, sc in each of first 32 sc, turn leaving last 2 sts unworked. (33 sc)

Row 56: Ch 1, sc2tog in first 2sc, sc in each sc to the end, turn. (32 sc)

Row 57: Ch 1, sc in each of first 30 sc, turn leaving last sc unworked. (31 sc)

Row 58: Ch 1, sc2tog in first 2 sts, sc in each sc across to last 2 sts, sc2tog in last 2 sts, turn (29 sc). Do not fasten off.

border

With RS of Front and Back facing up, place Front on top of Back, matching sts all around, with last st of each piece at top left-hand corner.

Joining Row: Insert hook in dropped loop of last st of both pieces, with 2 strands of yarn held together as one, leaving

last row of Front and Back open for top, ch 1, working through double thickness, sc evenly across side edge, bottom edge and remaining side edge, working 3 sc in each corner st as needed to keep work flat. Fasten off 1 strand of yarn.

handle

With 1 strand of yarn, sl st in each of first 6 sts along the top edge to where the edge begins to slope down. Turn.

Row 1: Ch 1, working over last 6 sl sts, sc in first sc, sc in each of next 5 sc in last row of Front, sc in each of next 6 sc onlast row of Back, turn. (12 sc)

Row 2: Ch 1, sc in each sc across, turn. (12 sc)

Row 3: Ch 1, sc2tog in first 2 sts, sc in each sc across to last 2 sts, sc2tog in last 2 sts, turn. (10 sc)

Rows 4-5: Rep Rows 2-3. (8 sc at end of Row 5)

Rows 6-80: Ch 1, sc in each sc across, turn. (8 sc)

Joining Row: Without twisting Handle, with WS of Handle and Purse facing, align last row of Handle with corresponding 8 sts centered over side seam on opposite side of top edge, working through double thickness of handle and top edge of Purse, ch 1, sc in each sc across. Fasten off.

Picot Edging: With WS facing, join 1 strand of yarn in first sc on Joining Row at top right-hand corner of Purse, ch 1, sc in first sc, *picot, skip next sc, sc in next sc; rep from * across sides and bottom edges to top right-hand corner, ending with sc in last sc. Fasten off. Weave in ends.

santa's
stocking

If you're ready to brighten up
your winter holidays with a fun
new look, this colorful stocking is
for you. A more traditional look
can be achieved, if desired, by
using only red, green, and white.

Marty Miller

instructions

stitches
chain st (ch)

single crochet (sc)

single crochet decrease
(sc2tog)

slip stitch (sl st)

NOTES: Wind one ball of each
of the Microspun colors (Cherry
Red, Lily White, Royal Blue,
Purple, Turquoise, Lime, and
Buttercup) into two balls, and
use two strands of yarn
throughout the stocking.

To change color: Complete last
sc of the rnd with next color in,
work last sc by working as fol-

skill level

Intermediate

finished size

7"/18cm wide at top x 21"/ 53cm long, excluding toes

materials

Lion Brand's *Microspun*, 100% microfiber acrylic, 2.5oz/71g = 168yd/62m, 3 balls of Cherry Red (A); 1 ball each of Lily White (B), Royal Blue (C), Purple (D), Turquoise (E), Lime (F), and Buttercup (G)

Lion Brand's *Fun Fur*, 100% polyester, 1.75oz/50g = 64yd/59m, 1 ball of White (H)

Crochet hook size I-9 US/5.5mm or size needed to obtain gauge.

gauge

15 sc and 16 rnds = 4"/10cm

lows: insert hook in next st, yo and draw yarn through st, drop first color, yo with next color, draw yarn through 2 loops on hook, sl st in first sc to join.

big toe

NOTE: Work each toe separately, then join them together while you crochet the body of the stocking.

With two strands of G, ch 2.

Rnd 1: 6 sc in the 2nd ch from hook, do not join, work in a spiral, place a marker in first st of rnd, move marker up as work progresses (6 sc).

Rnd 2: 2 Sc in each sc around (12 sc).

Rnds 3-7: Sc in each sc around (12 sc). At the end of Rnd 7, sl st to next sc to join. Fasten off.

little toe (make one each with c, d, e, and f)

With 2 strands of yarn held tog as one, ch 2.

Rnd 1: 6 sc in the 2nd ch from hook, do not join, work in a spiral, place a marker in first st of rnd, move marker up as work progresses (6 sc).

Rnd 2: *2 sc in the next sc, sc in the next sc; rep from * around (9 sc).

Rnds 3-6: Sc in each sc around (9 sc). At the end of Rnd 6, sl st to next sc to join. Fasten off.

stocking body

Rnd 1 (joining rnd): Join 2 strands A, in joining st in last rnd of C toe, ch 1, sc in same st, sc in each of next 4 sc, sc in joining st of D toe, sc in each of next 4 sc of D toe, sc in joining st of E toe, sc in each of next 4 sc of E toe, sc in joining st of F toe, sc in each of next 4 sc of F toe, sc in joining st of Big Toe, sc in each of next 11 sc of Big Toe, sc in same st as last st worked on F toe, sc in each of next 4 sc on F toe, sc in same st as last st worked on E toe, sc in each of next 4 sc on E toe, sc in same st as last st worked on D toe, sc in each of next 4 sc on D toe, sc in same st as last st worked on C toe, sc in each of next 4 sc on C toe, sl st to first sc to join (52 sc).

Rnds 2-4: Ch 1, sc in each sc around, sl st to next sc to join (52 sc). At end of last rnd, complete last st with C, fasten off A.

Rnds 5-74: Rep Rnd 2, working in the following color sequence: *2 rnds C, 2 rnds D, 2 rnds E, 2 rnds F, 2 rnds B, 4 rnds A; rep from * 4 times. Fasten off at end of Rnd 74.

Rnd 75: With WS facing, with 2 strands B and 1 strand H held together as one, join yarn in first sc, ch 1, sc in each sc around, sl st to next sc to join (52 sc).

Rnds 76-82: Ch 1, sc in each sc around, sl st to next sc to join (52 sc). Do not fasten off.

hanging loop

Sl st to center st at back of Stocking, sc in center sc, ch 20, skip 1 sc on edge, sc in next sc, sl st in next st, turn, sc in each of next 20 ch, sl st in next sc, sl st in next sc in Rnd 82. Fasten off. Weave in ends.

loads-of-texture scarf

Marty Mille

With so many lovely novelty yarns available, have you ever found it difficult to select which ones to use in a project? If so, then you'll love making this ultra-soft scarf! Start with a thick chenille and then add as many fun yarns in the same or complementary colors as you desire. The more yarns, the more interest.

instructions

stitches

chain st (ch)

single crochet (sc)

scarf

With A, leaving a 12"/30cm tail, ch 101 loosely.

Row 1: Sc in 2nd ch from hook and each ch across, turn. Fasten off, leaving 12"/30cm tail. Join second yarn, leaving 12" end. Ch 1, turn.

Row 2: Leaving a 12"/30cm tail, join B in first sc, ch 1, sc in each sc across. Fasten off, leaving a 12"/30cm tail.

Rows 3-12: Rep Row 2, working in the following color sequence, leaving a 12"/30cm tail at beg and end of each row: 1 row C; 1 row D; 1 row B & E held together as one; 1 row A; 1 row F; 1 row C; 1 row D; 1 row B & G held together as one; 1 row F; 1 row A. Fasten off.

Add more fringe to each end of each row if desired. Trim fringe to desired length. Knot the ends of the yarn.

skill level

Easy

finished measurements

6"/15cm wide x 68"/1.7m long plus fringe

materials

Lion Brand's *Chenille Thick & Quick*, 91% Acrylic/ 9% Rayon, 100 yd/90m, 1 ball of Terracotta (A)

Lion Brand's *Homespun*, 98% acrylic/2% polyester, 6oz/170g = 185yd/166m, 1 ball of Sierra (B)

Patons' *Bohemian*, 81% polyester/19% acrylic, 2.8oz/80g = 68yd/62m, 1 ball of Copper (C)

Patons' *Divine*, 79.5% acrylic/18% mohair/2.5% polyester, 3.5oz/100g = 142 yd/139m, 1 ball of Orangina (D)

Patons' *Brilliant*, 68% acrylic/19% nylon/12% polyester, 1.75 oz/50g = 166yd/152m, 1 ball of Gold Glow (E)

Bernat's *Frenzy*, 37% nylon/30% acrylic/12% polyester/10.5% alpaca/10.5% mohair, 1.75 oz/50g = 60yd/55m, 1 ball of Outrageous Orange (F)

Bernat's *Matrix*, 62% nylon/38% polyester, 1.75 oz/50g = 140yd/128m, 1 ball of Copper Wire (G)

Crochet hook size N-15 US/10mm or size needed to obtain gauge

gauge

6 sc = 4"/10cm

Remember, your gauge must match for the size to match.

think pink jacket

Crocheted in a spectrum of soft, pink loops with a sassy little kick pleat in the back, this jacket is sure to bring a smile to your face. The jacket is made in one piece, starting from the bottom edge.

Marty Miller

instructions

stitches

chain (ch)

single crochet (sc)

single crochet decrease (sc2tog)

slip stitch (sl st)

Note: Jacket is made in one piece, starting from the bottom edge. There is a little "kick pleat" at the back, so the bottom is started in two pieces which are then joined on the 8th row. Then you divide the fronts from the back and work each section separately. The shoulder seam in crocheted together on the right side of the fabric. The sleeves are then worked onto the jacket—so they may be made shorter or longer if you wish. The sleeves are worked in rounds, on the right side only. You do not turn each round.

skill level

Experienced

finished size

Women's size S, (M, L)

Finished bust: 36" (42, 48)/91cm (107, 122)

Back length: 17" (18, 20)/43cm (46, 51)

Sleeve length: 18" (18, 18.5)/46cm (46, 47)

Armhole depth: 8" (9, 10)/20cm (23, 25)

materials

Patons' *Pooch*, 63% acrylic/27% wool/10% nylon, 2.4oz/68g =

36yd/33m, 12 (15, 18) skeins of Spring Blush

Crochet hook size N-15US/10mm or size to needed to obtain gauge

Tapestry needle

Sewing needle and matching sewing thread

One 1"/25mm button to match (optional)

gauge

5 sts = 3"/8cm; 7.5 rows sc = 4"/10cm

Remember, your gauge must match for the size to match.

bottom edge first half

Starting at bottom edge, ch 31 (35, 37).

Row 1 (WS): Sc in 2nd ch from hook, sc in each ch across, turn. (30 [34, 36] sc)

Row 2-7: Ch 1, sc in each sc across, turn. (30 [34, 36] sc) Fasten off.

bottom edge second half

Work same as Bottom Edge First Half. Do not fasten off.

beg body

Row 8: Ch 1, sc in each sc across, with RS facing, sc in each sc across Row 7 of Bottom Edge First Half (60 [68, 72] sc), turn.

Work even on 60 (68, 72) sc for 8 (9, 11) rows.

first front

Row 1: Ch 1, sc in each of first 15 (17, 18) sc, turn, leaving remaining sts unworked. (15 [17, 18] sc)

Work even on 15 (17, 18) sc for 7 (8, 10) rows.

beg neck shaping

Next Row: Ch 1, sc2tog in first 2 sts, sc in each sc across, turn (14 [16, 17] sc).

Next Row: Ch 1, sc in each sc across, turn. (14 [16, 17] sc)

Rep last 2 rows (3 times) (11 [13, 14] sc at end of last row). Fasten off.

back

Row 1: With RS facing, join yarn in first st to the left of last st made in Row 1 of First Front, ch 1, sc in same st, sc in each of next 29 (33, 35) sc, turn, leaving remaining sts unworked. (30 [34, 36] sc)

Work even on 30 (34, 36) sc for 15 (16, 18) rows. Fasten off.

second front

Row 1: With RS facing, join yarn in first st to the left of last st made in Row 1 of Back, ch 1, sc in same st, sc in each sc across, turn. (15 [17, 18] sc)

Work even on 15 (17, 18) sc for 7 (8, 10) rows.

beg neck shaping

Next Row: Ch 1, sc in each sc across to last 2 sts, sc2tog in last 2 sts, turn. (14 [16, 17] sc)

Next Row: Ch 1, sc in each sc across, turn. (14 [16, 17] sc)

Rep last 2 rows (3 times) (11 [13, 14] sc at end of last row). Fasten off.

shoulder seam

With WS of Front and Back facing, matching sts across shoulders, join yarn in first st on armhole side of shoulder, ch 1, working through double thickness, sc in each st across shoulder. Fasten off. Rep Shoulder Seam across other shoulder.

sleeve

Rnd 1: With RS of jacket facing, join yarn at bottom of armhole, ch 1, work 32 (34, 38) evenly spaced around armhole, sl st in first sc to join. (32 [34, 38] sc)

Rnd 2: Ch 1, sc2tog in first 2 sts, sc in each sc around, sl st in first sc to join. (31 [33, 37] sc)

Rnd 3: Ch 1, sc in each sc around, sl st in first sc to join. (31 [33, 37] sc)

Rnd 4: Ch 1, sc in each sc around to last 2 sts, sc2tog in last 2 sts, sl st in first sc to join. (30 [32, 36] sc)

Rnd 5: Ch 1, sc in each sc around, sl st in first sc to join. (30 [32, 36] sc)

Rnds 6-25: Rep Rnds 2-5 (5 times) (20 [21, 25] sc at end of Rnd 25).

Work even on 20 (21, 25) sc for 7 (7, 9) more rnds. Fasten off.

Rep Sleeve in other armhole opening.

finishing

With sewing needle and sewing thread, sew button to Left Front edge at beg of neck shaping. Weave in ends.

yarn and pattern variation

To make the same jacket design in another yarn and stitch pattern, follow the directions below using Lion Brand's Wool Ease Thick & Quick and a size N/10mm Susan Bates crochet hook.

stitch pattern

UP/DOWN Pattern.

Ch an odd number of stitches.

Row 1: Sc in 2nd ch from hook and in each sc across. Ch 1, turn.

Row 2 (RS): Sc in first sc, dc in next sc, *sc in next sc, dc in next sc. Repeat from * across, ending with a dc. Ch 1, turn.

Row 3: Sc in first dc, dc in next sc, *sc in next dc, dc in next sc. Repeat from * across.

Repeat row 3 throughout.

festival poncho

Kathleen Sams

The new, variegated color tape yarn used in this poncho creates a garment that's quick to make and will complement most everything in your wardrobe.

skill level
Easy

finished size
One size fits most adults.

materials
Moda Dea's *Ticker Tape*, 100% nylon, 1.75oz/50g = 67yd/61m, 5 balls of Festival

Crochet hook size M-13US/9mm or size needed to obtain gauge

Tapestry needle

gauge
2 shells and 4 rows in pattern = 4"/10cm.

Remember, your gauge must match for the size to match.

NOTE: Pattern is worked over a multiple of 7 sts.

instructions

stitches
chain st (ch)

single crochet (sc)

double crochet (dc)

slip stitch (sl st)

rectangle
Ch 42.

Row 1 (RS): 2 dc in 3rd ch from hook, *skip next 3 ch, sc in next ch, ch 3, dc in each of next 3 ch; repeat from * across to last 4 ch, skip next 3 ch, sc in last ch, turn (6 shells made).

Row 2: Ch 3, 2 dc in first sc, *skip next 3 dc, [sc, ch 3, 3 dc] in next ch-3 space; rep from * across, skip next 2 dc, sc in top of turning ch, turn (6 shells made).

Rep Row 2 until Rectangle measures 45"/1.1m from beg. Fasten off.

finishing
Sew the short side of the rectangle to one end of the long side with RS facing. (See diagram.)

Double Fringe

Cut 12"/30cm lengths of yarn. Using 2 strands for Fringe, fold Fringe in half, insert hook from WS to RS in any ch-3 space on outer edge of Poncho, draw folded end of Fringe through space, draw ends through loop on hook and tighten. Place one Fringe in each space around outer edge of Poncho or as desired.

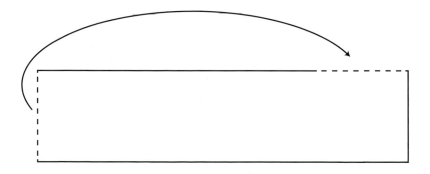

fruit & veggie hats for kids of all sizes

Cynthia Preston

Never will fruit and vegetables receive such a warm reception from little ones as when you serve up these delightful cotton caps. The vivid colors and fun designs are sure to be a hit. Can't decide? Crochet them all!

sizes

Child's size S (L)

finished measurements

Hat circumference: 16" (20)/41cm (51)

materials

Lily's Sugar 'n Cream, 100% cotton yarn, 2.5oz/71g = approx 120yd/109m, 1 ball each of Delft Blue and Hot Green

Crochet hook size F-5 US/3.75mm or size needle to obtain gauge

Tapestry needle

Stitch marker

gauge

15 sts/rnds sc = 4"/10cm

Remember, your gauge must match for the size to match.

instructions for blueberry baby hat

stitches

chain st (ch)

single crochet (sc)

double crochet (dc)

increase (inc)

reverse single crochet (reverse sc)

to start

Starting at stem at top of hat, in green, ch 6.

Rnd 1: Starting in second ch from hook, sl st 4 back down chain, ch 1, 8 sc in last ch, then go around the back of stem and join to ch 1, ch 1.

Rnd 2: 2 sc in each st, join, ch 1.

Rnd 3: Sc in each st, join, ch 1.

Rnd 4: (Inc, 1 sc) around, join, ch 1.

Rnd 5: Sc in each st, join, ch 1.

Rnd 6 (in FRONT loop only): (sk 2 st, 6 dc in one sp, sk 2 st, 1 sc) 4 times, join to first ch, fasten off green.

Rnd 7: With blue, in BOTTOM loop of previous rnd, ch 1 and 1 sc in same sp. (inc, 1 sc) around, place marker and move marker at end of each round to keep track of rounds.

Rnd 8: Sc in each st. (36 sc st)

Rnd 9: (Inc, 2 sc) around.

Rnd 10: Sc in each st.

Rnd 11: (Inc, 3 sc) around.

Rnds 12-28: For an infant size hat, stop increasing here and spiral down to rnd 28.

For a larger hat, make 1 rnd with 1 sc in each st, then make an increase rnd of (inc, 4 sc), pm. Spiral down to rnd 33.

Rnd 29: For small hat, reverse sc in each st, fasten off.

Rnd 34: For large hat, reverse sc in each st, fasten off.

finished size

Child's size S (L)

Hat circumference: 20" (22)/
51cm (56)

materials

Lily's *Sugar 'n Cream*, 100%
cotton, 2.5oz/71g = approx
120yd/109m, 1 ball each of
Yellow and Emerald

Crochet hook size F-5
US/3.75mm or size needed to
obtain gauge

Tapestry needle

Stitch marker

gauge

14 sts/16rnds = 4"/10cm

Remember, your gauge must
match for the size to match.

instructions for
hey lemonhead! hat

stitches

chain st (ch)

half double crochet (hdc)

single crochet (sc)

single crochet increase (sc
inc) = sc twice in same stitch

single crochet decrease (sc
dec) = sc2tog

reverse single crochet
(reverse sc)

stem and leaf

In green yarn ch 12.

Rnd 1: Starting in second ch from hook, sl st 7, ch 6 for leaf, starting in second ch from hook, 1 sl st, 1 sc, 2 hdc, sl st, (leaf made). On original ch, 3 sl st, ch 1.

Rnd 2: In ch 1 of original ch, make 6 sc, going around the back of the stem, join to first ch and fasten off.

hat

Rnd 3: Join yellow, ch 2, 1 sc in same sp as ch 2, then 2 sc in each st (12 sc around, counting ch 2 as a sc), join to ch 1 of beg ch and place marker to begin to spiral rnds.

Rnd 4: 2 sc in each st around, pm. (24 sts around)

Rnds 5-12: 1 sc in each st, move marker.

Rnd 13: (Inc, 2 sc) 8 times around, move marker. (32 sts)

Rnd 14: 1 sc in each st around, move marker.

Rnd 15: (Inc, 3 sc) around, move marker. (40 sts)

Rnd 16: 1 sc in each st, move marker.

Rnd 17: (inc, 4 sc) around, move marker. (48 sts)

Rnd 18: 1 sc in each st, move marker.

Rnd 19: (inc, 5 sc) around, move marker. (56 sts)

Rnd 20: 1 sc in each st.

Rnd 21: (Inc, 6 sc) around. (64 sts)

Rnd 22: 1 sc in each st.

Rnd 23: (Inc, 7 sc) around. (72 sts) Stop increases here for a small size hat; continue straight through round 36 without further increases.

Rnd 24: 1 sc in each st.

Rnd 25: (Inc, 8 sc) around. (80 sts)

Rnds 26-35: 1 sc in each st.

Rnd 36: 1 reverse sc in each st. Fasten off.

skill level
Intermediate

size
Child's size L

finished measurements
Hat circumference: 20"/51cm

materials
Lily's *Sugar 'n Cream*, 100% cotton yarn, 2.5oz/71g = approx 120yd/109m, 1 ball each of Pumpkin and Emerald or any worsted weight yarn

Crochet hook size F-5 US/3.75mm or size needle to obtain gauge

Tapestry needle

Stitch marker

gauge
14 sts/16 rnds sc = 4"/10cm

Remember, your gauge must match for the size to match.

instructions for carrot top hat

stitches

chain st (ch)

single crochet (sc)

single crochet decrease (sc2tog)

slip stitch cord (cord): Ch number indicated, sl st in 2nd ch from hook, sl st in each ch

across, sl st in front loop of last sc made

reverse single crochet (reverse sc)

to start

Starting at the top of the hat, at carrot root, in pumpkin yarn, ch 9.

Rnd 1: Sl st back 4, ch 3, sl st back down ch 3, continue sl sts down ch 9 (2 sl st), ch 1, 4 sc in last ch of ch 9, join to ch 1 to form circle, ch 1.

Rnd 2: (Inc, 1 sc) twice, place marker to indicate end of rnd and move it as each rnd is finished.

Rnd 3: Sc in each st.

Rnd 4: (inc, 2 sc) around. (8 sc)

Rnd 5: Sc in each st.

Rnd 6: (inc, 3 sc) twice around.

Rnd 7: 1 3-st cord, then sc in each st around.

Rnd 8: Go around back of cord to keep it on outside of hat, (inc, 4 sc) around. (12 sc)

Rnd 9: Sc in each st.

Rnd 10: (Inc, 3 sc) around.

Rnd 11: Sc in each st.

Rnd 12: (Inc, 2 sc) around.

Rnd 13: Sc in each st.

Rnd 14: (Inc, 1 sc) around. (30 sc)

Rnd 15: Sc in each st in each st.

Rnd 16: (Inc, 4 sc) around. (36 sc)

Rnd 17: Ac in each st.

Rnd 18: (Inc, 5 sc) around. (42 sc)

Rnd 19: 24 sc, 2-ch cord, 18 sc.

Rnd 20: (Inc, 6 sc) around. (48 sc)

Rnd 21: Sc in each st.

Rnd 22: (Inc, 7 sc) around. (54 sc)

Rnd 23: Sc in each st, make 4-ch cord.

Rnd 24: (Inc, 8 sc) around. (60 sc)

Rnd 25: Sc in each st.

Rnd 26: (Inc, 9 sc) around. (66 sc)

Rnd 27: Sc in each st.

Rnd 28: (Inc, 10 sc) around. (72 sc).

Rnds 29-38: Sc in each st.

Rnd 39: (dec, 10 sc) around. (66 sc)

Rnd 40: Sc in each st, 2 sl st, fasten off orange yarn.

Rnd 41: Join green for carrot leaves around bottom of hat. Ch 1, *1 sc, 5-ch cord, 1 sc, 6-ch cord, 1 sc, 7-ch cord, repeat from * around bottom of hat, fasten off.

instructions for beet-nik beret

stitches

chain st (ch)

single crochet (sc)

single crochet dec (sc2tog)

half double crochet (hdc)

double crochet (dc)

skill level

Intermediate

size

Child's size S (M, L)

finished measurements

Hat circumference: 19" (20, 21)/48 cm (51, 53)

materials

Lily's *Sugar 'n Cream*, 100% cotton, 2.5oz/71g = approx 120yd/109m, 1 ball of Dark Pine; 2 balls of Wine

Crochet hook size F-5 US/3.75mm or size needle to obtain gauge

Tapestry needle

Stitch marker

gauge

15 sts/16 rnds = 4"/10cm

Remember, your gauge must match for the size to match.

to start
Start at leaf cluster at top of hat in dark pine.

Row 1: Leaving a foot-long tail of yarn, ch 18, starting in second ch from hook, sc 17. Ch 7 and turn.

Row 2: Leaves will be crocheted onto the base just made: starting in 2nd ch from hook, sl st, 1 sc, 1 hdc, 1 dc, 1 hdc, 1 sc, turn work and sl st between second and third sc of base row. Make 1 more sl st along base.

Row 3: Ch 8, starting in 2nd ch from hook: 1 sl st, 1 sc, 1 hdc, 2 dc, 2 hdc, sk 2 sts along base and sl st onto next st on base. 1 more sl st.

Row 4: Ch 9, starting in 2nd ch from hook, 1 sl st, 1 sc, 1 hdc, 4 dc, 1 hdc, sk 2 st, sl st, sl st.

Row 5: Ch 10, starting in 2nd ch from hook, 1 sl st, 1 sc, 1 hdc, 5 dc, 1 hdc, sk 2 st, 2 sl st.

Row 6: Ch 11, starting in 2nd ch from hook, 1 sl st, 1 sc, 1 hdc, 6 dc, 1 hdc, sk 2 st, 1 sl st into very last loop of row 1. Fasten off.

finishing leaf cluster
Hide short tail end within first row. Thread long tail onto tapestry needle. Roll strip of leaves

starting at end with largest leaf. Hold cluster together and sew through all thicknesses to other side, go back in again to other side, being sure to catch all layers, and tie off.

hat

Rnd 1: Starting at bottom of leaf cluster, with top of leaves facing you, tie on wine at an outside loop. Ch 1 and 8 sc around base of cluster, join to ch 1 and ch 1.

Rnd 2: 2 sc in each st, place marker to indicate end of rnd and move it as each rnd is finished.

Rnd 3: (Inc, 1 sc) around. (24 sc)

Rnd 4: Sc in each st.

Rnd 5: (Inc, 2 sc) around.

Rnd 6: Sc in each st.

Rnd 7: (Inc, 3 sc) around.

Rnd 8: Sc in each st.

Rnd 9: (inc, 4 sc) around.

Rnd 10: Sc in each st.

Rnd 11: (Inc, 5 sc) around.

Rnd 12: Sc in each st.

Rnd 13: (Inc, 6 sc) around.

Rnd 14: Sc in each st.

Rnd 15: (Inc, 7 sc) around.

Rnd 16: Sc in each st.

Rnd 17: (inc, 7 sc) around.

Rnd 18: Sc in each st, pm.

Rnd 19: (inc, 8 sc) around. (For small hat, make this your last increase and go ahead to rnds 22-24.)

Rnd 20: Sc in each st.

Rnd 21: (inc, 9 sc) around.

Rnds 22-24: Sc in each st. (For large hat, make (inc, 10 sc) at round 23. Then make 3 rounds of 1 sc in each st. Decrease accordingly in following rnds.)

Rnd 25: (dec, 9 sc) around.

Rnd 26: Sc in each st.

Rnd 27: (dec, 8 sc) around.

Rnd 28: Sc in each st.

Rnd 29: (dec, 7 sc) around.

Rnd 30: Sc in each st.

Rnd 31: (dec, 6 sc) around.

Rnd 32: Sc in each st.

Rnd 33: For inner hat band: in back loop only, 1 sc in each st.

Rnd 34: Sc in each st, 2 sl st, fasten off.

finishing

Lightly damp press hatband to inside beret, folding in at back loop ridge.

striped baby blanket

Nothing showers a new baby with love more than a handcrafted gift. The colorful pattern in this striped baby blanket is ideal for varying shades of color.

Nanette Seale

skill level
Intermediate

finished measurements
35 x 35"/89 x 89cm

materials
Red Heart *Baby Clouds*, 100% acrylic, 6oz/170g = 148yd/135m, 4 skein Pale Blue (A)

Red Heart *Super Saver*, 100% acrylic, 8oz/226g = 425yd/389m, 1 skein Blue (B) and 1 skein Light Blue (C)

Crochet hook size J-10US/6mm or size needed to obtain gauge

Tapestry needle

gauge
10 sts/8 rows in pattern = 4"/10cm

Remember, your gauge must match for the size to match.

instructions

stitches
chain st (ch)

single crochet (sc)

half double crochet (hdc)

front post double crochet (fpdc)

back post half double crochet (bphdc)

slip stitch (sl st)With A ch 85.

to start
Row 1: Hdc in 2nd ch from the hook, hdc in each ch across, turn.

Row 2: Ch 1, hdc in each st across, turn. Drop A.

Row 3 (RS): With B, ch 1, sc in 4 sts, long fpdc in corresponding st from 2 rows below, *sc in next 4 sts, long fpdc in next st from 2 rows below, rep from * across, end with sc in last 4 sts, turn.

Row 4: Ch 1, sc in first 4 sts, *bphdc in the next long fpdc, sc in next 4 sts, rep from * across, end with sc in last 4 sts, turn. Drop B.

Row 5: Pick up A, ch 1, hdc in each st across, turn.

Row 6: Ch 1, hdc in each st across, turn. Drop A.

Row 7: With C, ch 1, sc in 4 sts, long fpdc in corresponding st from 2 rows below, *sc in next 4 sts, long fpdc in next st from 2 rows below, rep from * across, end with sc in last 4 sts, turn.

Row 8: Ch 1, sc in first 4 sts, *bphdc in the next long fpdc, sc in next 4 sts, rep from * across, end with sc in last 4 sts, turn. Drop C.

Row 9: Pick up A, ch 1, hdc in each st across, turn.

Row 10: Ch 1, hdc in each st across, turn. Drop A.

Rows 11-76: Rep rows 3-10, ending with an A row. Fasten off B and C. Do not fasten off A.

border
Rnd 1: With right side facing and using A, hdc evenly around with 3 hdc in each corner, join. Fasten off.

Weave in all loose ends.

flirty poncho

Kathleen Sams

The stitch pattern in the body of this poncho showcases the two distinct yarns—a chenille blend and a variegated nylon fur—chosen by the designer. The fringe brings the yarns together in a celebration of color and fiber.

skill level

Intermediate

finished size

One size fits most adults.

24"/61cm long from shoulder to center front point.

materials

Moda Dea's *Dream*, 57% nylon/43% acrylic, 1.75oz/50g = 93yd/85m, 4 balls Winter White (A).

Moda Dea's *Wild!*, 100% nylon, 1.75oz/50g = 103yd/94m, 3 balls Denim (B).

Crochet hook size M-13US/9mm or size needed to obtain gauge.

Yarn needle

gauge

2 shells in pattern = 4"/10cm; 8 rows in pattern = 4"/10cm.

Remember, your gauge must match for the size to match.

NOTE: Pattern is worked over a multiple of 5 + 4 sts.

instructions

stitches

chain st (ch)

single crochet (sc)

double crochet (dc)

slip stitch (sl st)

rectangle (make 2)

With A, ch 69.

Row 1 (RS): Dc in 4th ch from hook, *ch 3, skip next 3 ch, dc in each of next 2 ch; rep from * across, turn (13 ch-3 spaces). Fasten off A.

Row 2: With WS facing, join B in first dc, ch 1, sc in first dc, 5 dc in each ch-3 space across, ending with sc in top of turning ch, turn (13 shells made). Fasten off B.

Row 3: With RS facing, join A in first sc, ch 3, working over sts in last row, dc in next corresponding dc 2 rows below, *ch 3, skip next shell, dc in each of

next 2 dc 2 rows below; rep from * across, turn. Fasten off A.

Rows 4-21: Rep Rows 2-3 (9 times). Fasten off.

finishing

Sew the short side of one rectangle to the one end of the long side of the other rectangle. (See diagram.)

neck edging

With RS facing, join A at side seam on neck edge, ch 1, sc evenly around working sc in each dc and each ch-3 space, sl st in first sc to join. Fasten off A.

Weave in ends.

fringe

Cut 12"/30cm lengths of A and B. Using 2 strands for Fringe, fold Fringe in half, insert hook from WS to RS in any ch-3 space on outer edge of Poncho, draw folded end of Fringe through space, draw ends through loop on hook and tighten. Place one Fringe in each space around outer edge of Poncho or as desired. Trim Fringe to desired length.

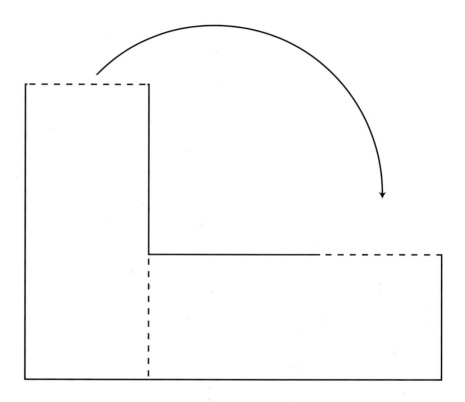

arm warmers

Carrie McWithey

These mutely striped arm warmers harken back to the romantic renaissance age but with a modern twist. They're perfect for when the occasion calls to go sleeveless on a chilly evening. Use a simple, elegant yarn to make a striking eveningwear accessory or go mod by turning up the contrast between the stripes and pairing them with matching leg warmers.

instructions

stitches

chain st (ch)

single crochet (sc)

slip stitch (sl st)

arm warmer

Starting at bottom edge, with A, ch 15 and close into a ring with 1 sl st in first ch. Note: Arm Warmers are worked on WS and will be turned inside out to be worn. Carry all colors on outside of work.

Rnd 1 (WS): Ch 1, work 14 sc in ring, do not join, work in a spiral, place a marker in first st, move marker up as work progresses (14 sc).

Rnd 2-4: Sc in each sc around (14 sc).

Rnd 5: Ch 3, skip next 2 sc, sc in each of next 12 sc. Drop A to WS to be picked up later, join B.

Rnd 6: With B, work 3 sc in ch-3 space, sc in each of next 12 sc (15 sc).

Rnd 7: Sc in each sc around (15 sc). Drop B, pick up A.

Rnds 8-20: Sc in each sc around, working in the following color sequence: *3 rnds A, 2 rnds B; rep from * once, then work 3 rnds A (15 sc). Drop A, pick up B.

Rnd 21: With B, 2 sc in next sc, sc in each of next 15 sc (16 sc).

Rnd 22: Sc in each sc around (16 sc). Drop B, pick up A.

Rnd 23-28: With A, 2 sc in next sc, sc in each of next 16 sc (17 sc). At end of Rnd 28, sl st in next sc to join. Fasten off. Weave in ends. Turn inside out to wear.

skill level

Intermediate

finished size

7"/18cm around wrist

8.5"/22cm around top

14"/36cm long

materials

Paton's *Allure*, 100% nylon, 1.75oz/50g = 47yd/43m, 2 ball of Amethyst (A); and 1 ball of Mink (B)

Crochet hook size J-10 US/ 6mm or size needed to obtain gauge

Tapestry needle

Stitch marker or contrasting yarn for marker

gauge

8 sts and 8 rnds sc = 4"/ 10cm

Remember, your gauge must match for the size to match.

girl's muff & headband

Carrie McWithey

Headbands are all the rage; add a matching muff and you're sure to please that special little girl. Alternate rows of soft mohair and chenille for the body of each project, then complete the fun look with an eyelash yarn trim.

instructions for muff

Row 1: Using two strands of (A) together, ch 18, join with slip stitch.

Row 2: Sc 17 around.

Row 3: Drop 1 strand of (A), pick up 1 strand of Suede, sc 17 around.

Row 4: Drop (A), pick up other Suede, sc 17 around.

Row 5: Drop 1 (B), pick up 1 Divine, sc 17 around.

Row 6: Drop (B), pick up other (A), sc 17 around. Repeat rnds 3-6 three times. Fasten off. Sc around ends with 1 strand of (C) and 1 strand of (B). Tie ends in front, then flip inside out.

instructions for headband

Row 1: Using 1 strand (A), ch 8, turn, sc in 2nd chain from hook, sc 6, turn.

Row 2: Ch1, sc 6, drop (A), pick up (B).

Row 3: Ch 1, sc 6, turn.

Rows 4 – 40: Repeat Row 3, changing yarn every two rows, ending with (B).

To join ends of headband, use (A) sc across going through both ends.

Cut and fasten off, then tie ends.

Sc (C) around both edges. Cut, fasten off, and tie. Turn inside out.

skill level
Easy

finished measurements

Muff: 10"/25cm in circumference and 8"/20cm wide

Headband: 17"/43cm circumference and 3"/7.5 wide

materials

Paton's *Divine*, 79.5% acrylic/18% mohair/2.5% polyester, 3.5oz/100g = 142yds/129m, 1 ball of Floral Fantasy (A)

Lion Brand's *Fun Fur*, 100% polyester, 1.75oz/50g = 64yd/59m, 1 ball Raspberry (B)

Lion Brand's *Lion Suede*, 100% polyester, 3oz/85g = 122yd/112m, 1 ball Rose (C)

Crochet hook size J or size needed to obtain gauge

gauge

Muff: 7 sts/8 rnds = 4"/10cm

Headband: 8 sts/7 rows = 3"/7.5cm

Remember, your gauge must match for your size to match.

ribbon-trimmed cloche

Marty Miller

The style may have been revived from the 20s & 30s, but this is definitely not your grandmother's cloche. The thick wool yarn guarantees warmth and durability while the novelty ribbon yarn around the soft brim and hatband areas adds a touch of festive color.

skill level
Easy

finished size
Fits most adults, 20"/50cm stretchable circumference

materials
Lion Brand's *Wool-Ease Thick & Quick*, 80% acrylic/20% wool, 6oz/170g = 108yd/97m, 1 ball Grass (A)

Lion Brand's *Incredible*, 100% nylon, 1.75oz/50g = 110yd/100m, 1 ball Copper Penny (B)

Crochet hook size N-15 US/10mm or size needed to obtain gauge

Yarn needle

Contrasting yarn for markers

gauge
7 sts = 4"/10cm

Remember, your gauge must match for the size to match.

instructions

stitches
chain st (ch)

single crochet (sc)

cloche
With A, Ch 2.

Rnd 1 (RS): 6 sc in 2nd ch from hook, do not join, work in a spiral, place a marker in first st, move marker up as work progresses (6 sc).

Rnd 2: 2 sc in each sc around (12 sc).

Rnd 3: *2 sc in next sc, sc in next sc; rep from * around (18 sc).

Rnd 4: *2 sc in next sc, sc in each of next 2 sc, rep from * around (24 sc).

Rnd 5: *2 sc in next sc, sc in each of next 3 sc, rep from * around (30 sc).

Rnd 6: *2 sc in next sc, sc in each of next 4 sc, rep from * around (36 sc).

Hat should measure 6.5"/17cm across at end of Rnd 6.

Rnds 7-14: Sc in each sc around (36 sc). At end of last row, sl st in next sc to join. Do not fasten off.

Rnd 15: Join B in first sc, with one strand each of A and B held together as one, ch 1, *sc in sc, ch 1, skip next sc; rep from * around, sl st in first sc to join (18 ch-1 spaces).

Rnd 16: Ch 1, sc in sc, (sc, ch 1) in each ch-1 space around, ending with sc in last ch-1 space, sl st in first sc to join (17 ch-1 spaces). Fasten off B.

Rnd 17: With A only, ch 1, counting each sc and each ch-1 space as a st, *2 sc in next st, sc in each of next 5 sts; rep from * around, sl st in first sc to join (42 sc).

Rnd 18: Ch 1, sc in each of first 3 sc, *2 sc in next sc, sc in each of next 6 sc, rep from * around, ending with sc in each of last 3 sc, sl st in first sc to join (48 sc).

Rnd 19: *2 sc in next sc, sc in each of next 7 sc, rep from * around (54 sc).

Rnd 20: Ch 1, sc in each of first 3 sc, *2 sc in next sc, sc in each of next 8 sc, rep from * around, ending with sc in each of last 4 sc, sl st in first sc to join (48 sc). Fasten off A.

Rnd 21: With RS facing, join B in first sc, ch 1, sc in each sc around (48 sc). Fasten off. Weave in ends.

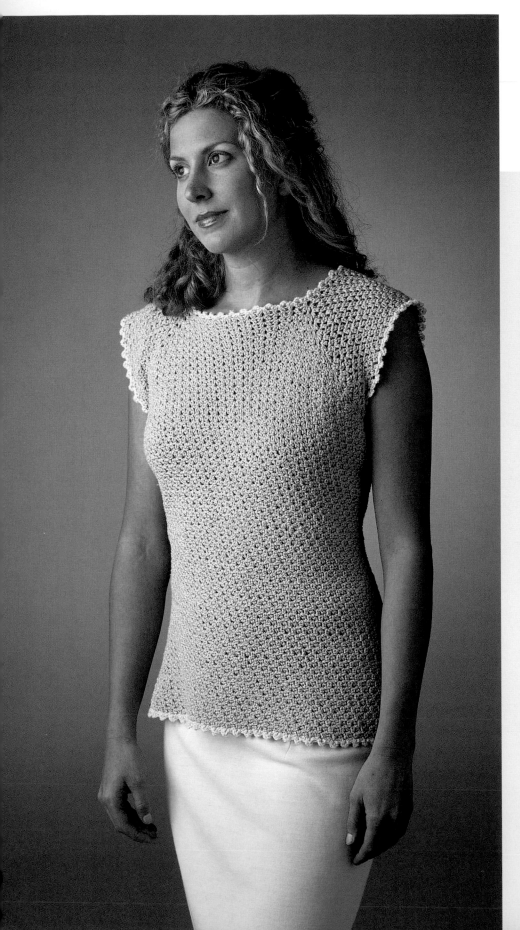

skill level

Intermediate

sizes

Women's size S, (M, L, XL) to fit bust 32-34" (36-38, 40-42, 44-46)

Finished bust: 38" (42, 46, 50)/107cm (117, 124, 132)

Back length: 20.5" (21, 22, 22.5)/52cm (54, 57, 59)

Directions are given for Small. Changes for Medium, Large, and X-Large are in parentheses. When only one number is given, it applies to all sizes.

materials

Patons' *Brilliant*, 69% acrylic/19% nylon/12% polyester, 1.75 oz/50g = approx 166yd/152m, 6 (7, 8, 9) balls Glitter Green (A) and 1 ball of White Twinkle (B)

Crochet hooks H-8/5mm for body and F-5/3.75mm for edging or size to needed to obtain gauge

Tapestry needle

Stitch markers

gauge

7 v-sts/12 rows = 4"/10cm &

Remember, your gauge must match for the size to match.

simply elegant evening top

This cap sleeve evening top features a picot edging in a contrasting color. The construction is seamless, and is crocheted in a spiral from the top down.

Donna May

instructions

stitches

Extended single crochet (esc): Insert hook in stitch, yo and pull up a loop, yo and pull yarn through one loop (2 loops on hook), yo and pull through both loops.

Extended Single Crochet v-stitch (v-st): (esc, ch 1, esc) worked in same stitch or space (referred to in directions simply as v-st).

Slip Stitch (sl st)

Picot: (sl st, ch 2, sl st)

V-st increase (inc v-st): (v-st, ch 1, v-st) worked in v-st

V-st decrease (dec v-st): (1 esc in next v-st) twice

to start

Beginning at Neckline (right back shoulder)

With H hook and color A, ch 64 (68, 72, 76). Taking care not to twist the piece, sl st in first ch to join.

Mark the beginning of rnd 1 (the right back shoulder) with a marker or by tying a short length of contrasting color of yarn around the first stitch in the rnd so you can easily count the rounds as you spiral around.

Rnd 1: (3 ch, 1 esc) in same st as joining [counts as 1 v-st], (sk 1 st and work v-st in next st) 31 (33, 35, 37) times. [32 (34, 36, 38) v-sts]

Rnd 2: The increases will start in this round. (V-st in next v-st) 5 (5, 5, 5) times; inc v-st in ch-1 sp; (v-st in next v-st) 9 (10, 11, 12) times; inc v-st in next ch-1 sp; (v-st in next v-st) 5 (5, 5, 5) times; inc v-st in ch-1 sp; (v-st in next v-st) 9 (10, 11, 12) times; inc v-st in ch-1 sp. [36 (38, 40, 42) v-sts]

Continue spiraling around through rnd 13 (14, 15, 16), making 1 v-st in each v-st along the sides of the raglan rectangle and working an inc v-st in each corner in the ch 1 space between the 2 v-sts in the inc v-st of the previous round. [124 (134, 144, 154) v-sts]

for all sizes

With WS facing you, lay piece flat with long edge as lower edge and right back shoulder (where the marker is) on the lower left as you look at the piece. Your yarn marker will be on the RS against the table. Pick up top edge of the piece (folding to place WS inside) and match to lower edge (creating neck and armholes). Mark ch-1 sp that is at the lower edge of right front of armhole.

size small

Rnd 14: Pick up the piece and with RS facing, continue from your last st worked. Begin rnd 14 by working 1 v-st in the next ch-1 sp to join sides. Work 1 v-st in ea of the next 33 v-sts; work 1 v-st in ch-1 sp to join sides; work 1 v-st in ea of the next 33 v-sts. (68 v-sts)

Rnds 15-19: Work 1 v-st in ea v-st around.

Rnd 20: Work 1 v-st dec over next 2 v-sts, work 1 v-st in ea v-st around to second side (directly under armhole), work 1 v-st dec over two sts, work 1 v-st in ea rem v-st around. (66 v-sts)

Rnds 21–23: Work 1 v-st in ea v-st around.

Rnds 24–35: Rep rnds 20-23 three times. (60 v-sts)

Rnds: 36–37: Work 1 v-st in ea v-st around.

Rnd 38: Inc 1 v-st in next st, work 1 v-st in next v-st around to second side (directly below armhole) and inc 1 v-st, work 1 v-st in ea rem v-st around. (62 v-sts)

Rnd 39: Work 1 v-st in ea v-st around.

Rnds 40–49: Rep rnds 39–40 four times. (70 v-sts)

Rnds 50-61: Rep rnd 39. Join, then fasten off and weave in ends.

size medium
Rnd 15: Pick up the piece and with RS facing, continue from your last st worked. Begin rnd 15 by working 1 v-st in the next ch-1 sp to join sides. Work 1 v-st in ea of the next 36 v-sts; work 1 v-st in ch-1 sp to join sides; work 1 v-st in ea of the next 36 v-sts. (74 v-sts)

Rnds 16-20: Work 1 v-st in ea v-st around.

Rnd 21: Work 1 v-st dec over next 2 v-sts, work 1 v-st in ea v-st around to second side (directly under armhole), work 1 v-st dec over two sts, work 1 v-st in ea rem v-st around. (72 v-sts)

Rnds 22–23: Work 1 v-st in ea v-st around.

Rnds 24–35: Rep rnds 21–23 three times. (64 v-sts)

Rnds: 36–38: Work 1 v-st in ea v-st around.

Rnd 39: Inc 1 v-st in next st, work 1 v-st in next v-st around to second side (directly below armhole) and inc 1 v-st, work 1 v-st in ea rem v-st around. (66 v-sts)

Rnd 40: Work 1 v-st in ea v-st around.

Rnds 41–59: Rep rnds 39–40 five times. (76 v-sts)

Rnds 51-63: Work 1 v-st in ea v-st around. Join, then fasten off and weave in ends.

size large
Rnd 16: Pick up the piece and with RS facing, continue from your last st worked. Begin rnd 16 by working 1 v-st in the next ch-1 sp to join sides. Work 1 v-st in each of the next 39 v-sts; work 1 v-st in ch-1 sp to join sides; work 1 v-st in ea of the next 40 v-sts. (80 v-sts)

Rnds 17–21: Work 1 v-st in ea v-st around.

Rnd 22: Work 1 v-st dec over next 2 v-sts, work 1 v-st in ea v-st around to second side (directly under armhole), work 1 v-st dec over two sts, work 1 v-st in ea rem v-st around. (78 v-sts)

Rnds 22–25: Work 1 v-st in ea v-st around.

Rnds 26–37: Rep rnds 22–25 four times. (72 v-sts)

Rnds: 38–43: Work 1 v-st in ea v-st around.

Rnd 44: Inc 1 v-st in next st, work 1 v-st in next v-st around to second side (directly below armhole) and inc 1 v-st, work 1 v-st in ea rem v-st around. (74 v-sts)

Rnd 45: Work 1 v-st in ea v-st around.

Rnds 46–55: Rep rnds 44-45 five times. (84 v-sts)

Rnds 56-66: Rep rnd 44. Join, then fasten off and weave in ends.

size x-large

Rnd 17: Pick up the piece and with RS facing, continue from your last st worked. Begin rnd 18 by working 1 v-st in the next ch-1 sp to join sides. Work 1 v-st in ea of the next 40 v-sts; work 1 v-st in ch-1 sp to join sides; work 1 v-st in ea of the next 40 v-sts. (82 v-sts)

Rnds 18-22: Work 1 v-st in ea v-st around.

Rnd 23: Work 1 v-st dec over next 2 v-sts, work 1 v-st in ea v-st around to second side (directly under armhole), work 1 v-st dec over two sts, work 1 v-st in ea rem v-st around. (80 v-sts)

Rnds 24–26: Work 1 v-st in ea v-st around.

Rnds 27–38: Rep rnds 23–26 twice. (74 v-sts)

Rnds: 39–44: Work 1 v-st in ea v-st around.

Rnd 45: Inc 1 v-st in next st, work 1 v-st in next v-st around to second side (directly below armhole) and inc 1 v-st, work 1 v-st in ea rem v-st around. (76 v-sts)

Rnd 46: Work 1 v-st in ea v-st around.

Rnds 47–56: Rep rnds 45–45 four times. (86 v-sts)

Rnds 57-68: Rep rnd 46. Join, then fasten off and weave in ends.

picot edging for all sizes

With RS facing and using size F hook and B, sl st to join yarn in a stitch under arm. Ch 1, sc in same st as joining; 1 ch, sk 1 st and work *(sl st, 2 ch, sl st) in next st (one picot made), 1 ch, sk 1 st; rep from * around; sl st to join. Fasten off, weave in ends.

Repeat as above for other arm-hole.

Repeat for neckline, joining yarn at back shoulder.

Repeat in same manner for lower edge, joining yarn at one side.

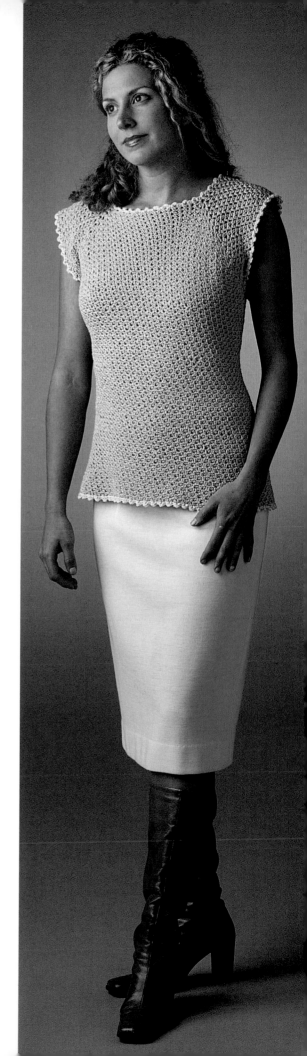

baby clouds overalls

Cute and comfy, these overalls make a great handmade gift. The decorative pockets are trimmed and outlined with a contrasting yarn, and can be embellished further if desired with appliqués or patches.

Nanette Seale

skill level
Intermediate

finished size
12 months

Finished waist = 21"/53cm

Length from waist to cuff edge of pant legs = 17"/43cm

Length from top edge of Bib to waist = 5.5"/14cm

materials
Red Heart *Baby Clouds*, 100% acrylic, 6oz/170g = 148yd/135m, 2 skeins Blue Sky (A)

Red Heart *Super Saver*, 100% acrylic, 8oz/226g = 425yd/389m, 1 skein each of Light Blue (B) and White (C)

Crochet hook sizes G-6US/4cm and J-10US/6mm or sizes needed to obtain gauge

Yarn needle

20"/51cm long polyester zipper to match

Sewing needle

Matching sewing thread

gauge
10 sts and 9 rows sc = 4"/10cm

instructions

stitches
chain st (ch)

single crochet (sc)

slip stitch (sl st)

pants
Starting at waist, with J-10 hook and A, ch 54 and without twisting ch, sl st in first ch to join.

Rnd 1 (RS): Sc in each ch around, sl st in first sc to join (53 sc).

Rnds 2-18: Ch 1, sc in each ch around, sl st in first sc to join (53 sc).

First Leg
Work now progresses in rows.

Row 19: Ch 1, sc in each of first 27 sc, turn (27 sc).

Rows 20-39: Ch 1, sc in each sc across, turn (27 sc). Fasten off at end of Row 39.

Second Leg
Row 19: With RS facing, join A in same st in Rnd 18 where last st of Row 19 of First Leg is worked, ch 1, sc in same sc, sc in each of next 26 sc, turn (27 sc).

Rows 20-39: Ch 1, sc in each sc across, turn (27 sc). Do not fasten off.

Inseam Edging
Row 1: Ch 1, working across row-end st of Second Leg, sc in each row-end st across to crotch, sc in each row-end sc on same side of First Leg. Fasten off.

Rep Inseam Edging across back side edges of Legs.

front bib
Mark center front and center back stitches and sides with stitch markers. On waist edge, locate 15 sts on front of Pants, place a marker in first and last sts.

Row 1: With RS facing, join A in first marked st, ch 1, sc in same sc, sc in each st across to 2nd marker, turn (15 sc).

Rows 2-10: Ch 1, sc in each sc across, turn (15 sc).

Row 11: Ch 1, sc in first sc, ch 1, skip next sc, sc in each of next 9 sc, ch 1, skip next sc, sc in last sc, turn. (The ch-1 spaces are buttonholes.)

Row 12: Ch 1, sc in each st and space across, turn (15 sc). Fasten off A.

First Strap

Row 1: With RS facing, skip first 5 sc on waist edge to the left of last st made in Row 1 of Front Bib (marked st), join A, ch 1, sc in next 3 sts, turn (4 sc).

Row 2: Ch 1, sc in each sc across, turn (4 sc).

Rep Row 2 until Strap measures 12.5"/32cm or desired length. Fasten off A.

second strap

Row 1: With WS facing, skip first 5 sc on waist edge to the left of first st made in Row 1 of Front Bib (marked st), join A in next st, ch 1, sc in same sc, sc in next sc, turn (2 sc).

Work same as First Strap.

edging

With RS facing, using G-6 hook, join C in ch at center back of waist edge, ch 1, sc evenly across working 3 sc in each outside corner st, working across waist edge, around 3 sides of Strap, across Front Bib, around 3 sides of other Strap, and across remainder of waist edge, sl st in first sc to join. Fasten off.

pocket (make 5)

Starting at bottom edge, with G-6 hook and B, ch 11.

Row 1: Sc in 2nd ch from hook, sc in each ch across (10 sc).

Rows 2-10: Ch 1, sc in each sc across, turn (10 sc).

Pocket Edging

Rnd 1: Ch 1, sc evenly around, working 3 sc in each corner st, sl st in first sc to join. Fasten off leaving a sewing length.

finishing

With yarn needle and sewing length, sew one Pocket across sides and bottom edge to center of Front Bib. Sew 2 Pockets to seat of Pants. Sew one Pocket to front of each Leg approximately 3.5" above the last row.

With sewing needle and sewing thread, sew one button to RS of end of each Strap. Sew zipper to WS from cuff edge of one Leg to cuff edge of other leg.

pink clouds
baby sweater

Nanette Seale

This baby sweater is made in two types of yarn:
a fluffy pale pink for the main areas, and a darker pink
for contrasting accent areas.

instructions

stitches

chain st (ch)

single crochet (sc)

half double crochet (hdc)

slip stitch (sl st)

to start

Starting from the top, ch 36 with A.

Row 1: Hdc in 2nd ch from hook, hdc in each ch across, turn.

Row 2 (RS rw): Ch 1, hdc in first st, *2 hdc in next st, hdc in next st, repeat from * across, turn.

Row 3: Ch 1, hdc in each st across, turn. Drop A.

Row 4: Join B, ch 1, hdc in 2 sts, *2 hdc in next st, hdc in next 2 sts, repeat from * across, turn.

Row 5: Ch 1, sc in each st across, turn. Drop B.

Row 6: Pick up A, ch 1, hdc in 3 sts, *2 hdc in next st, hdc n next 3 sts, rep * across, turn.

Row 7: Ch 1, hdc in each st across, turn.

Row 8: Ch 1, hdc in 4 sts, *2 hdc in next st, hdc in next 4 sts, repeat from * across, turn. Drop A.

Row 9: Pick up B, ch 1, sc in each st across, turn.

separating body

Row 10: Ch 1, sc in 12 sts, sk next 25 sts, sc in next 26 sts, sk next 25 sts, sc in last 12 sts, turn. Fasten off B.

Row 11: Pick up A, ch 1, hdc in each st across, turn.

Row 12: Ch 1, hdc in first 4 sts, *2 hdc in next st, hdc in next 4 sts, repeat from * across, turn.

Rows 13-21: Ch 1, hdc in each st across, turn. At end of last row, turn. Fasten off A.

edging

Rnd 1: With RS facing, join B in top stitch of left front edge. Sc

skill level

Intermediate

finished size

12 months

Finished chest = 22"/56cm

Back length = 12"/30cm

Length from shoulder to cuff edge of sleeve = 12"/30cm

materials

Red Heart's *Baby Clouds*, 100% acrylic, 6oz/170g = 148yd/135m, 2 skein Pale Pink (A)

Red Heart's *Super Saver*, 100% acrylic, 8oz/226g = 425yd/389m, 1 skein of Baby Pink (B)

Crochet hook size J-10US/6mm or size needed to obtain gauge

Tapestry needle

gauge

10 sts/8 rows hdc = 4"/10cm

Remember, your gauge must match for the size to match.

evenly around edges—down the front, across the bottom, up the other front, across the neck, with 3 sc in each corner joined.

Rnd 2: Ch 1, sc around evenly with 3 sc in each corner st. Join in first st.

Row 3: Sl st down one side of front, across the bottom edge and sl st on other side of front.

collar

Row 1 (Continue with B): Sc in first st next to the 3 sc corner, *sc in 4 sts, 2sc in next st, repeat from * across neckline, end with sc in last 2 sts before the 3 sc corner, turn.

Row 2: Ch 1, 2 sc in first st, *sc in next 5 sts, 2 sc in next st, repeat from * across, sc in last st, turn.

Row 3: Ch 1, sc in each st across, turn.

Row 4: Ch 1, sc in 6 sts, *2 sc in next st, sc in next 6 sts, repeat from * across, sc in last 3 sts, turn.

Row 5: Ch 1, sc in each st across, turn.

Row 6: Ch 1, (sc 2 sts tog) 2 times, sc across to the last 4 sts, (sc 2 sts tog) 2 times, turn. Fasten off.

Row 7: With RS facing, join B again at bottom of collar and sl st evenly all around collar edge. Fasten off.

sleeves

Rnd 1: Join B, sc 29 sts evenly around sleeve top. Join in first st. Fasten off.

Rnd 2: Join A with a sl st in first st, ch 1, hdc in same st, hdc in each st around. Join in first st.

Rnd 3: Ch 1, hdc in each st around. Join in first st.

Rnd 4: Ch 1, hdc in first st, hdc 2 sts tog, (hdc in next 4 sts, hdc next 2 sts tog) 4 times, hdc in last 2 sts. Join in first st.

Rnd 5: Ch 1, hdc in each st around. Join in first st.

Rnd 6: Ch 1, hdc in first st, hdc next 2 sts tog, (hdc in next 3 sts, hdc next 2 sts tog) 4 times, hdc in last st. Join in first st.

Rnds 7-10: Ch 1, hdc in each st around. Join in first st. Fasten off at end of rnd 10.

Rnd 11: Join B with a sl st in first st, sc in each st around. Join in first st.

Rnd 12: Ch 1, sc in first st, *sc next 2 sts tog, sc in next 2 sts, repeat from * around. Join in first st.

Rnds 13-14: Ch 1, sc in each st around. Join in first st.

Rnd 15: Sl st in each st around. Join in first st. Fasten off.

Repeat for 2nd sleeve.

ties

make 1 for each end of both yarn B stripes = 4

Join B at edge of edging with a sl st, ch for 8"/20cm, sl st back down the chain to the joining. Fasten off.

granny square tote

Marty Miller

Warning: this is not your grandma's tote. While this bag has the forti-
tude and spaciousness of granny's, gone is the gingham, replaced by
saucy citrus-green eyelash yarn. This tote is comprised of nine rounds
of the basic granny square but if you desire a larger or smaller bag, simply make more or less rounds in the squares.

instructions

stitches

chain st (ch)

single crochet (sc)

double crochet (dc)

square (make 2)

With one strand each of A and
B held together as one, ch 4
and close into a ring with 1 sl st
in first ch.

Rnd 1 (RS): Ch 3, 2 dc in ring,
ch 1, [3 dc, ch 1] 3 times in
ring, sl st in 3rd ch of turning ch
to join (4 ch-1 corner spaces).

Rnd 2: Sl st to first corner ch-1
space, ch 3, [2 dc, ch 1, 3 dc,
ch 1] in same ch-1 space [3 dc,
ch 1, 3 dc, ch 1] in each corner
ch-1 space around, sl st in 3rd
ch of turning ch to join (4 ch-1
corner spaces and 1 ch-1 space
on each side).

Rnd 3: Sl st to first corner ch-1
space, ch 3, [2 dc, ch 1, 3 dc] in
same ch-1 space, ch 1, [3 dc,
ch 1] in next ch-1 space, [3 dc,
ch 1, 3 dc, ch 1] in next corner

ch-1 space, [3 dc, ch 1] in next
ch-1 space; rep from * around,
sl st in 3rd ch of turning ch to
join (4 ch-1 corner spaces and 2
ch-1 spaces on each side).

Rnds 4-9: Sl st to first corner
ch-1 space, ch 3, [2 dc, ch 1, 3
dc] in same ch-1 space, ch 1, [3
dc, ch 1] in each ch-1 space
across to next corner, [3 dc, ch
1, 3 dc, ch 1] in next corner ch-
1 space, [3 dc, ch 1] in each ch-
1 space across to next corner;
rep from * around, sl st in 3rd
ch of turning ch to join (4 ch-1
corner spaces and 8 ch-1
spaces on each side at end of
Rnd 9).

gusset and handle

Rnd 10: Ch 1, sc in each dc and
each ch-1 space around, sl st in
first sc to join.

Rnd 11: Ch 1, sc in each of first
4 sc (ending in corner sc), ch 80
(for Handle), skip 35 sc, without
twisting ch, sc in next sc (next

corner sc), sc in each sc around
to beg, sl st in first sc to join.

Rnd 12: Ch 1, sc in each sc and
each ch around, sl st in first sc
to join.

Rnds 13-14: Ch 1, sc in each sc
around. Fasten off.

finishing

With WS of Front and Back
Facing, working through double
thickness of Front and Back,
matching sts in last rnd, join
one strand each of A and B in
first sc below beg of Handle, ch
1, sc in each sc around 3 sides
of Bag to last sc before beg of
Handle on opposite side. Fasten
off. Weave in ends.

skill level
Advanced

finished measurements
12 x 12"/30 x 30cm
plus Handles

materials
Lily's *Sugar 'n Cream*, 100%
cotton yarn, 2.5oz/71g =
120yd/109m, 1 ball of
Hot Green or any worsted
weight yarn (A)

Lion Brand Yarn's *Fun Fur
Prints*, 100% polyester,
1.5oz/40g = 57yd/52m, 5
balls Citrus (B)

Crochet hook size K10.5
US/6.5mm or size needed to
obtain gauge

Yarn needle

gauge
With one strand each of A
and B held together as one,
11 sc = 4"/10cm; square = 12
x 12"/30 x 30cm.

Remember, your gauge
must match for the size to
match.

beach cover-up

A loose-fitting cover-up in a bright cotton yarn is the perfect choice for casual wear on hot summer days. The cover up is crocheted vertically in two identical pieces that are then crocheted together.

Marty Miller

instructions

stitches

chain (ch)

double crochet (dc)

double crochet decrease (dc2tog)

single crochet (sc)

slip stitch (sl st)

body (make 2)

Ch 82 (86, 90).

Row 1: Sc in second ch from hook and each ch across, turn. (81, [85, 89] sc)

Row 2: Ch 4, skip first 2 sc, dc in next sc, *ch 1, skip next sc, dc in next sc. Repeat from * across, ending with dc in last ch-4 sp, turn. (41, [43, 45] dc, including 1st ch-3)

Row 3: Ch 4, skip first dc. Dc in next dc, *ch 1, dc in next dc. Repeat from * across, ending with dc in last ch-4 sp, turn.

Row 4: Ch 4, dc in first dc (increase made), ch 1, dc in next dc, *ch 1, dc in next dc.

Repeat from * across, ending with dc in last ch-4 space, turn. (42, [44, 46] dc)

Rows 5-10: Repeat rows 3 and 4 alternately 3 times. (At the end of row 10 you will have 45, [47, 49] dcs)

Row 11: Repeat row 3.

Small Size Only

At the end of row 11, ch 13 to reach shoulder height. Turn.

Medium Size Only

Rows 12 and 13: Repeat Row 3. At the end of row 13, ch 13 to reach shoulder height. Turn.

Large Size Only

Rows 12 – 15: Repeat Row 3. At the end of row 15, ch 13 to reach shoulder height. Turn.

Row 12 (14, 16): Dc in 6th ch from hook, *ch 1, skip 1 ch, dc in next ch, repeat from * 2 more times. **Ch 1, dc in next dc. Repeat from ** across. Ch 4, turn. (42. [44. 46] dc)

Rows 13 (15, 17)–21(23, 25): Repeat row 3. Fasten off.

Turn the material. You will now be starting the back and connecting the back to row 21 (23, 25).

Row 22 (24, 26): With another strand of yarn, ch 34. Skip 17 dc on row 21. Sc in next dc and every ch-1 space and dc on row 21, until last 5 ch-1 sps, ending with a sc in the 6th dc from the end of row 21 to leave slit at bottom edge. Ch 13, turn.

Row 23 (25, 27): Dc in 6th ch from hook, *ch 1, skip 1 ch, dc in next ch. Repeat from * 2 more times. Ch 1, dc in 1st sc, **ch 1, skip 1 sc, dc in next sc. Repeat from ** until last sc. ***Ch 1, skip 1 ch, dc in next ch, repeat from *** to the end. Ch 4, turn. (42, [44. 46] dc)

Rows 24 (26, 28)–42 (46, 50): Repeat row 3.

Row 43 (46, 51): Sc in each dc and ch-1 sp across, working 2 sc in last ch-4 sp. Fasten off. Make a second piece exactly the same way, but do not fasten off.

back seam
Sl st both sides together at the middle of the back, working one sl st in each sc. This is now the right side of the cover-up. Fasten off.

sleeves (make 2)
You will be working the sleeves directly onto to the right side of the fabric at the opening between the back and the front.

Row 1: With the right side of the fabric facing you, starting at the shoulder edge, join yarn in first st. Ch 4. (You will now be working your stitches in the dc, ch sp, or bottom loops of foundation ch that form the sleeve/armhole edge.) The pattern stitch is *dc, ch 1, skip one st. Repeat from * across. Do not join to first ch-4, turn. (35 dc)

Row 2: Ch 4, skip first dc, *dc in next dc, ch 1. Repeat from * 15 more times. Dc2tog in the next 2 dc, **ch 1, dc. Repeat from ** to end, turn. (34 dc)

Row 3: Ch 4, skip first dc. *dc in next dc, ch 1. Repeat from * across, turn. (34 dc)

Row 4: Ch 4, skip first dc, *dc in next dc, ch 1. Repeat from * 14 more times. Dc2tog, **ch 1, dc in next dc. Repeat from ** across, turn. (33 dc)

Row 5: Repeat row 3.

Row 6: Repeat row 4, but only repeat from the first * 13 times. (32 dc)

Row 7: Repeat row 3.

Row 8: Repeat row 4, repeating from the first * 12 times. (31 dc)

Row 9: Repeat row 3.

Row 10: Repeat row 4, repeating from the first * 11 times. (30 dc)

Rows 11–32 (or longer): Repeat row 3.

Row 33: Ch 1, sc in each dc and ch-1 sp across until last ch-4 sp. 2 sc in last ch-4 sp. Ch 1.

shoulder/sleeve seam
Working on the right side of the sweater with wrong sides together, match the top edges of the sleeve and shoulders, starting at the end of the sleeve and ending at the neck edge. Sc through both layers, making 2 sc in each space at the end of the row so that the seam lies flat. Fasten off.

collar band
Working on the right side of the sweater, join yarn at the right front corner.

Row 1: Ch 1, sc evenly around the neck edge of the sweater, making 2 sc in the space at the end of every row. Sc2tog at each of the 2 front corners and 6 stitches from each shoulder seam in the back. (4 sc2tog total) Turn. (Place a marker at each dec.)

Row 2: Ch 1, sc in each sc to first marker, sc2tog at marker, move marker to this st, sc to next marker behind shoulder seam. Sc2tog at marker. Move marker to this st. Sc to right before center back seam, sc2tog, place new marker. Rght after center seam, sc2tog. Place new marker. *Sc to next marker. Sc2tog. Repeat from * across, ending with sc to end. Turn.

Rows 3-4: Ch 1, sc across, working sc2tog at each marker.

Row 5: Sc across, working sc2tog at first two and last two markers, turn.

Rows 6–8: Repeat Row 5. Fasten off.

hood

Row 1: From wrong side, connect yarn in front corner, of neck edging, ch 4, skip next sc, dc in next sc. *Ch 1, skip next sc, dc in next sc. Repeat from * across, turn.

Row 2: Ch 4, dc in next dc, *ch 1, dc in next dc. Repeat from * across, ending with dc in last ch-4 sp. Turn.

Rows 3–36 (38, 40): Repeat row 2.

seam

Fold hood in half so that one half of the top edge meets the other half of the top edge. Working from the side with the yarn attached (A) to the other side (B), ch 3, sl st in 1st ch-4 sp on side B, sl st in same sp, sl st in next dc, ch 3.

*Sl st in next dc on side A, sl st in next ch-1 sp, sl st in next dc, ch 3,

Sl st in next dc on side B, sl st in next ch-1 sp, sl st in next dc, ch 3.

Repeat from * to end. Fasten off.

collar option

If you want a collar instead of a hood, simply work the hood pattern for 8 rows, or however wide you want the collar.

edging

From the right side, join yarn at a bottom corner. Ch 1, sc in same sp and evenly around, making 3 sc in each of the outside corners, 2 sc in the sp at the ends of the rows, and 1 sc in each dc and ch-1 sp between them in order to keep the edge flat. If you want to add a tie at the neck edge, when you reach the top of the collar band on each side, ch 56 to measure about 15"/40cm, skip 1 ch, sl st in each ch back to the edge, and then continue around. Fasten off.

infant one-piece romper

Made from 100% cotton in gender-neutral colors, this romper makes a lovely gift that's both practical and adorable.

Nanette Seale

skill level

Intermediate

finished size

0-3 months

Finished chest = 15"/38cm

Finished length = 19"/48cm

materials

Paton's *Grace*, 100% cotton, 1.75oz/50g = 136yd/125m, 1 ball each of Snow (A), Apricot (B), and Sky (C)

Crochet hook size E-4US/3.5mm or size needed to obtain gauge

Yarn needle

Three small buttons to match

3 medium/large snaps

Sewing needle

Matching sewing thread

gauge

20 sts and 24 rows sc = 4"/10cm; [2 rows sc, 2 rows hdc] twice in pattern = 2"/5cm or size needed to obtain gauge.

Remember, your gauge must match for the size to match.

instructions

stitches

chain st (ch)

half double crochet (hdc)

half double crochet decrease (hdc2tog)

single crochet (sc)

single crochet decrease (sc2tog)

slip stitch (sl st)

back

Starting at crotch, with C, ch 12.

leg openings

Row 1 (WS): Sc in 2nd ch from hook, sc in each ch across, turn. (11 sc)

Rows 2-3: Ch 1, sc in each sc across, turn. (11 sc)

Row 4: Ch 1, 2 sc in first sc, sc in each sc across to last sc, 2 sc in last sc, turn. (13 sc)

Rows 5-16: Rep Rows 2-4 (4 times). (21 sc at end of Row 16)

Rows 17-18: Rep Row 2. (21 sc)

Row 19: ch 4, sc in 2nd ch from hook, sc in each of next 2 sc, sc in each st across. (24 sc)

Rows 20-24: Rep Row 19. (39 sc)

body

Rows 25-53: Rep Row 2 (39 sc). Fasten off C.

Row 54: With RS facing, working in back loops of sts, join A in back loop of first sc, ch 1, hdc in same st, hdc in each st across, turn. (39 hdc)

Row 55: Ch 1, working in both loops of sts, hdc in each st across, turn. (39 hdc) Drop A to be picked up later.

Row 56: With WS facing, join B in first hdc, ch 1, sc in each st across, turn. Fasten off B.

Row 57: With RS facing, join C in first sc, ch 1, sc in each sc across, turn. (39 sc)

Fasten off C, pick up A.

Rows 58-60: With A, ch 1, hdc in each st across, turn. (39 hdc) Fasten off A.

Row 61: With RS facing, skip first 3 sts, join B in next st, ch 1, sc in same st, sc in each st across to last 3 sts, turn leaving remaining sts unworked. (33 sc) Drop B, join C.

Row 62: With C, ch 1, sc in each st across, turn. (33 sc) Drop C, join A.

Rows 63-65: With A, ch 1, hdc in each st across, turn. (33 hdc) Drop A, pick up B.

Row 66: With B, ch 1, sc in each sc across, turn. (33 sc) Drop B, pick up C.

Row 67: With C, ch 1, sc in each sc across, turn. (33 sc) Drop C, pick up A.

Rows 68-72: Rep Rows 63-67. (33 sts)

Rows 73-74: Rep Rows 63-65. (33 hdc)

right shoulder

Row 75: Ch 1, sc in each of first 11 sts, turn leaving remaining sts unworked. (11 sc) Fasten off A, join B.

Row 76: With B, ch 1, sc in each sc across, turn. (11 sc) Fasten off B, pick up C.

Row 77: With C, ch 1, sc in each sc across, turn. (11 sc) Fasten off C.

left shoulder

Row 75: With RS facing, skip first 11 sts to the left of last st made in Row 75 of Right Shoulder, join A in next sc, ch 1, sc in each sc across, turn. (11 sc) Fasten off A, join B.

Rows 76-77: Rep Rows 76-77 of Right Shoulder.

right front

Work same as Back through Row 67.

Row 68: With A, ch 1, hdc in each of first 15 sts, turn leaving remaining sts unworked. (15 hdc)

Rows 69-70: Ch 1, hdc in each st across, turn. (15 hdc) Drop A, pick up B.

Row 71: With B, ch 1, sc in each sc across, turn. (15 sc) Drop B, pick up C.

Row 72: With C, ch 1, sc in each sc across, turn. (15 sc) Drop C, pick up A.

Rows 73-75: Ch 1, hdc in each st across, turn. (15 hdc) Drop A, pick up B.

right shoulder

Row 76: With B, ch 1, sc in each of first 11 sts, turn leaving remaining sts unworked. (11 sc) Drop B, pick up C.

Row 77: With C, ch 1, sc in each sc across, turn. (11 sc) Fasten off C.

left front

Row 68: With WS facing, skip 3 sts to the left of last st made in Row 68 of Left Front, join A in next st, ch 1, hdc in each of first 18 sts, turn leaving remaining sts unworked. (18 hdc)

Rows 69-75: Rep Rows 69-75 of Right Front. Fasten off A.

left shoulder

Row 76: With WS facing, skip first 4 sts, join B in next st, ch 1, sc in each st across, turn. (11 sc) Drop B, join C.

Row 77: With C, ch 1, sc in each sc across, turn. (11 sc) Fasten off C.

right front band

Row 1: With RS facing, join B in row-end st at end of Row 68 on right-hand side of Right Front, ch 1, work 11 sc evenly spaced across to corner st at end of row 77, turn. (11 sc)

Rows 2-3: Ch 1 sc in each sc across, turn. (11 sc)

Row 4: Sl st in each st across. Fasten off.

left front band

Row 1: With RS facing, join B in row-end st at end of Row 77 on top left-hand side of Left Front, ch 1, work 11 sc evenly spaced across to row-end st in Row 68, turn. (11 sc)

Rows 2-4: Rep Rows 2-4 of Right Front Band.

sleeve (make 2)

Starting at cuff edge, with A, ch 41.

Row 1 Hdc in 2nd ch from hook, hdc in each ch across, turn (40 hdc).

Rows 2-3: Ch 1, hdc in each st across, turn (40 hdc). Drop A, join B.

Row 4: With B, ch 1, sc2tog in first 2 sts, sc in each sc across to last 2 sts, sc2tog in last 2 sts, turn (38 sc). Drop B, join C.

Row 5: With C, ch 1, sc in each sc across, turn (38 sc). Fasten off C.

begin cap

Row 6: With WS facing, skip first 3 sts, join A in next st, ch 1, hdc in same st, hdc in each st across to last 3 sts, turn (32 hdc).

Rows 7-8: Ch 1, hdc2tog in first 2 sts, hdc in each st across to last 2 sts, hdc2tog in last 2 sts, turn (28 hdc at end of Row 8). Drop A, join B.

Row 9: With B, ch 1, sc2tog in first 2 sts, sc in each sc across to last 2 sts, sc2tog in last 2 sts, turn (26 sc). Drop B, join C.

Row 10: With C, ch 1, sc2tog in first 2 sts, sc in each sc across to last 2 sts, sc2tog in last 2 sts, turn (24 sc). Drop C, pick up A.

Rows 11-13: With A, rep Row 7 (18 hdc at end of Row 13).

Rows 14-15: Rep Rows 9-10 (14 sc at end of row 15). Fasten off all colors.

assembly

Weave in ends. With yarn needle and matching yarn, sew shoulder seams. Sew Front to Back across sides from Row 23 to Row 61. With Left Front Band over Right Front Band, sew bottom edges of Front Bands to skipped sts in Row 67. Sew Sleeve seams from cuff edge to Row 5. Sew Caps of Sleeves into armholes, matching stripes on Sleeves to Front and Back stripes.

sleeve band

Rnd 1: With RS facing, working across opposite side of foundation ch on cuff edge of one Sleeve, join B in any ch, ch 1, *sc in each of next 3 ch, sc2tog

in next 2 ch; rep from * around, sl st in first sc to join. (32 sc.

Rnds 2-3: Ch 1, sc in each sc around, sl st in first sc to join. (32 sc)

Rnd 4: Sl st in each st around, sl st in first sl st to join. (32 sl sts) Fasten off B.

Rep Sleeve Band around cuff edge of other Sleeve.

leg band

Row 1: With RS facing, join B in first row-end st to right of crotch, ch 1, work 62 sc evenly spaced across Front and Back leg openings to last row-end st before other side of crotch, turn. (62 sc)

Row 2: Ch 1, *sc in each of next 5 sc, sc2tog in next 2 sts; rep from * across, ending with sc in each of last 6 sc, turn. (54 sc)

Row 3: Ch 1, *sc in each of next 5 sc, sc2tog in next 2 sts; rep from * across, ending with sc in each of last 5 sc, turn. (47 sc)

Row 4: Sl st in each sc across. (47 sl sts) Fasten off B.

Rep Leg Band across left leg opening.

collar

Row 1: With RS facing, join B in first st on neck edge to the left of Right Front Band, ch 1, work 34 sc evenly across neck edge to last st before Left Front Band, turn. (34 sc)

Row 2: Ch 1, *sc in each of next 3 sc, 2 sc in next sc; rep from * across, ending with sc in each of last 2 sc, turn. (42 sc)

Row 3: Ch 1, sc in each sc across, turn. (42 sc)

Row 4: Ch 1, *sc in each of next 4 sc, 2 sc in next sc; rep from * across, ending with sc in each of last 2 sc, turn. (50 sc)

Row 5: Rep Row 3. (50 sc)

Row 6: *sc in each of next 5 sc, 2 sc in next sc; rep from * across, ending with sc in each of last 2 sc, turn. (58 sc) Fasten off B.

Row 7: With RS facing, join B in row-end st in Row 1 on left side of Collar, sl st up side edge, across Row 6, then down other side edge of Collar to row-end st on right-hand side of Row 1. Fasten off.

waistband trim

Rnd 1: With RS facing, join C in remaining loop of first st in Row 53 of Back, ch 1, sc in remaining loop of each st around Back and Front, sl st in first sc to join.

Rnd 2: Sl st in each sc around, sl st in first sl st to join. Fasten off. Weave in ends.

Sew buttons evenly spaced across Left Front Band. Use spaces between sts on Right Front Band for buttonholes. With sewing needle and sewing thread, sew snaps to crotch.

close-fit hat

Carrie McWithey

This hat crochets up so quickly you'll want to make one for each day of the week. Big stitches make up the open-weave design and the multicolored novelty yarn is shot with gold metallic threads for added flair.

instructions

stitches

chain st (ch)

single crochet (sc)

double crochet (dc)

increases dc (inc dc): 2 dc in same st (shell)

slip stitch (sl st)

hat

Starting at center top, with 2 strands of yarn held together as one throughout, ch 5 loosely and close into a ring with 1 sl st in first ch.

Rnd 1 (WS): Ch 1, work 12 sc in ring. Do not join, work in a spiral, and place a marker in first st of rnd, move marker up as work progresses (12 sc).

Rnd 2: DC 22, including 10 inc dc.

Rnd 3: *Ch 1, skip next dc, 2 dc in next dc: rep from * around (22 dc; 11 ch-1 spaces).

Rnd 4: Dc in each st and space around, increasing 5 dc evenly spaced around (38 dc).

Rnd 5: Ch 1, skip next dc, 2 dc in next dc, *ch 1, skip next 2 dc, 2 dc in next dc, ch 1, skip next dc, 2 dc in next dc; rep from * 6 times (30 dc; 15 ch-1 spaces).

Rnd 6: *Ch 1, skip next ch-1 space, 2 dc in space bet next 2 dc; rep from * around (30 dc; 15 ch-1 spaces).

Rnd 7: Dc in each st and space around (45 dc).

Rnd 8: *Ch 1, skip next 2 dc, 2 dc in next dc; rep from * 14 times (30 dc; 15 ch-1 spaces).

Rnds 9-10: Rep Rnd 6 (30 dc; 15 ch-1 spaces in each rnd).

Rnd 11: *Sc in each of next 8 sts or spaces, skip next st or space; rep from * 4 times (40 sc).

Rnd 12: *Ch 1, skip next st, shell in next st, ch 1, skip next 2 sts, shell in next st; rep from * 7 times, skip next st, sl st in next st to join (16 shells; 8 ch-1 spaces). Fasten off. Weave in ends.

skill level

Intermediate

finished size

One size fits most adults; circumference = 22"/56cm

materials

Moda Dea's *Cache*, 75% wool/22% acrylic/3% polyester, 1.76oz/50g = approx 72 yd/66m, 3 balls

Crochet hook size J US or size needed to obtain gauge

Stitch marker

Yarn needle

gauge

3 shells = 4"/10cm

Remember, your gauge must match for the size to match.

crochet trimmed top

Spice up ordinary store-bought clothes with simple crocheted fringe borders. Repeat more rows and shorten fringe for an interesting variation.

Glenda Larsen

instructions

stitches

chain st (ch)

double crochet (dc)

slip stitch (sl st)

trim

With sewing needle and crochet cotton, work a row of running sts around neck edge, approximately .5"/1cm in from edge, working approximately 3 sts per 1"/2.5cm.

Rnd 1: Join cotton in edge of shirt, below any running st, ch 1, *sc over running st, ch 3; rep from * around, sl st in first sc to join.

Rnd 2: Sl st in first ch-3 sp, ch 1, (sc, ch 5) in each ch-3 sp around, sl st in first sc to join.

Rnd 3: Rep rnd 2.

Fasten off. Weave in ends.

fringe

Cut 5"/13cm lengths of cotton. Using 5 strands of cotton each group in each loop of last rounds. Fold in half, insert hook from WS to RS in any ch-5 loop last rnd of trim, draw folded end of Fringe through loop, draw ends through loop on hook and tighten. Place one Fringe in each loop around Trim.

Trim Fringe to desired length.

skill level
Easy

finished size
3"/7.5cm wide

materials
J&P Coats' *Royale*, 100% mercerized cotton, size 10, 300 yd/275m, 1 ball Mexicana

Steel crochet hook size 8US/1.4mm or size needed to obtain gauge

Tapestry needle

Sewing needle big enough for size 10 cotton

Cotton shirt

gauge
3 loops = 1"/2.5cm

Remember, your gauge must match for the size to match

picot lace shawl

Donna May

This delicate-looking lace shawl exudes elegance with whatever it accompanies. The beauty of the open picot stitch is enhanced by the use of metallic yarn. Soft scalloped edging makes a graceful border for the triangle shape. Shawl also looks great worn as neck scarf, as triangle tip conceals well within folds.

skill level

Intermediate

finished size

Fits most adults 65"/165cm wide at top x 28"/71cm from center top to bottom tip of triangle.

materials

Patons' *Brilliant*, 69% acrylic/19% nylon/12% polyester, 1.75 oz/50g = 166yd/152m, 4 balls of #3023 Gold Glow

Size H / 5.0 mm crochet hook or size to obtain gauge

gauge

([sc, ch 3, sc], ch 5) 3 times and 11 rows in pattern = 4"/10cm

instructions

stitches

chain st (ch)

picot: [sc, ch 3, sc] in same st or space

single crochet (sc)

slip stitch (sl st)

to start

Starting at top edge, ch 233.

Row 1: Work [sc, ch 3, sc] in 8th ch from hook, ch 5, *skip next 4 ch, [sc, ch 3, sc] in next ch, ch 5; repeat from * across, ending with sc in last ch, turn. (45 pattern repeats)

Row 2: Ch 7, *[sc, ch 3, sc] in center ch of next ch-5 loop, ch 5; rep from * across to last ch-7 loop, sc in 3rd ch of last ch-7 loop, turn (45 ch-5 loops).

Rows 3-4: Rep Row 2.

Row 5 (dec row): Ch 7, *[sc, ch 3, sc] in center ch of next ch-5 loop, ch 5; rep from * across to last ch-5 loop, sc in center ch of last ch-5 loop, turn, leaving rem ch-7 loop unworked (44 ch-5 loops).

Row 6 (dec row): Rep Row 5 (43 ch-5 loops).

Rows 7-8: Rep Row 2.

Rows 9-16: Rep Rows 5-8 (twice) (39 ch-5 loops at end of last row).

Rows 17-55: Rep Row 5 (1 ch-5 loop at end of last row).

Row 56: Ch 7, *[sc, ch 3, sc] in center ch of next ch-5 loop, sl st in next sc. Do not fasten off. Do not turn.

right side edging

Working across side edge of Shawl, ch 1, [sc, ch 3, sc] in next ch-3 space, *3 sc in next space, [sc, ch 3, sc] in next ch-3 space; rep from * 18 times, **3 sc in next space, 1 sc in next space, [sc, ch 3, sc] in ch-3 space; rep from twice, 3 sc in next space, sc in next space, sl st in next space (corner).

top edging

Working across top edge of Shawl, ch 1, [sc, ch 3, sc] in same space, ch 3, [sc, ch 3, sc] in next ch (directly over picot), *ch 5, skip next 4 ch, [sc, ch 3, sc] in next st (directly over picot); rep from * across to next corner, [sc, ch 3, sc] in next space (corner).

leftside edging

Working across other side edge of Shawl, sc in next space, 3 sc in next space, [sc, ch 3, sc] in next ch-3 space, *skip next space, sc in next space, 3 sc in next space, [sc, ch 3, sc] in next ch-3 space; rep from * twice, **sc in next space, 3 sc in next space, [sc, ch 3, sc] in ch-3 space; rep from ** 18 times, sl st in next st to join. Fasten off. Weave in ends.

his 'n her onesies and booties

Donna May

This comfortable baby onesie design features two neck options: a ruffled edge for a girl, and a sailor collar for a boy. The wraparound ties add color to the front of the onesie and make diaper changes a snap.

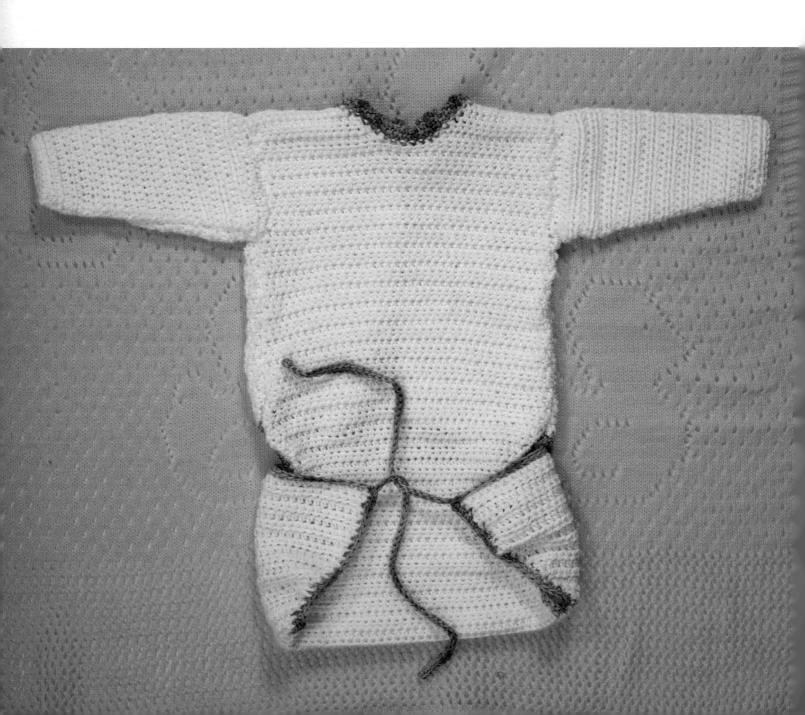

instructions for onesies

stitches

chain st (ch)

single crochet (sc)

half double crochet (hdc)

half double crochet decrease (hdc2tog)

half double crochet increase (hdc inc): 2 hdc in 1 st

single crochet decrease (sc2tog)

slip stitch (sl st)

picot stitch (p): (sl st, 3 ch, sl) all in the same stitch

front and flap

Front and flap are crocheted starting at flap edge and ending at shoulders.

When beginning a new piece, mark right side on first or second row.

With D (E, F) hook and Snow, ch 62.

skill level

Intermediate

sizes

Newborn (3, 6) months

Finished Measurements

Chest = 17.5" (18.5, 19.5)/44cm (43, 46);

Finished length from shoulder to crotch = 12.5" (13.5, 14.5)/44cm (43, 46);

NOTE: The larger sizes are made with larger hooks.

materials

Ruffled Collar Version: Paton's *Grace*, 100% cotton, 1.75oz/50g = approx 136yd/125m, 4 (4, 5) balls of Snow; 1 ball of Tangelo or Spearmint

Square Collar Version: Add 1 more ball of Snow

Crochet hook sizes C-2US/3mm and D-3US/3.25mm (D-3US/3.25mm and E-4US/3.5mm, E-4US/3.5mm and F-5US/4mm) or sizes needed to obtain gauge for size chosen

Tapestry needle

Stitch markers

6 small buttons

Sewing needle and matching sewing thread

gauge

Newborn: 18 hdc/14 hdc rows = approx 4"/10cm using size D-3/3.25mm hook

3 Months: 17 hdc/13 hdc rows = approx 4"/10cm using size E-4/3.5mm hook

6 Months: 16 hdc/12 hdc rows = approx 4"/10cm using size F-5/3.7mm hook

Remember, your gauge must match for the size to match.

NOTE: In this project, the turning chain does NOT count as a stitch.

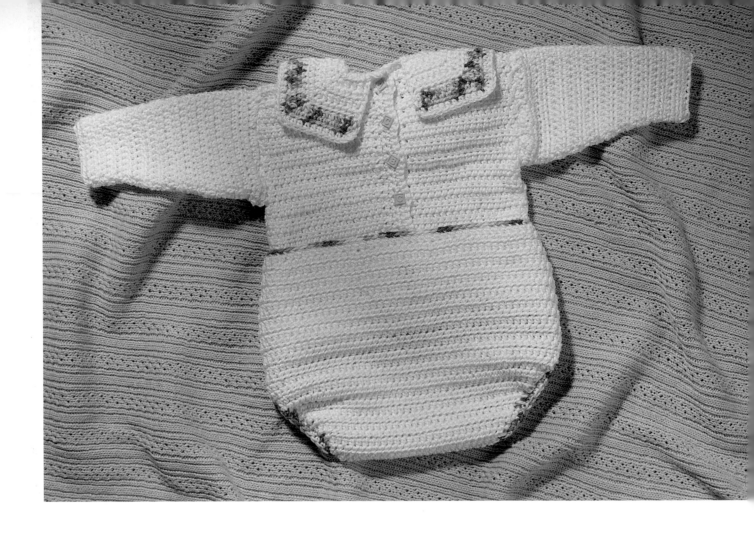

Row 1: Hdc in 3rd ch from hook and 1 hdc in each st across; ch 1, turn. (60 sts)

Row 2: Work 1 hdc in first st and in next 3 sts, 2 hdc in next st, (1 hdc in ea of next 9 sts, 2 hdc in next st) five times; 1 hdc in ea of next 5 sts; ch 1, turn. (6 hdc inc, 66 sts)

Rows 3-8 (work even): 1 hdc in first and in ea st across; ch 1, turn.

Row 9: Working hdc across, dec 1 hdc at ea end of row (sk first st and leave last st unworked); ch 1, turn. (2 dec, 64 sts)

Rows 10-32: Rep row 9. (18 sts in row 32)

Row 33: Work hdc in first st, 2 hdc in next st; hdc in ea rem st across to last 2 sts and then work 2 hdc in next to last st, ch 1, turn. (2 hdc inc. 20 sts)

Rows 34-43: Rep row 33 (inc 2 hdc ea row). (40 sts in row 43)

Rows 44-63 (work even): Hdc in first st and in ea st across; ch 1, turn.

Row 64: Sl st first 2 sts, ch 1, and work hdc across to last 2 sts; leave last 2 sts unworked; ch 1, turn. (4 dec, 36 sts)

Row 65-72 (work even): Hdc in first st and in ea st across; ch 1, turn.

left neck shaping

Row 1: Work hdc in first st and hdc in ea of next 15 sts; ch 1, turn. (16 sts)

Row 2: Sl st in first st and work hdc in second st and hdc in rem 14 sts; ch 1, turn. (1 dec, 15 sts)

Row 3: Work hdc in 1st st and hdc in ea of next 13 sts; leave last st unworked; ch 1, turn. (1 dec, 14 sts)

Row 4: Sl st in first st, ch 1, work hdc in next st and in rem

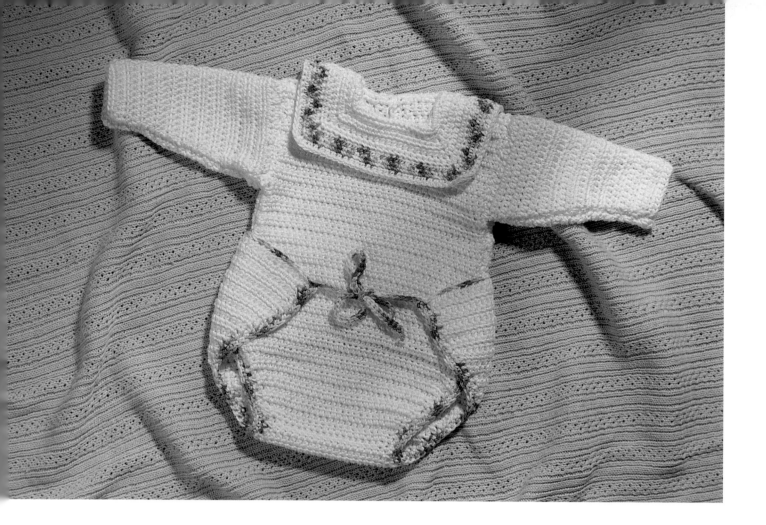

12 sts across; ch 1, turn. (1 dec, 13 sts)

Row 5: Work 1 hdc in first st and in ea of next 11 sts; leave last st unworked; fasten off and weave in ends. (1 dec, 12 sts)

right neck shaping

Row 1: With RS facing, sk 4 sts for neck and with sl st, attach yarn. Work 1 ch, 1 hdc in same st as joining and ea st across; ch 1, turn. (16 sts)

Row 2: Hdc in first st and in next 14 sts; leave last st unworked, ch 1, turn. (1 dec, 15 sts)

Row 3: Sl st in first st, ch 1, hdc in next 14 sts, ch 1, turn. (1 dec, 14 sts)

Row 4: Hdc in first st and in next 12 sts, leaving last st unworked, ch 1, turn. (1 dec, 13 sts)

Row 5: Sl st in first st, ch 1, hdc in next 12 sts; fasten off and weave in ends. (1 dec, 12 sts)

sleeves (make 2)

Starting from the top, ch 42.

Row 1: Hdc in 3rd ch from hook and 1 hdc in ea ch across; ch 1,

turn. (40 sts)

Row 2 (work even): Hdc in first st and in ea st across; ch 1, turn.

Row 3 (dec 1 st ea end): Sl st in first st, ch 1, hdc in ea of next 38 sts; leave last st unworked. (2 dec, 38 sts)

Rows 4-17: Rep rows 2 and 3 7 times. (dec 2 ea row, 24 sts in row 17).

Rows 18-22: Rep row 2; fasten off, weave in ends.

right back

Ch 22.

Row 1: Hdc in 3rd ch from hook and in ea ch across, ch 1, turn. (20 sts)

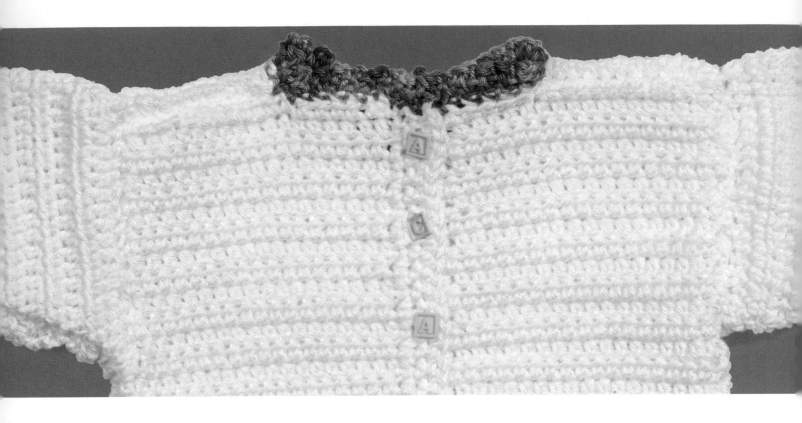

Rows 2-19 (work even): Hdc in first st and 1 hdc in ea st across, ch 1, turn.

Row 20: Work 1 hdc in first st and in next 17 sts; leave last 2 sts unworked; ch 1, turn. (2 dec, 18 sts)

Rows 21-32 (work even): Hdc in first st and in ea rem 17 sts, ch 1, turn. Fasten off at end of row 32. Weave in ends.

button band on right back

Row 1: With RS facing, at top left corner attach yarn with sl st in last neckline st. Work 1 ch and sc in same sp as joining; work 1 sc in end of ea row along center edge of right back piece; ch 1, turn. (32 sts)

Rows 2-3 (work even): Sc in first and in ea st across, ch 1, turn. Fasten off at end of row 3. Weave in ends.

left back
Ch 22.

Row 1: Hdc in 3rd ch from hook and in ea ch across, ch 1, turn. (20 sts)

Rows 2-19 (work even): Hdc in first st and hdc in ea st across, ch 1, turn.

Row 20: Sl st in first 2 sts, ch 1, hdc in rem 18 sts, ch 1, turn. (2 dec, 18 sts)

Rows 21-32 (work even): Hdc in first st and in rem17 sts, ch 1, turn. Fasten off at end of row 32. Weave in ends.

buttonhole band on left back

Row 1 (RS): With sl st attach yarn at bottom right edge (center line of garment). Ch 1 and work 1 sc in same place as joining; work 1 sc in end of each row; ch 1, turn. (32 sts)

Row 2 (work even): Hdc in first st and in ea st; ch 1, turn.

Row 3: Work 1 sc in first st, (2 ch, sk 1 st, 1 sc in ea of next 4 sts) 6 times; end with 1 sc in

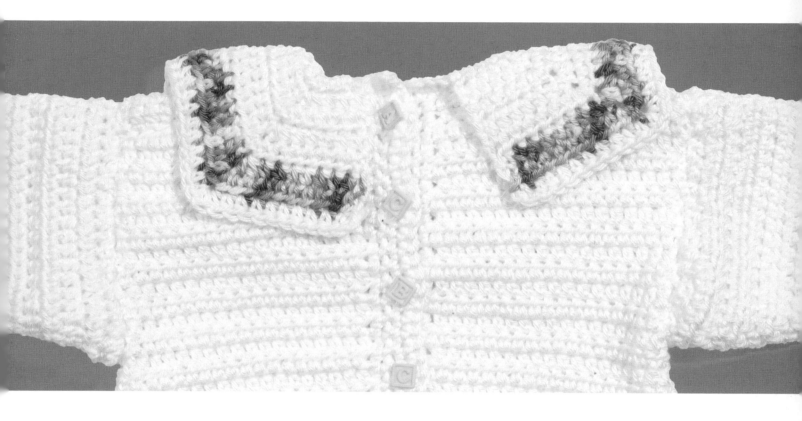

last st; ch 1, turn. (6 button holes begun)

Row 4: Work 1 sc in ea of first 5 sts, then 2 sc in next ch-2 sp, (1 sc in ea of next 4 sts, 2 sc in next ch-2 sp) five times; end with 1 sc in last st; fasten off and weave in ends. (6 button-holes completed)

assembly

With RS together and using back stitch, sew shoulder seams, then sew in sleeves. For each side, starting at cuff edge of sleeve, sew sleeve seam and continue down, sewing side seam. Weave in all

ends. Finger press seams to flatten.

ruffled neck edging

Row 1: With RS facing and D (E, F) hook, attach Tangelo with sl st in end of button hole band at neckline edge, ch 1, and work 34 sc evenly across; ch 1, turn. (34 sts)

Row 2 (work 34 picots): 3 ch, then sl st in first st [counts as first picot]; (sl st in next st, 3 ch, sl st in same st) 33 times. (34 picot sts) Fasten off and weave in ends.

flap edging and ties

Row 1: With RS facing and D (E, F) hook, with sl st, attach Tangelo or Spearmint with a sl st at lower edge of button band and work 1 ch and 1 sc in same sp as joining. Work sc evenly across to side seam. Do not fasten off.

Change to C (D, E) hook and sc in end of ea row until you reach top corner of flap, then begin tie by working 43 ch. Work 1 sl st in front lp of 2nd ch from hook and in front lp of ea rem ch of tie. When you reach top of flap, sc in ea st across to cor-ner. At corner (begin second tie), ch 43. As for first tie, sl st in front lp of 2nd ch from hook and in front lp of ea rem ch of tie. Do not fasten off.

When end of tie is reached, work 1 sc in end of ea row of flap back to other side seam. At side seam, change to D (E, F) hook and work 1 sc in ea st across right back, ending with 1 sc in corner st of buttonhole band. Fasten off and weave in ends.

Row 2 (second row of leg band): With RS facing you and using C (D, E) hook, with sl st attach Tangelo or Spearmint in last sl st of tie. Work 1 sc in first st of leg band section (below tie). Work 1 ch, then work 1 sc in same sp as joining; work 1 sc in ea sc across to side seam. Sl st into first st on back section; fasten off and weave in ends.

Repeat for other leg band: with RS facing, attach yarn with sl st in last st on lower band of right back. Work 1 sc in first st of leg band and in ea st across to tie. Sl st in first sl st of tie. Fasten off and weave in ends.

sew on buttons
Sew six buttons on RS of button band, placing each button directly under a button hole when buttonhole band is lapped over button band.

alternate square collar
Row 1: With RS facing, attach Snow with sl st in end of button hole band at neckline edge and ch 1, work 34 sc evenly across; ch 1, turn. (34 sts)

Row 2: Work hdc in first st and in ea of next 4 sts; 3 hdc in next st; 1 hdc in ea of next 5 sts; 3 hdc in next st; 1 hdc in ea of next 10 sts; 3 hdc in next st; 1 hdc in ea of next 5 sts; 3 hdc in next st; 1 hdc in ea of next 5 sts; ch 1, turn. (8 hdc inc, 42 sts)

Row 3: Sl st in ea of first 3 sts, ch 1, work hdc in ea of next 3 sts; 3 hdc in next st; 1 hdc in ea of next 7 sts; 3 hdc in next st; 1 hdc in ea of next 12 sts; 3 hdc in next st; 1 hdc in ea of next 7 sts; 3 hdc in next st; 1 hdc in ea of next 3 sts; leave last 3 sts unworked; ch 1, turn. (44 sts)

Row 4: Work 1 hdc in first st and in ea of next 3 sts; 3 hdc in next st; 1 hdc in ea of next 9 sts; 3 hdc in next st; 1 hdc in ea of next 14 sts; 3 hdc in next st; 1 hdc in ea of next 9 sts; 3 hdc in next st; 1 hdc in ea of next 4 sts; ch 1, turn. (8 hdc inc, 52 sts)

Row 5: Work 1 hdc in first st and 1 hdc in ea of next 4 sts; 3 hdc in next st; 1 hdc in ea of next 11 sts; 3 hdc in next st; 1 hdc in ea of next 16 sts; 3 hdc in next st; 1 hdc in ea of next 11 sts; 3 hdc in next st; 1 hdc in ea of next 5 sts; ch 1, turn. (8 hdc inc, 58 sts)

Row 6: Work hdc in first st and in ea of next 5 sts; 3 hdc in next st; hdc in ea of next 13 sts; 3 hdc in next st; 1 hdc in ea of next 18 sts; 3 hdc in next st; 1 hdc in ea of next 13 sts; 3 hdc in next st, hdc in ea of next 6 sts, ch 1, turn. (8 hdc inc, 66 sts)

Row 7: Work 1 hdc in first st and in ea of next 6 sts; 3 hdc in next st; 1 hdc in ea of next 15 sts; 3 hdc in next st; 1 hdc in ea of next 20 sts; 3 hdc in next st; 1 hdc in ea of next 15 sts; 3 hdc in next st; 1 hdc in ea of next 7 sts. YO Spearmint and pull through loop on hook. Cut Snow, leaving a tail for weaving in; turn. (8 hdc inc, 74 sts)

Row 8: Work 1 hdc in first st and in ea of next 7 sts; 3 hdc in next st; 1 hdc in ea of next 17 sts; 3 hdc in next st; 1 hdc in ea of next 22 sts; 3 hdc in next st; 1 hdc in ea of next 17 sts; 3 hdc in next st; 1 hdc in ea of next 8 sts; ch 1, turn. (8 hdc inc, 84 sts)

Row 9: Work 1 hdc in first st and in ea of next 8 sts; 3 hdc in next st; 1 hdc in ea of next 19 sts; 3 hdc in next st; 1 hdc in ea of next 24 sts; 3 hdc in next st; 1 hdc in ea of next 19 sts; 3 hdc in next st; 1 hdc in ea of next 9 sts; ch 1, turn. YO Snow, pull through loop on hook, cut Spearmint, leaving a tail for weaving in. (8 hdc inc, 90 sts)

Row 10: Work 1 hdc in first st and in ea of next 9 sts; 3 hdc in next st; 1 hdc in ea of next 21 sts; 3 hdc in next st; 1 hdc in ea of next 26 sts; 3 hdc in next st; 1 hdc in ea of next 21 sts; 3 hdc in next st; 1 hdc in ea of next 10 sts. Fasten off and weave in ends.

Tack down back corners of collar to garment if desired. Optional blocking of collar corners is easily achieved by dampening collar with water and pulling corners to a point.

Lay flat to dry.

instructions for booties (make 2)

With Snow, ch 20.

Row 1: Hdc in 3rd ch from hook and in ea ch across. (18 sts)

Rows 2-12: Work hdc even.

At end of row 12, fasten off, leaving a tail of yarn about 15"/38cm long to gather toe together and stitch top of foot.

Use a tapestry needle to sew tail through one short end of fabric with running stitches. With right sides together, pull

skill level

Intermediate

sizes

Newborn (3 months, 6 months)

materials

Paton's Grace, 100% cotton, 1.75oz/50g = approx 136yd/125m, small amounts Snow and a trim color

Crochet hook size D-3/2.25mm for Newborn

Crochet hook size E-4/3.5 for 3 months

Crochet hook size F-5/3.75mm for 6 months

or size to obtain gauge

Tapestry needle

gauge

Newborn: 18 hdc/14 hdc rows = approx 4"/10cm using size D-3/3.25mm hook

3 Months: 17 hdc/13 hdc rows = approx 4"/10cm using size E-4/3.5mm hook

6 Months: 16 hdc/12 hdc rows = approx 4"/10cm using size F-5/3.7mm hook

Remember, your gauge must match for the size to match.

thread to gather. Do not fasten off, but continue sewing 8 sts on the long edges together to form top of bootie. Fasten off and weave in ends.

Thread tapestry needle with a 12"/30cm length of yarn and gather the heel as you did the toe. Fasten off and weave in ends.

ankle trim

Rnd 1: Attach Snow with sl st to top edge of bootie in 1st st to the left of center of the top seam. Ch 1 and sc around, increasing 6 sc evenly; insert hook in first st of rnd, yo trim color and pull through. Join and color change.

Rnd 2: Ch 1 and sc around, joining turn.

Row 3: Ch 3 and work 1 dc in same place as joining; (ch 1, sk 1 st and dc in next st) around. Do not work the 3 center sc. Turn.

Row 4: (Sl st, ch 2, sl st) in ea ch-1 space across. Fasten off and weave in ends.

ties (make 2)

Ch 75 with trim color and sl st across in front loop only. Fasten off, leaving a long tail, then draw the already done tail through tie for several inches.

Thread ties through ch-1 spaces around ankle on bootie and tie in front.

retro granny squares

Fashion favorites from the 70s have come roaring back into style as illustrated here with boldly colored granny squares showcased against a black background. The asymmetrical design on one-sleeve echoes the colors in the squares and boasts of the uniqueness of the wearer.

Cynthia Preston

skill level
Intermediate

sizes
Small: 36"/91cm bust*

*Note: This sweater can be made in size XL by adding two more granny squares and increasing the sides and sleeves to match.

materials
Lion Brand's *Lion Suede*, 100% polyester, 3oz/85g = 122yd/110m, 1 ball each of Denim, Fuchsia, Eggplant, and Teal, and 3 (5) balls of Ebony

Size I crochet hook or size needed to obtain gauge

Tapestry needle

gauge
7dc/rows = 3"/7.5cm

Remember, your gauge must match for the size to match.

instructions

stitches

Slip stitch (sl st)

Single crochet (sc)

Double crochet (dc)

granny squares

Make one 2nd row granny squares in each of the following color combinations (inner/outer colors): Eggplant/Fuchsia, Fuchsia/Denim, Eggplant/Teal, Teal/Fuchsia, Teal/Eggplant, Teal/Denim, Denim/Eggplant, Fuchsia/Teal, Fuschia/Eggplant, and Denim/Eggplant.

Rnd 1: With inner color, ch 4, join to first ch to form circle, ch 3, 2 dc in circle, (ch 2, 3 dc in circle) 3 times, ch 2, join to ch 3 with sl st. Fasten off.

Rnd 2: Join outer color 2 at corner, ch 3, 2 dc, ch 2, 3 dc all in same corner sp. (3 dc, ch 2, 3 dc) in the other 3 corners. Join to first ch 3 with sl st. Fasten off.

Using Ebony yarn, sew the 10 granny squares together with right sides facing in a strip, then sew both ends of the strip together to form a border for the front and back neckline of the sweater.

sweater

Sweater Front Neckline Edge (Rnd 1) and Top-of-Shoulder Gussets (Rows 2-4)

Rnd 1: Starting at far right at end of square 5, with right side facing, tie on ebony, ch 1 and make 1 sc in each st along the strip of granny squares, (8 sc along the top of each square), ch 3 and turn.

Row 2: To make shoulder gussets: 5 dc in sp at bottom of ch 3, sk 2 st along side of square and sl st to side of granny square, ch 3, sk 2 st and sl st to side of granny square, turn.

Row 3: (Dc inc, 1 dc) across row just made, sl st to side of square, skipping 2 st. Ch 3 and sk 2 st on side of granny square and sl st. Turn.

Row 4: Dc in same sp as ch 3, 7 dc across row, 1 dc inc in last st, sk 2 st up side of seam and sl st into granny square. Fasten off. Make gusset on other side.

sweater front and back

Row 1: With right side of the squares facing you, tie on ebony yarn at end of first square. Ch 3 and 23 dc across row, ch 3 and turn. (Counting turning ch, there should be 24 sts in the row.)

Rows 2-5: 1 dc inc, dc across row, in last st make 1 dc inc. Ch 3 and turn.

Rows 6-8: 2 dc inc, dc across row, last 2 st make 2 dc inc. Ch 3 and turn.

Row 9: 1 dc inc, dc across row, in last st make 1 dc inc. Ch 3 and turn.

Rows 10-21: 1 dc in each st, ch 3, turn. Repeat for front.

Row 22: Dc across. Fasten off.

Sew up side seams when front and back are done.

sleeves

Make one sleeve in Ebony yarn.

For sleeve with colored yarns, see color notes; rows without color notes are in Ebony. Sleeves are worked from the top down.

Row 1: Ch 19. In 3rd st from hook, dc across row, ch 3 and turn.

Rows 2-6: In base of ch 3 make 1 dc (a dc inc), dc across row, dc inc, ch 3, and turn.

COLOR NOTE: For colored sleeve make 1 sc row in fuchsia, 1 sc row in ebony, 1 dc row in ebony, 1 sc row in eggplant, 1 sc row in teal, 2 rows dc in ebony. (2 rows of sc equals 1 of dc, increase in sc in increase rows when called for.)

Rows 7-9: 2 dc inc, dc across row, and dc inc in last 2 sts, ch 3, and turn. Color Note: 1 sc row in denim, 1 sc row in ebony, then 2 dc row in ebony.

Row 10: 1 dc in each st, ch 3 and turn.

Row 11: 1 dc decrease, then dc in each st, 1 dc dec, ch 3, and turn. Color Notes: 1 sc row in fuchsia, 1 sc row in ebony.

Row 12: 1 dc in each st, ch 3, and turn.

Row 13: 1 dc in each st, ch 3, and turn. Color note: 1 sc row in denim, and 1 sc row in teal.

Rows 14-29: Repeat rows 10-13, ending with 2 non-decreasing rows. Color notes: 1 sc row in magenta, 1 sc row in black.

Sew sleeve sides together, sew sleeves to body. Hide all ends.

embroidery

Welcome to the embroidery chapter! Whether you're looking for a new craft or just looking for great ways to add pizzazz to ordinary items, you'll find lots of great projects.

Once relegated to very traditional styles, embroidery is now one of the hottest embellishment trends. From home decor items such as sheets and towels to casual and formal clothing to greeting card and scrapbooking papers, no surface is safe!

Embroidery materials have also come a long way. The color palettes of today's silk ribbons and flosses are simply amazing, and inspire more than their share of projects. When shopping for materials, spend a few minutes in the knitting and crochet sections, also—many yarns make great substitutes for traditional embroidery floss.

Enjoy!

embroidery basics

tools & supplies

needles

Embroidery needles are made in a variety of sizes. Ideally, you want the smallest possible needle for the job to prevent creating larger-than-necessary holes in your fabric or paper surfaces. Since they're relatively inexpensive, the easiest thing to do is just purchase a variety package or two to give yourself an assortment of choices. When buying individual needles, note the size number on the package: the higher the number, the thinner the needle.

designs

Every great embroidery project begins with a great design. The patterns in this book are available to you, of course, but you can also find a host of great designs in embroidery books, copyright-free pattern books and websites, and in the stenciling departments. Don't be afraid to enlarge or reduce the sizes of your patterns, or to mix and match elements from different sources.

embroidery floss

The best part of shopping for embroidery floss or silk ribbon will be savoring all of the available colors.

Embroidery floss is now available in several finishes. There's even a metallic floss that's great for holiday embroidery projects.

If your embroidery design is extra fine or if you're working on a thin fabric, you may wish to separate the embroidery floss into three strands (instead of the usual six). Separating the floss is a simple task: just trim the floss to the desired length, pull the threads into two groups at one end with one group in each hand, and pull gently to separate them all the way down the stand. If you have trouble separating floss without tangling problems, try using a shorter length of floss.

silk ribbon

Silk ribbon is available in a variety of widths and beautiful array of colors. Generally, narrower ribbon is used for smaller, more detailed stitches.

Although embroiderers used to work in floss OR silk ribbon, many crafters now combine the two materials in projects with great results. (See the embroidered afghan on page 301 as an example.)

yarns and crochet threads

Stumped about which type of floss or ribbon is perfect for your next project? Don't decide until you take a peek in the yarn department. Many of the new yarns are perfect for embroidery, especially when you're working on knit or woven garments or a thick fabric.

embroidery hoop

Hoops are available in many sizes and materials. To use a hoop, disassemble the two circles (or ovals) and place the plain one underneath the fabric, centering the area you plan to embroider. Smooth any folds or wrinkles from the fabric, then place the remaining circle on over the bottom one so the fabric is sandwiched in the middle. Adjust the tension on the top hoop so the fabric is taut. When you've finished working in that area, release the tension and move the hoop to a new location.

fabrics

Many fabrics are suitable for embroidery. Linen, cotton, and cotton blends are ideal. Be sure to wash and iron them before use.

The embroidery aisle also offers a great selection of evenly woven fabrics that work well for needlework, as well as items such as afghans and towels that are designed specifically for embroiderers.

paper

Any craft-weight paper will give good results. Look for papers with printed patterns that can be embroidered over, as well as solid colors.

paper piercer

Although paper makes a great embroidery surface, a paper piercer is usually needed to make small, clean holes for your needle to go in and out of. Look for this small tool in the paper crafts section.

clear-drying craft glue

A small dab of craft glue is placed over knots and loose threads on the wrong side of paper embroidery.

transferring patterns

Once you've found the perfect design to embroider, you need to decide how to transfer the design to your embroidery surface. There are several good techniques available—choose the one that most suits your project and your personal preference.

mother nature
If your fabric or paper is even slightly transparent, you can tape the right side of the pattern to the wrong side of the embroidery surface, then hold it up to a glass window on a sunny day and trace the pattern with a chalk pencil or disappearing ink pen.

chalk pencil
Turn the paper your pattern's on face down and trace over the design with a chalk pencil. Turn the paper right side up and place it on your embroidery fabric or paper. Tape or pin the paper in place, then trace over the design with a ballpoint pen. (Note: This is not a good transfer choice when working with light-colored fabrics.)

craft transfer paper
This paper works the same way carbon paper does, but is far less messy. To use, Tape or pin the transfer paper to the embroidery surface, then trace over the pattern with a ballpoint pen as directed by the manufacturer.

tulle
Tulle netting can also be used to easily transfer patterns. First tape a piece of trimmed tulle over your design. Trace over the pattern with a waterproof pen, then baste it to your embroidery surface. When you've finished embroidering, remove the basting stitches and gently tear and cut away the tulle.

basic stitches

A repertoire of surface stitches represents the basis of almost every type of embroidery. Learning fundamental stitches will give you the means to create different effects.

Also called freestyle embroidery, surface embroidery calls for stitches worked independently of the weave of the background fabric. You can stitch in any direction and with a variety of threads.

Stitches can be grouped in a number of ways: lines (running stitch, backstitch, stem stitch, and split stitch), couching, chains (chain stitch), band and border stitches (buttonhole stitch and herringbone stitch), featherstitch, satin stitch, and detached stitches (French knot, bullion knot, and fly stitch).

no absolutes

Conventional use of surface stitches is not absolute. The beauty is their adaptability to produce an array of shapes, patterns, and textures. Once you master a stitch, experiment. Alter the scale and direction by working haphazardly or using different thicknesses of thread. You'll discover that some stitches can be overlapped, just as others can be worked in twists, spirals, and circular motifs.

backstitch

This makes a smooth, continuous row of stitching suitable for outlines, fine-line borders, and stems.

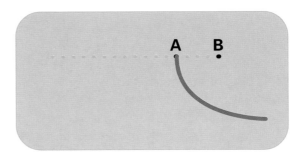

1 Bring the needle up at A, a short distance from B (starting point).

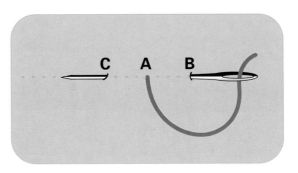

2 Bring the needle into B and bring it out at C.

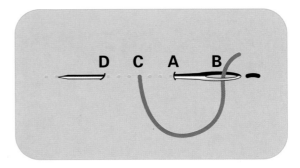

3 Bring the needle into A and bring it out at D.

4 Repeat, making sure the stitches are uniform in size.

bullion knot

A raised stitch of twisted thread, the bullion knot is often used as a flower center. Work it with "tails" to simulate stamens of tiny trees.

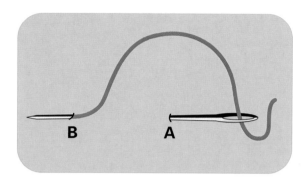

1 Bring the needle down at A then bring needle up at B.

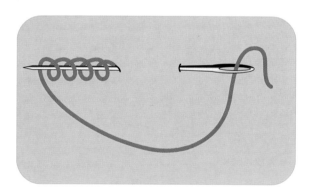

2 Twist the thread around the needle about six times (the number of twists should equal the length between A and B).

3 Holding the twist with your finger and thumb, pull the needle and thread through the fabric and the twist.

4 To ensure that the twist stays flat against the fabric, place the needle against the end of the twist and pull on the thread. Flatten any bumps in the twist with the needle.

5 Bring the needle down at B (at the end of the twist).

buttonhole stitch

Formed of tight loops, this stitch can be used for edgings in cutwork, appliqué, or as a decorative stitch. If the stitches are widely spaced they are called blanket stitch.

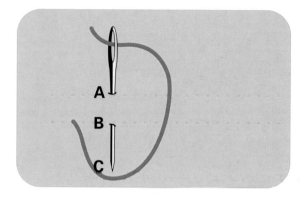

1 Bring the needle down at A, then bring the needle up at B, forming a small loop.

Bring the needle out at C through the loop. (Be sure to keep the thread under the needle.)

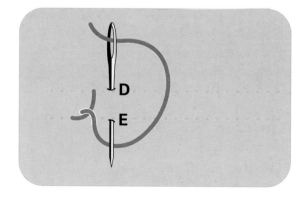

2 Bring the needle down at D and bring it up at E.

3 Repeat, spacing stitches evenly. Pull loops securely but not so tightly that the stitch goes awry. To finish, secure with a small stitch to hold the loop.

chain stitch

Quick and easy, this stitch brings the working thread though the loop to produce a slightly raised effect. Use chain stitch for thick outlines or repeat rows of it to fill an area.

1 Work this stitch from top to bottom. Bring the needle up and make a loop. Holding the loop with your finger, bring the needle down.

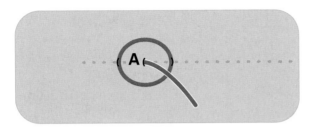

2 Bring the needle up through the loop on the stitching line at A. (Make sure the thread is under the needle.) Pull the thread gently to tighten the loop.

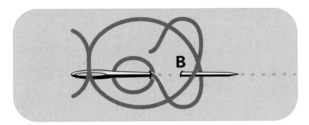

3 Bring the needle up at B, taking care to insert where the thread emerged in the previous loop.

4 Repeat. Make a vertical stitch to finish the loop.

couching

Couching, which creates outlines or shapes for filling, involves securing a thread or several threads to the fabric with small, evenly spaced stitches.

1 Place the thread to be couched at the start of the stitching line; remove the needle and use your nonstitching hand to hold the thread taut on the fabric.

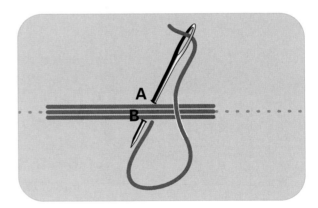

2 Bring the couching thread down at A (a little way along the stitching line) and take a small vertical stitch over the laid thread, bringing the needle up at B.

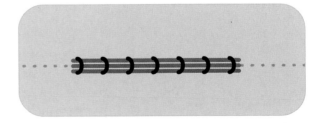

3 Repeat step 2 to the end of the stitching line and fasten off.

detached chain stitch

Also known as daisy stitch or lazy daisy, this stitch is usually embroidered in a flower shape. You can design daisies with five to eight petals, incorporating French knots as flower centers. Use the stitch to make leaves as well.

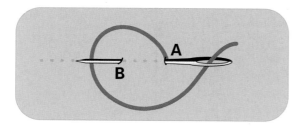

1 Bring the needle up at A and insert it as close as possible to A, forming a loop. Bring the needle up through the loop on the stitching line at B. (Make sure that the thread is under the needle.

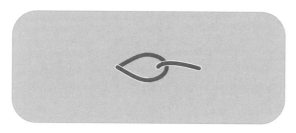

2 Make a vertical stitch to secure the loop. This stitch may be tiny or long.

3 To make an eight-petal daisy, draw a tiny circle for the center. Working from the center, make four detached chain stitches in a cross shape.

4 Add four more petals between the existing petals.

feather stitch

Use this delicate stitch for decorative borders as well as trees and shrubbery.

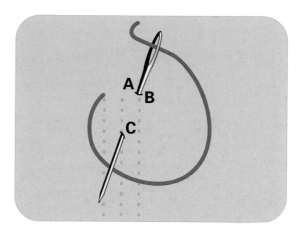

1 Bring the needle up at A. Holding down the thread with your thumb, bring the needle in at B and bring it up at C, making a modest loop. (Keep the loop under the needle.)

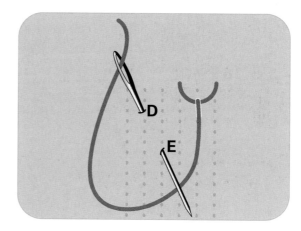

2 Repeat the stitch below and to the left. Bring the needle up at D. Holding down the thread with your thumb, bring the needle in at E, making a modest loop. (Keep the loop under the needle.)

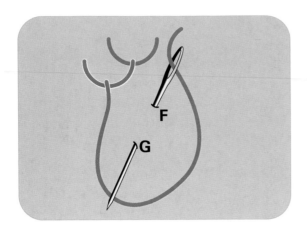

3 Repeat the stitch below and to the right. Bring the needle down at F. Holding down the thread with your thumb, bring the needle in at G, making a modest loop. (Keep the loop under the needle.)

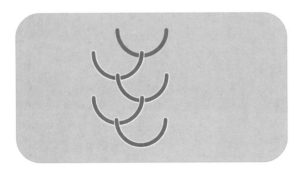

4 Repeat, alternating stitches as seen in steps 2–3. To finish, make a vertical stitch over a loop.

fly stitch

Seemingly ordinary, this stitch allows for different shapes, as the length of the "tail" can be varied. Fly stitch can be used to fill space or form rows.

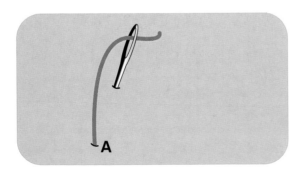

1 Bring the needle up at A.

2 Insert it a small distance away at B and bring the needle up at C, forming a loop at. (Keep the thread under the needle.)

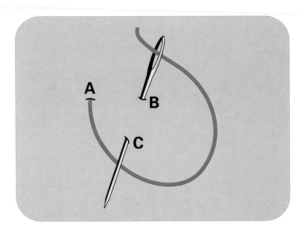

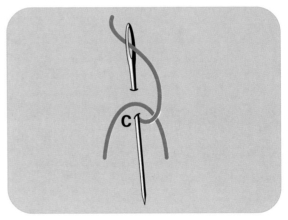

3 Bring the needle up through the loop at C.

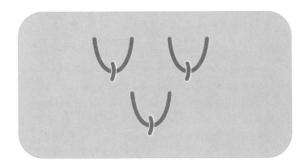

4 The fastening stitch may be long or short.

french knot

Like the bullion knot, this stitch works nicely as a flower center.

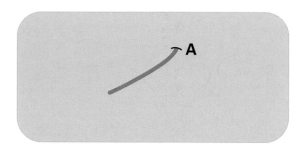

1 Bring the needle up at A.

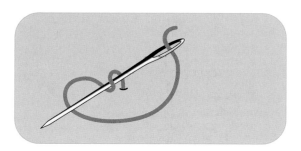

2 Hold the thread taut between the index finger and thumb of your nonstitching hand and twist the needle around the thread twice. (If you prefer a fine knot, twist the thread around the needle once.)

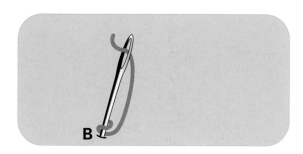

3 Insert the needle halfway at B (right next to A) and slide the twist down the needle so that it lies on the fabric. Slowly push the needle through.

herringbone stitch

Frequently used for decorative borders, this stitch can be embroidered in a regular fashion, with even spaces apart or close together.

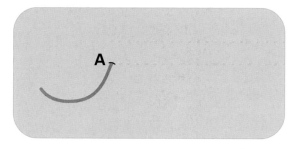

1 Working from left to right, bring the needle up at A on the lower stitching line.

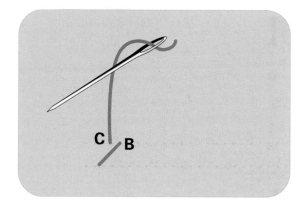

2 Make a diagonal stitch, bringing the needle down at B and up at C (a short distance left of and even with B).

3 Bringing the needle down at D, make a diagonal stitch in the other direction.

4 Bringing the needle up at E (a short distance left of and even with D). Make a diagonal stitch, bringing the needle down at F.

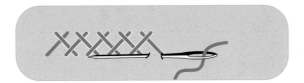

5 Repeat, making sure that the stitches are consistently spaced and diagonal lines are parallel.

long and short stitch

Use this stitch to shade petals and leaves for a realistic effect. Long and short stitch typically uses the same color, with a gradation of one shade on each row. Covering a rectangular area is easy, as the stitches go in one direction and are uniform. However, shapes that diminish in size, such as petals are trickier to execute.

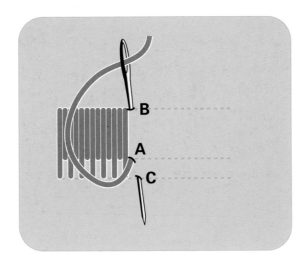

1 Bring the needle up at A and down at B. Bring the needle up at C and down at B. Continue the row, alternating stitches.

2 Bring the needle up at K to begin the second row. This and subsequent rows are made with stitches of equal length fitting into the spaces.

repeating long and short stitch

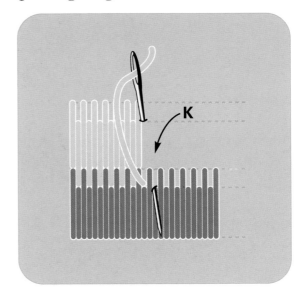

1 Begin in the center. Bring the needle up at A and down at B. Continue working to the right. Then return to the center and work to the left. (The stitches should converge toward the center.)

2 For subsequent rows, work stitches of equal length. As the shape diminishes, you'll find it necessary to eliminate some stitches.

open cretan stitch

When worked evenly, this stitch forms a zigzag line. However, you can overlap stitches to build interesting textures. Cretan stitch often depicts grasses.

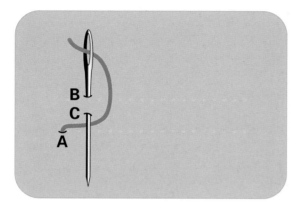

1 Bring the needle up at A.

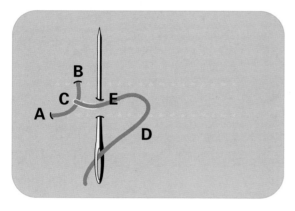

2 Bring the needle in at B and out at C (slightly to the right and below), keeping the thread to the right.

3 Bring the needle in at D and out at D.

running stitch

Often seen in hand quilting, this simple stitch makes a broken line that may be curved or straight. It also works well as flower stems or as veins in leaves.

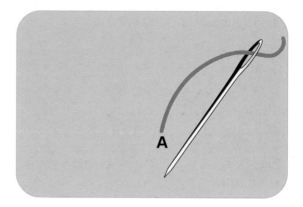

1 Bring the needle up at A.

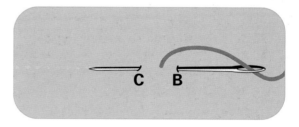

2 Working right to left, bring the needle in at B and out at C, making a small stitch along the stitching line.

3 Make another stitch the same length as the first. Repeat until reaching the end of the row.

satin stitch

Although simple in appearance, this stitch requires careful work. The individual stitches need to be embroidered exactly parallel to one another. To ensure a well-defined shape, satin stitch should be embroidered at an angle wherever possible. Limit the length of the stitches; otherwise they become unwieldy and may snag. Consider outlining the shape with a split stitch beforehand. This step will keep the edge smooth.

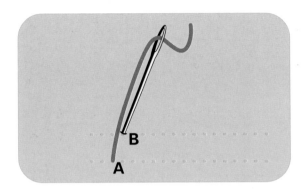

1 Bring the needle up at A on one edge of the shape to be covered and bring it down at B, diagonally across on the opposite edge.

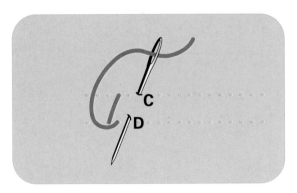

2 Bring the needle down at C, immediately next to A, and bring it up at D.

split stitch

This stitch creates a thin line to fill spaces or to outline a shape before it is filled by satin stitch.

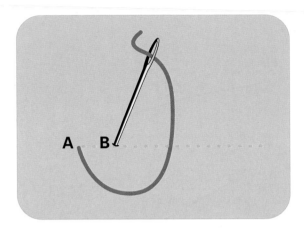

1 Bring the needle up at A and down at B.

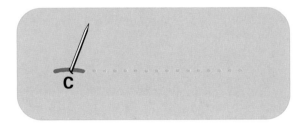

2 Bring the needle up at C, splitting the stitch in the middle.

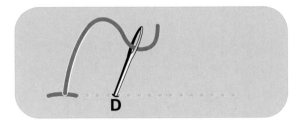

3 Bring the stitch down at D (ahead of B). The length between C and D should equal that between A and B.

4 Repeating, ensuing that stitches are uniform.

stem stitch

This stitch results in ropelike lines that vary in thickness according to the angle of needle insertion. While working, keep the thread above or below the stitching line.

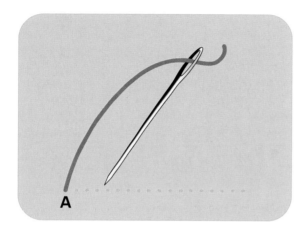

1 Working from left to right, bring the needle up at A.

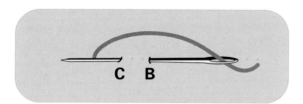

2 Bring the needle in at B along the stitching line and bring it up at C (halfway between A and B).

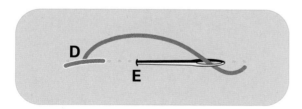

3 Pull the thread through. For the second stitch, bring the needle in at D and bring it out at E.

woven spider's web

This circular stitch is embroidered on a foundation of straight stitches radiating from a central point. Use it to create flowers, berries, or wheels. For different effects, vary the number and length of the foundation threads. Or leave them partially uncovered. Changing colors and textures also adds interest.

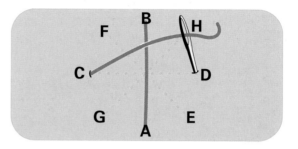

1 Bring the needle up at A and in at B. Bring the needle up at C and in at D; then repeat to finish the foundation threads.

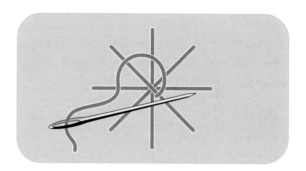

2 Bring the needle up near the center of the circle and under foundation threads AB and EF (but not through the fabric.

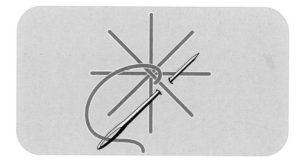

3 Bring the needle back over EF then under it and CD.

4 Continue until the foundation stitches are covered.

wheatear stitch

This stitch can be used to produce floral motifs or a continuous decorative line.

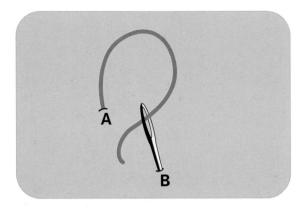

1 To make a V, bring the needle up at A and down at B (below A and to the right).

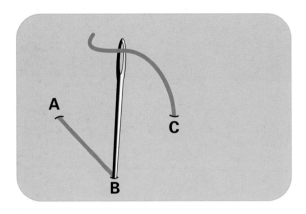

2 Bring the needle up at C (opposite A, and above and to the right of B) and down at B.

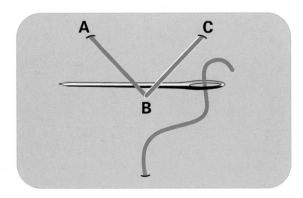

3 Bring the needle up at D (below B) and and insert the needle behind the V.

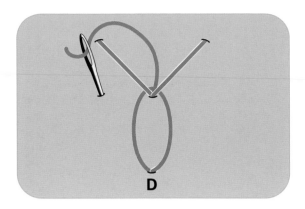

4 Bring the needle down at D and out at E to begin the first leg of the next V.

5 Repeat until completing the desired line length.

whipped running stitch

Whipped running stitch works well to create straight lines or curves. Try variations by using a contrasting thread or ribbon for whipping. Or alter the length and spacing of the running stitches.

1 From right to left, work a row of evenly spaced running stitches for the foundation.

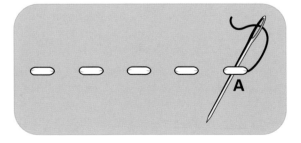

2 Thread a tapestry needle with a blunt end, which will prevent splitting foundation-row stitches. Bring up the tapestry needle at A next to the first stitch (to the right) in the foundation row.

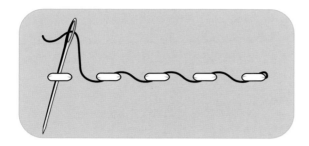

3 Whip the needle over then under the next stitch.

4 Repeat to the end of the row.

paper embroidery

Embroidering on paper will give you pleasure, especially if you enjoy paper arts or scrapbooking. Although delicate in appearance, this technique is not difficult and offers the opportunity for self-expression. Using a variety of threads, you can execute a number of surface embroidery stitches. Like fabric, papers are available in a range of weights, textures, and colors.

Attention to selection of materials contributes to success. Cardstock, a medium-weight paper, is a practical choice. Mulberry paper, rag paper, and silk paper are other examples. Containing cotton or linen fibers, these papers withstand wear. The higher the content of fibers, the stronger the paper. Corrugated cardboard, brown paper, wallpaper, suede paper, and velvet paper are popular with some crafters.

Most embroidery threads—cotton, rayon, polyester, linen, and silk—are suitable. Heavy or coarse thread, such as yarn and heavy crewel, are not as practical; large needles make large holes in the paper, and the threads may tear it. Use certain threads, such as metallic, for decorative effect. For stitching, choose the smallest needle possible, such as embroidery or crewel needle.

To begin, carefully mark where the stitches will be embroidered. Lightly draw the design with a pencil. If you're a beginner, test your design on cardstock; keep it basic and work with the outline. Or transfer your pattern to tracing paper, which you can then secure to the cardstock with tape that is low tack.

Poke holes about 1/8"/3mm apart, using a very fine piercing to make small holes and a coarse piercing tool for large holes that accommodate more than one thread. As you gain experience, you may opt to vary the distance between holes for creative effect. Remove the design.

Experiment with your surface embroidery repertoire. Many of these stitches work well when applied to paper, including backstitch, buttonhole stitch, chain stitch, couching stitch, detached daisy stitch, feather stitch, French knot, Herringbone stitch, open Cretan stitch, straight stitch, and running stitch. In general, choose stitches with wide spacing, as closely spaced stitches tend to cause tears.

For a decorative flourish, incorporate ribbon embroidery.

ribbon embroidery

Fun and fast to complete, ribbon embroidery lends itself to a range of artistic expression, from tiny delicate stitches to large, bold strokes.

The mid-18th century—when embroidered ribbons adorned the fashions of the French court—marked its first heyday. Ribbon embroidery spread to England, Australia, New Zealand, and the United States. It flourished once more in the 1880s and 1890s, when Victorians fussed with decoration. In the late 1980s, the practice underwent another revival in Australia, where needlework has remained popular. With a wealth of readily available ribbon, novice and expert needleworkers around the world enjoy this splendid art.

no-fuss, no-muss ribbon work

- Silk ribbon creases easily. If a brand is not available wrapped around storage reels, cut cardboard tubes from paper towels or bathroom tissue and wrap the ribbon around them.

- The more frequently you pull ribbon through fabric, the more it frays. Work with short lengths—10-14"/26-36cm.

- For easier use, lock the ribbon into the needle. Thread the ribbon through the eye of the needle. Pierce the just-threaded ribbon end in the center of the ribbon and about 1/4"/6mm from the end. Pull the long end, locking the strand in place.

- Before stitching, knot the end of the ribbon. After threading the needle, lay the long end of the ribbon over the needle. Wrap the ribbon around the needle. Pull the needle though to make a knot.

- Run the needle under a few stitches on the back of the fabric; end the ribbon toward the center of the stitching. For security, take through a ribbon piece on the back.

- Avoid pulling the ribbon too tightly or letting it twist when it should not.

- Avoid letting the ribbon twist on the back; that causes it to twist on the next front stitch.

- Use your free thumb to hold the ribbon flat against the fabric, releasing it at the last minute.

backstitch

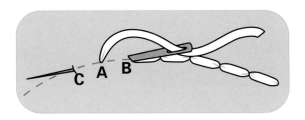

1 Bring the needle up at A and down at B. Bring the needle out at C and down at D. Repeat.

so many stitches

More than one hundred stitches are used in ribbon embroidery. A number are adapted from surface embroidery. However, the use of ribbon instead of thread affects execution. You'll find tips on handling the ribbon for optimum results.

buttonhole stitch

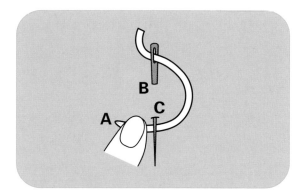

1 Bring the needle up at A. Holding the ribbon down with your thumb, bring the needle down at B and up at C.

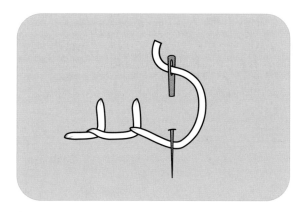

3 Bring the needle over the ribbon and pull the stitch into place. Repeat.

chain stitch

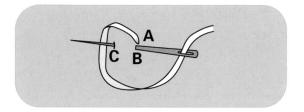

1 Bring the needle up at A and shape the ribbon into a loop; then bring the needle down at B and out at C. (Keep the needle over the ribbon.) Gently pull until the loop is the desired size.

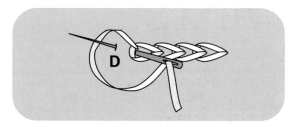

2 To make the next stitch, bring the needle up at D, taking care to insert where the thread emerged in the previous loop. Repeat until the desired length.

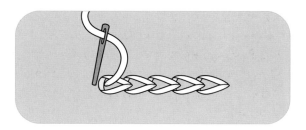

3 To end, bring the needle down over the end of the last loop.

couching

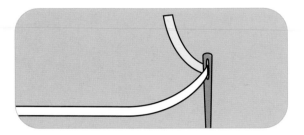

1 You will need two ribbons and two needles for this stitch. Working the ribbon that will lie flat, bring the needle up on the left side of the area to be covered. Stretch the ribbon over to the right and use your left thumb to hold it flat.

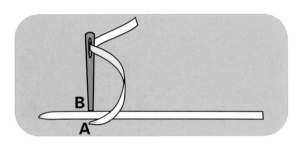

2 Bring the second needle up at A, over the laid ribbon, and down at B.

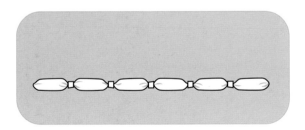

3 Repeat until the flat ribbon is secured. At the end of the row, bring the first needle down through fabric.

detached daisy

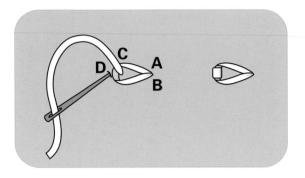

1 Bring the needle up at A and down at B, forming a loop. (Make sure the distance between A and B is close without piercing the ribbon.) Gently pull the loop to the desired size.

2 Bring the needle up at C. (Make sure that the loop is under the needle.) Bring the needle down at D to secure the loop.

Create a ribbon rosebud with a detached daisy stitch. For the calyx, make one fly stitch underneath the bud; you may want to use floss.

fern stitch

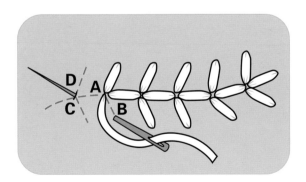

1 Lightly pencil the length and shape of the frond.

2 Bring the needle up at A and down at B. Bring the needle up C and down at D. Repeat to make additional sections of the fern.

fly stitch

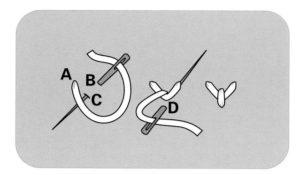

1 Bring the needle up at A and down and B. (Avoid pulling the ribbon too tightly.)

2 Bring the out at C, forming a loop. (Make sure that the loop is under the needle.) Pull the ribbon toward you, forming a V; then bring the needle down at D.

french knot

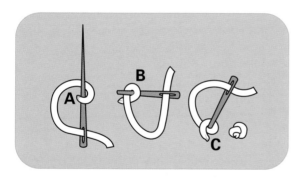

1 Bring the needle up at A and wrap the ribbon once or twice around it.

2 Turn the point of the needle clockwise and bring it down at B (close to A).

3 Keep the ribbon wrapped around the needle as you bring the needle down at C. Avoid pulling the knot too tightly, as ribbon knots should looser than those worked with embroidery thread.

herringbone stitch

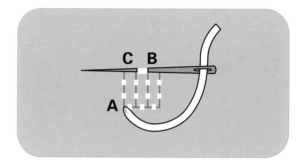

1 Working from left to right, bring the needle up at A, down at B, and out at C.

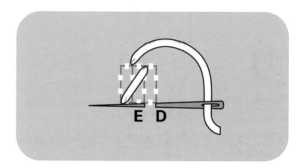

2 Bring the needle down at D and out at E.

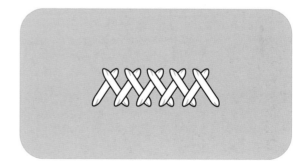

3 Repeat, continuing the row.

japanese ribbon stitch

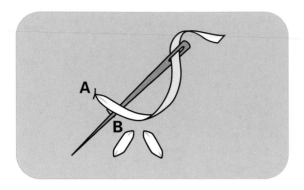

1 This stitch is also called ribbon stitch. Bring the needle up at A and flatten the ribbon with your fingers. Just below the length of the stitch, bring the needle down through the ribbon at B.

2 Slowly pull the ribbon through the fabric; the sides will curl inward, forming a point. Avoid pulling the ribbon tightly, as the curls should be visible—ideal for producing leaves and flower petals.

loop stitch

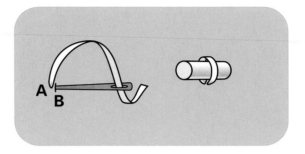

1 Bring the needle up at A and down at B, leaving a sizable loop.

2 To keep each loop uniform, insert a pencil (pen straw, toothpick, or large needle) through the loop. Pull until the loop is snug.

loop stitch flowers

1 Pencil a small circle.

2 Make the first three petals in a Y shape then fill in the two remaining petals.

3 Anchor the center with a French knot.

stem stitch

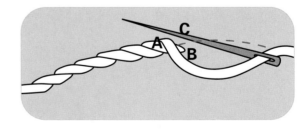

1 Working from left to right, bring the needle up at A.

2 Bring the needle in at B along the stitching line and bring it up at C (halfway between A and B).

3 Pull the thread through.

spider web rose stitch

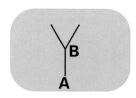

1 Use perle cotton or embroidery floss to form the spokes of the web. Bring the needle up at A and down at B. (Avoid pulling the thread too tightly.) Add a bar of equal length on each side.

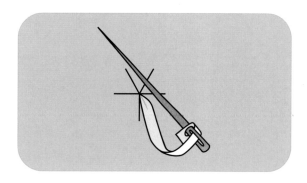

2 Now work with ribbon. Bring the needle up at the center of the web.

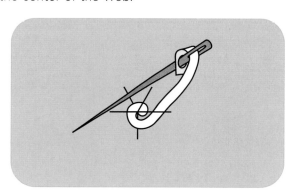

3 In counterclockwise direction, weave the ribbon over and under the spokes, keeping it loose and allowing it to twist.

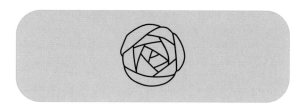

4 Continue until the spokes are covered.

straight stitch

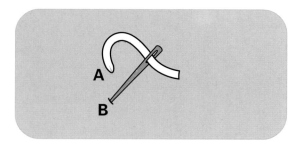

1 Bring the needle up at A and use your thumb to flatten the ribbon along the propose length of the stitch.

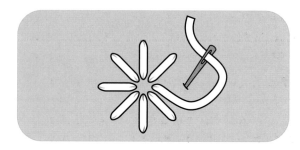

2 Bring the needle down at B and pull gently. Produce a multi-petal flower with eight stitches.

NOTE: For a more basic flower, slant three straight stitches so they meet at the bottom. Use the same color ribbon or a different color for the center stitch.

hardanger

Hardanger refers to a type of openwork counted-thread embroidery most often used for table linens. It typically calls for white or cream threads or threads that harmonize with the background fabric. Stitches called kloster blocks are arranged diagonally or in straight lines across evenweave fabric. Then the threads are cut within the blocks and removed, leaving straight threads that can be woven or wrapped and embellished with filling stitches. Other embroidery, such as satin stitch and backstitch, often decorates the fabric around the cutwork.

There are a variety of stitches in Hardanger, and all are easy to learn and execute. Combining different stitches results in an intricate design.

Practice stitches before starting a project. For flawless Hardanger, follow these tips:

- Work from the right, holding the fabric in your hand instead of using a hoop.

- Do not use knots to secure the thread. To begin, leave a 3"/7.5cm tail secured by two backstitches. You can unpick and weave them under some stitches or on the reverse side later.

- Always use enough thread to finish a block of five stitches. Avoid changing thread in the middle of a block. Fasten off threads on the back of the work.

- To ensure accuracy and avoid eyestrain, use a magnifying lamp for stitching and cutting.

- Work methodically, making sure stitches and blocks line up.

- Before cutting threads, complete all surface stitches and double check alignment of blocks.

- Work diagonally when stitching from one bar to the next. Always work Hardanger in sequence.

kloster blocks in a straight line

To make square and rectangular motifs, create kloster blocks—groups of horizontal and vertical stitches that enclose areas subsequently cut away. The simplest form is a square made of groups of five stitches worked over four fabric threads and placed at right angles to one another. Count threads carefully so that the last block will touch the first.

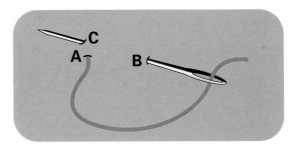

1 Make two small backstitches, leaving a tail of thread to secure later. Work five satin stitches over four threads of linen. Bring the needle up at A, in at B, and out at C. Repeat until completing block.

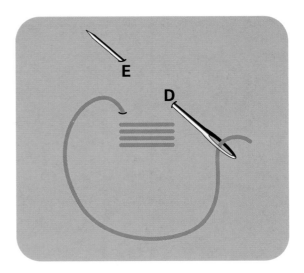

2 To make another block, bring the needle down at D and make a large diagonal stitch, bringing the needle out at E (four threads from the top of the previous block). Work the next block.

3 To turn a corner (at a right angle), bring the needle down at E, out at F (four threads away). Work the next block.

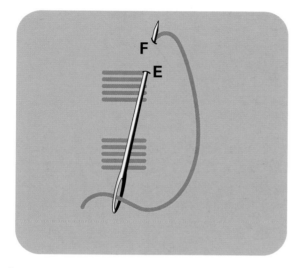

4 Continue working around the sides, stitching three kloster blocks on each side of the square.

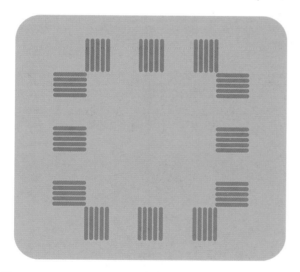

5 To finish, slip the needle under two blocks of stitches on the back of the fabric and trim the thread. Unpick the backstitches and sew the ends on the back of the fabric.

kloster blocks on the diagonal

Use kloster blocks to produce other patterns such as diamonds.

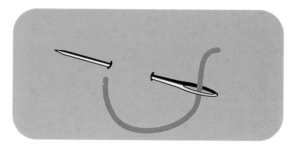

1 Make two small backstitches, leaving a tail of thread to secure later. Work five satin stitches over four threads of linen.

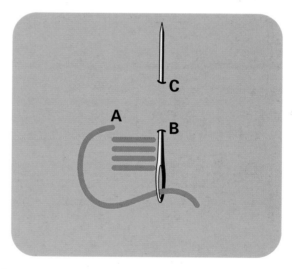

2 To turn a corner (at a right angle), bring the needle up at A, in at B, and out at C. Work the next block.

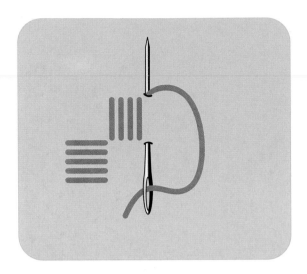

3 To turn the next corner, make a backstitch to bring the needle out at the opposite end of the last stitch. Work the next block at a right angle to the first.

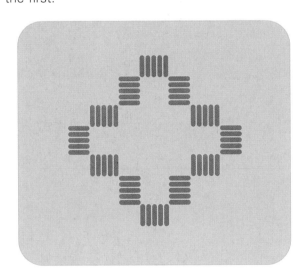

4 Work four blocks on each side to the diamond. Change the stitch angle by alternating steps 2 and 3 until you end up at the starting point.

cutting threads

Avoid cutting threads until completing all kloster blocks and surface embroidery. Make sure that the blocks are precisely opposite one another and that no threads have been skipped. (If you end up where you started, your stitching is accurate.) Cut the threads with fine pointed scissors.

cutting threads on a diamond pattern

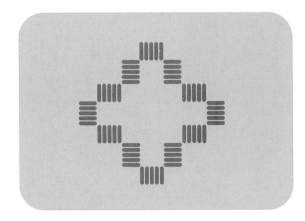

1 Cut threads between satin stitches, not at the end of the block. (Per block there are five satin stitches and four fabric threads to cut.)

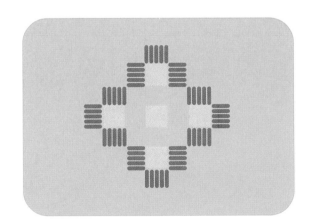

2 Use tweezers to pull out the cut threads, leaving a grid of threads arranged in a square pattern. (On a square pattern, the remaining threads will form a cross.)

cutting threads on larger motifs

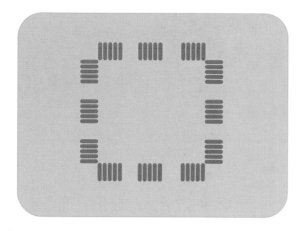

1 Follow the cut threads across and cut the other end on the opposite side of the motif. Cut the threads in groups of four instead of trying to cut across eight or twelve threads at once.

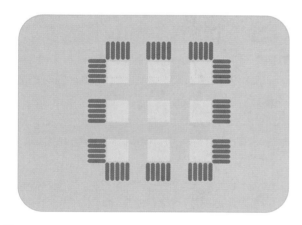

2 Cut the remaining threads. Pull out the cut threads, leaving a grid of threads.

wrapped bars

Wrapping threads that are left once the cutwork is done adds a decorative touch and strengthens the fabric.

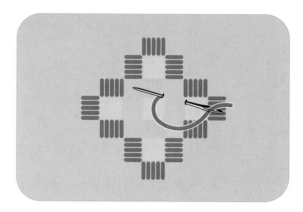

1 Secure the thread on the back of the fabric by slipping the needle under two or three kloster blocks. Keep your finger behind the fabric thread to tension them, and then wrap them tightly.

2 Take the needle across the back of the fabric to wrap the next bar. Work around the motif and secure the thread on the back.

woven bars

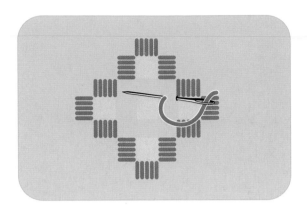

1 Secure the thread on the back of the fabric by slipping the needle under two or three kloster blocks. Bring the needle out in the middle of the group of fabric threads and backstitch over the first two threads.

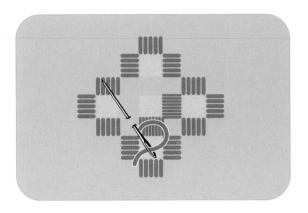

3 To continue to the next bar, bring the needle out in middle of the group of threads to be woven.

2 Weave over and under two threads (figure-eight pattern). Pull the thread tightly with each stitch. Continue weaving in a figure-eight pattern until the bar is fully covered. The stitches should be tight and even.

4 Continue until all the bars are woven. Sew in the ends on the reverse side of the fabric.

satin stitch

Satin stitch in particular gives Hardanger much of its character. Worked horizontally, vertically, or diagonally, this stitch can be used to produce a variety of motifs around or adjoining cut areas.

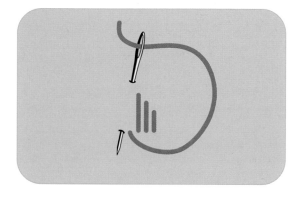

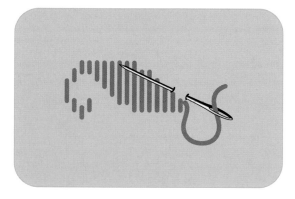

duplicate stitch

Duplicate stitch, also called Swiss darning, is a pleasing alternative for needleworkers who love the look of knits but have little time to devote to knitting. This technique involves duplicating a stitch already knitted into a garment to produce a motif, usually in a different color, and sometimes in a different yarn. And it's relatively easy.

If embroidery is a new pastime, choose a sweater that was knit in a large or medium gauge so the stitches will be easier to identify. Before trying the technique on a new sweater, purchase a secondhand sweater for practice. Make sure that the sweater is knitted in stockinette stitch (a knit with Vs created by knit and purl rows). Look for a light-colored sweater, as the stitches are easier to see than dark ones. Inspect it for straight, smooth rows of well-defined stitches. Stitches on a frequently washed sweater tend to blend together, making them hard to work with.

1 With basting thread, mark the area to be embroidered. Insert a tapestry or yarn needle (threaded) from the inside (wrong side) to the outside (right side of the sweater) at the base of a stitch and pull the needle through to the outside, leaving a tail of yard on the inside.

2 With the needle, trace the right side of the V (as compared to the left side), and insert the needle at the top of the right side of the V under the base of the stitch above, reinserting the point of the needle at the top of the left leg of the V.

3 Insert the needle at the point of the entry and through the point of the next stitch.

4 Adjust the tension on the thread so as to cover the stitch below. (Avoid pulling so tightly that you pucker the knitting underneath.)

5 To start the next row, insert the needle at the base of the stitch above the last stitch that you made. (Some needlecrafters ensure coverage of knitted stitches by alternating their rows: On one row, they cover the knitted stitch from the right side of the V to the left side. On the next row, they stitch from the left side of the V to the right side.

You can appropriate surface embroidery stitches for use in duplicate stitch. For example, outline stitch and stem stitch function as thin lines.

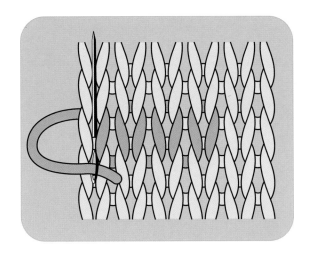

embroidery rescue tips

What do you do if the tip of a Japanese ribbon stitch is accidentally pulled too tight and disappears to the back of the fabric?

Insert the eye end of a chenille needle or the tip of a blunt tapestry needle under the ribbon and use it as a tool to gently wiggle and pull the stitch back up to the surface of the fabric.

If this doesn't work, make a second Japanese ribbon stitch right over the first one. The first stitch acts as padding, the second stitch hides it. The second stitch will be a tiny bit longer since you must begin the second stitch just beyond the original starting point and complete it just slightly past the end point of the one you are covering.

What do you do if a French knot is too tight?

If the French knot was stitched with silk ribbon, cover it with a second, looser French knot stitched directly over the first one. The first stitch acts as padding. Begin the second knot right next to one side of the first stitch and complete it on the other side so the first knot is completely covered and not visible. Another trick: Instead of hiding the tight knot, stitch two or three additional French knots of different sizes close to the first one. A cluster of French knots fools your eye into thinking you intended to have different sizes.

If the French knot was stitched with floss or wool it is difficult, but not impossible, to hide with a second knot stitched right over the first one if you are careful. The first knot acts as padding, the second knot covers and hides the first one. Alternatives: Stitch two or three more French knots of different sizes, just like the suggestion for ribbon embroidery. Seed beads look much like French knots so you can add them, too.

What do you do if a French knot is too loose?

If the French knot was stitched with silk ribbon, bring the needle and silk up right in the middle of it and stitch down over the side of the knot that is too loopy.

If the French knot was stitched with floss or wool carefully bring the needle and thread right up into the middle of the stitch and make one or more tiny stitches to catch and tack the loopy part of the knot. Use a single strand of floss or wool to avoid getting a lumpy, large knot and to keep the repair stitches from showing. Alternatively, snip off (or "behead") the errant French knot, secure the thread tails on the back of the project, and begin again.

bead embroidery

Bead Embroidery embellishes wearables, accessories, and wallhangings. Use beads to produce interesting textures and to highlight small details. Sequins, spangles, shisha glass, and jewel-like pieces imbue surfaces with sparkle and dramatic color. Although dazzling, bead embroidery is achievable, even for novices. In fact, most familiar stitches adapt readily to this technique, including backstitch, couching, chain stitch, detached chain stitch, feather stitch, fern stitch, fly stitch, herringbone stitch, satin stitch, and open Cretan stitch.

You can attach beads to any fabric, although chiffon and voile require need lightweight backing such as lawn. Frame the work for stitching.

Select a strong thread such as sewing cotton or polyester that is still fine enough to pass through the hole in the bead or sequin. Pull the thread through a block of beeswax to strengthen the thread and prevent if from twisting.

Beading needles are long and fine. They have a tendency to bend, so replace them whenever this happens.

To create textures and patterns sew on masses of beads and sequins one at a time. You may need to a secure sequin with two or three stitches or with a bead sewn in the center.

To form a loop, bring the needle up through the fabric and thread on the beads. Bring the needle down as close as possible to where it emerged.

To produce a fringed effect, bring the needle up through the fabric and thread on several beads. Take the needle back through each one except the one at the bottom.

For stitching in rows, try lazy stitch, couching, and backstitch.

couching

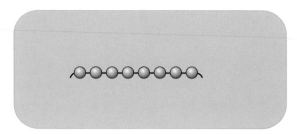

1 Knot the thread end and bring the needle up. Thread on the beads and lay them on the fabric.

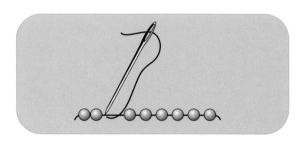

2 Knot the couching threads. Bring the needle up and secure the foundation thread.

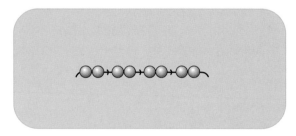

3 Continue securing the foundation thread at even intervals such as every two to three beads.

backstitch

1 Knot the thread end and bring the needle up. Thread on four beads and bring the needle down by the last bead.

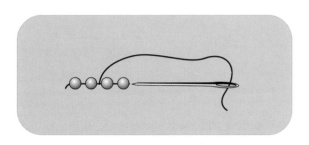

2 Bring the needle up between the second and third beads. Insert the needle in the third and fourth beads, taking a stitch.

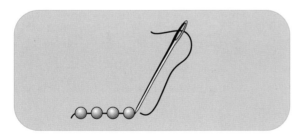

3 Repeat with four more beads.

lazy stitch

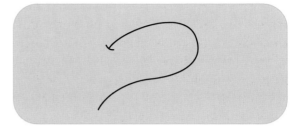

1 Knot the thread end and bring the needle up.

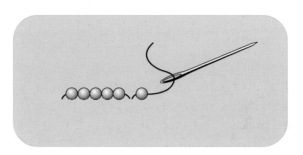

2 Thread on five beads. Bring the needle down and immediately back up (no more than the width of half of a bead).

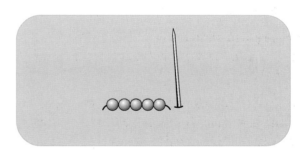

3 Repeat with five more beads.

flower jeans and purse

With ready-made appliqué flowers and a little simple embroidery, you can give your favorite jeans and accessories a look that's fresh and fun.

Joan K. Morris

skill level
Easy

materials
2 packages of iron-on flower appliqués

Pair of blue jeans

Blue-jean purse

Fabric glue (optional)

2 skeins of light green cotton pearl floss

Iron and ironing board

Dressmakers pen

Scissors

Large-eye embroidery needle

instructions

1 Use the iron and follow package directions to apply the flower appliqués to the jeans, purse, or gloves. If necessary, use the fabric glue as well. Let glue dry.

2 Use the dressmakers pen to draw the vines and the leaves onto jeans and purse.

3 Cut a piece of floss, knot the end, and use the embroidery needle to stitch vines and leaves. Use the stem stitch for the vines and the satin stitch for the leaves; create a vein on the leaf by stitching from the center to the edge, leaving the leaf's center slightly open.

NOTE: Since the jeans will be washed, you might want to dab a bit of fabric glue on the knots on the inside to keep them from coming undone.

bloomin' gloves

Appliqué flowers and embroidery are as at home on knit gloves as they are on denim. It's so easy to make a coordinated outfit!

Joan K. Morris

skill level

Easy

materials

1 packages of iron-on flower appliqués

Pair of knit gloves

Fabric glue (optional)

1 scrap piece of cardboard, slightly larger than

the gloves

1 skeins of light green cotton pearl floss

Iron and ironing board

Dressmakers pen

Scissors

Large-eye embroidery needle

instructions

1 Use the iron and follow package directions to apply the flower appliqués to the gloves. (Be careful when applying appliqués to the gloves; the iron can scorch the knit.) If necessary, use the fabric glue as well. Let glue dry.

2 Insert a piece of scrap cardboard cut to be a little larger than the glove. (This will stretch the knit so that you can draw (and stitch) your design easily.) Use the dressmakers pen to draw the vines and the leaves onto the gloves.

3 Cut a piece of floss, knot the end, and use the embroidery needle to stitch vines and leaves. Use the stem stitch for the vines and the satin stitch for the leaves; create a vein on the leaf by stitching from the center to the edge, leaving the leaf's center slightly open.

NOTE: You might want to dab a bit of fabric glue on the knots on the inside to keep them from coming undone.

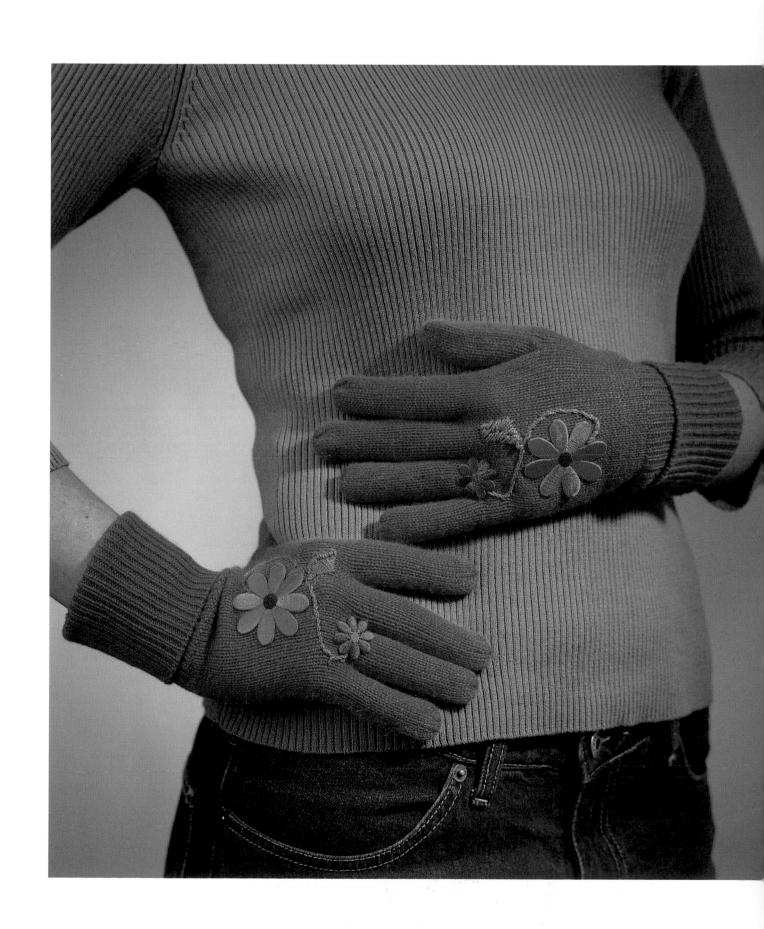

beaded trim top

Beth Fielding

Beaded ribbon trims offer needleworkers an easy, quick way to add the sparkle of colorful beads to necklines, cuffs, pockets, and more.

instructions

1 Pin the beaded trim to the top neckline, beginning at the center back and working your way back around to the starting point. Do not cut any excess trim.

2 Baste the trim in place with a sewing needle and thread, then embroider over the ribbon with a running, chain, or stem stitch. If the beads are especially heavy, you may need to embroidery both the top and bottom edges of the ribbon. In the top shown here, a running stitch done at the top edge of the ribbon was sufficient. Stop embroidering about half an inch (13mm) before you reach the end.

3 Remove the basting stitches and remove any excess beaded trim, allowing a small amount for overlap.

4 Fold under the cut trim edge and embroider over the fold to prevent unraveling and hide any raw edges.

5 Press the ribbon with a low-heat iron if needed. For best laundering results, wash the garment by hand, not machine.

skill level

Easy

materials

Pullover top or sweater

Beaded ribbon trim

Sharp-tipped sewing pins, needle, and thread

Scissors

Embroidery floss in complementary color

Embroidery needle

confetti scarf set

Cathy Maguire

Here's a fun approach to beading and embroidery. Using a simple sewing technique, you can scatter sequins and beads like falling confetti on a purchased scarf set. Feel free to experiment with different color combinations.

skill level
Easy

materials

Metallic flat sequins in silver and pink, 9mm

Knit hairband, gloves, and scarf

Rayon thread (to match the scarf set)

Glass seed beads in lilac and silver, 10/0

Clear cupped sequins, 5 and 10mm

Acrylic jewels, 4.5mm

Fabric glue

Straight pins

Ruler

Scissors

Small-eye needle

instructions

1 Use the straight pins to mark where you want to place the 9 mm silver sequins on the hairband, gloves, and scarf. As shown in the photograph, you'll embellish the entire headband, the gloves' edges, and the area measuring about 9"/23 cm up from each end of the scarf.

2 Double-thread the needle with a long length of thread, and tie the two thread ends into a knot twice. Trim the ends so they're completely covered by the sequin.

3 Here's a simple technique that will attach the sequins and beads firmly. Insert the needle into the right side, taking care to catch only the material's top layer. Make a short double stitch, ending with the thread on the right side. Thread on one sequin and one lilac bead. Keeping the thread taut so the bead sits over the sequin hole, bring your needle back down through the sequin hole (but not through the bead hole) and

make another double stitch over the first one. Knot the thread ends twice on the right side; make sure you get the first knot as close to the material as you can. Trim thread ends.

4 Repeat the process with the remaining silver sequins.

5 Mark where you want to place the 9 mm pink sequins with straight pins. Use the same technique as above to secure the pink sequins and silver beads.

6 Mark where you've decided to place the small and large cupped sequins. At this point, start creating clusters of sequins. Pair the cupped sequins with either a lilac or a silver bead, and secure in the same fashion.

7 Scatter the remaining acrylic jewels, using a small dab of fabric glue to attach them.

geometric tote

Perk up a dull denim tote with a scattering of colorful felt circles and sparkling sequins.

Joan K. Morris

instructions

1 To make the circular patterns, start with the four round objects you've assembled; for example, you can use cups, small cans, or pill bottles. Use the pencil to draw around each of the objects on the scrap paper, and then cut out the circles.

2 Pin the four patterns onto one of the pieces of colored felt and cut out the shapes. Repeat for the other three colors. You'll have 16 felt circles in all.

3 Lay the tote on a flat surface. Arrange the felt circles on the tote until you are pleased with the result. (Don't feel obligated to use all 16 circles.) Use a straight pin to mark each spot where you've decided to place a circle.

4 Thread the embroidery needle with the black floss, and knot the end. Embroider a blanket stitch edge around each circle. The top of the stitch will range from about 1/2"/1.3cm

from the edge of the larger circles to 1/4"/6mm from the edge of the smaller ones.

5 Follow the manufacturer's instructions and apply the iron-on adhesive to the backside of each circle (i.e., the side with the knot). Next apply each circle to the tote. If necessary, reinforce any loose spots with fabric glue. Let dry.

6 With the black floss, stitch a sequin in a matching color to the center of each circle, making sure that the knots are on the inside of the tote. Apply a dab of fabric glue to each knot to keep it from unraveling. Allow to completely dry before handling.

skill level
Easy

materials
Scrap paper

4 pieces of felt, measuring 9 x 12"/23 x 30cm each in a different color

1 denim tote bag

1 skein of black cotton pearl embroidery floss

Iron-on adhesive (ultra bond for felt)

Fabric glue

1 package of multicolor sequin bangles

tools
4 assorted round objects, ranging from 1"/2.5cm to 3.5 "9cm in diameter

Pencil

Scissors

Straight pins

Large-eye embroidery needle

Ruler

Iron and ironing board

embroidered child's sweater

Beth Fielding

Sweaters make great canvases for embroidery and a variety of stencil patterns are available to make it easy. Although needle-work departments often have good selections of stencils, don't be shy about investigating stencils in scrapbooking, glass etching, and craft painting departments for more choices.

instructions

1 Working on an inconspicuous area of the sweater, experiment to determine the embroidery floss thickness most complementary to your sweater. If the fabric in thin, you may need to split the floss into a two- or three-thread strand. If the fabric is thick, you may need to stitch with two or three thicknesses of floss.

2 Position the stencil on one side of the sweater front. Pin in place and transfer the stencil pattern with a transfer pen or chalk pencil.

3 Embroider the stencil pattern in flattering stitches. French knots, the chain stitch, and the lazy daisy stitch were used in this project.

4 If desired, choose a single element or two from the stencil's design and repeat it around the hem, neckline, or sleeve.

5 Press the stitching flat from the back side of the sweater. Launder by hand as needed.

skill level
Easy

materials
Purchased child's sweater

Stencil

Embroidery floss in several complementary colors

Tapestry needle

Sewing pins

Transfer pen or chalk pencil

ribbons and roses sheets

Cathy Maguire

Add a few delicate flowers and a little ribbon, and you've turned a simple sheet set into something simply stunning. If you're short on time, consider embellishing just the pillowcases.

skill level

Intermediate

materials

2 spools of thread, burgundy and pink

5 yds/4.6m burgundy organza ribbon, 1/4"/6mm wide

Set of pink percale sheets with ruffles

6 yards (5.5 m) pink variegated ribbon, 3/16"/5mm wide

2 skeins of embroidery floss in medium green and light green

Package of organza sheer roses, assorted colors

Sewing machine with needle for fine fabrics

Straight pins

Scissors

Ruler

Fine point disappearing ink pen

2 tapestry needles, size 26

Small-eye needle

NOTE: Be sure to alter the thread, ribbon, and sheet colors to suit your personal taste.

instructions

1 Thread the burgundy thread through the sewing machine's needle and the bobbin with pink thread. Set the stitch size for 1/16"/1.5mm.

2 Cut the burgundy ribbon approximately 1/2"/12mm longer than the flat sheet's width. Pin the ribbon just under the ruffles so it extends a little past the sheet's edge on each side. Fold the ribbon ends and pin flush with the sheet's edges.

3 Sew the ribbon to the sheet, stitching as close as possible to the ribbon's top and bottom edges. (Don't worry if the organza's weave becomes distorted; you actually want to produce a ribbed effect.)

4 To attach ribbon to the pillowcase, pin the ribbon just

under the ruffles so it starts a little past a seam. Stitch along the ribbon's top edge around the case until you've almost reached your starting point. Cut the ribbon so it extends beyond the seam, fold the end, and pin so the folded edge is flush with the near seam edge. Finish the row of stitches. Sew along the ribbon's bottom edge to secure.

5 Thread the machine with pink thread. Measure 3/4"/2cm below the burgundy ribbon, and use the same techniques in Steps 3 and 4 to attach the ribbon to the flat sheet and pillowcases. Periodically make sure you're maintaining the 3/4" gap.

6 To create stems on the flat sheet and on one side of the pillowcases, use the fine point pen to trace 6"/15 cm long S-shapes between the ribbons, working from the center out-

ward and spacing the stems 1"/2.5cm apart.

7 Thread one tapestry needle with the medium green floss and the other with the light green. Beginning on the wrong side of the flat sheet, embroider the first stem with small, evenly spaced running stitches in medium green, finishing on the wrong side. Use light green for the next S-shape, and continue embroidering stems, alternating between the medium and light greens.

8 Wrap the medium green running stitches in light green and vice versa by bringing your needle up to the right side slightly above one end of a stem. Weave the thread through the running stitches, always entering the running stitch from above. Don't pull the floss too

taut; you want a rope effect. Finish on the wrong side.

9 Embroider three lazy daisy leaves at each end of the stem, alternating the leaves above and below the stem.

10 To make the flowers, cut 12 lengths of the pink ribbon and nine of the burgundy, each measuring 8"/20cm. Using a 1/4" seam allowance, sew the ribbon into a closed loop. Finger press seams. Double-thread the small-eye needle with thread to match the ribbon and sew running stitches close to the ribbon's edge. Pull tight to gather, then secure the gathering with a backstitch and double knot.

11 Double-thread the small-eye needle with pink thread. Sew a single stitch next to the stem's midpoint and then attach a handmade flower with two or three stitches. Finish with a double knot on the right side of the fabric and trim ends. Be sure to alternate colors.

12 Apply a ready-made organza rose to each end of the stem by looping that thread through the rose's green ribbon and then stitching the flower to the sheet, alternating the colors in a pattern you find pleasing.

a sweet little drawstring bag

Joan K. Morris

Velvet drawstring bags are simple to make, require minimal sewing skills, and make great embroidery surfaces. They make great evening purses.

skill level
Easy

materials
Small piece of black velvet

Skein gold embroidery floss

Package of small pearl beads

Black thread

1/4"/6mm black satin ribbon

tools
Scissors

Ruler

Straight pins

Large-eye embroidery needle

Sewing machine

Pencil

Safety pin

instructions

1 Cut the black velvet fabric so that you have a piece measuring 11 x 18"/28 x 46cm.

2 Place the fabric on a flat surface with the right side facing up and the short end at the top. Temporarily fold both the top and bottom edges over 2.5"/6 and pin in place. Next fold the piece in half widthwise, wrong sides together, so that the folded edges meet at the top. This step will give you a sense of the finished size of bag so you can place your designs. Place a pin where you want the center of each design to be. Don't place the designs too close to the side edges since you'll need to allow for 1/2"/12mm seams on each side.

3 For each arm of the design, separate a length of floss into three strands; thread the neede and knot the end. Starting at the design's center, do a chain stitch for 1", referring to the photo as a guide, then place a pearl. On the wrong side, run the thread back through the stitches to the center. Bring the thread up to the right side and start the chain stitch for the next arm. Repeat until you have six arms in all. Tie off the thread on the wrong side.

4 Repeat Step 3 until you have completed all your designs.

5 Now fold the bag widthwise with right sides together, and unpin the top folds. With the black thread, machine-stitch the sides, using a 1/2" seam allowance. Stitch one side completely from top to bottom. On the other side, stitch down 3.5"/9cm from the top, leaving a 1/2" gap before resuming the seam to the bottom. (The gap will allow you to run the ribbon through the drawstring casing.) Use your fingers to press the seams open. (If you iron the seams open when working with velvet, you risk losing a lot of the nap.)

6 Turn the top edge over 1/4" and machine-stitch.

7 Fold the top over 2"/5cm with wrong sides together, and machine-stitch close to the edge. Create the drawstring casing by measuring 1/2" above this first line of stitches and machine-stitching around the purse again. (Before you start, make sure the opening you left in the side seam falls between these two lines of stitches.)

8 Turn the bag right side out. Push out the corners with a pencil.

9 Place the safety pin on one end of the ribbon. Push the safety pin into the hole in the seam, and slide the ribbon and safety pin all the way around the bag. When you reach the other seam; just keep wiggling the pin until it goes through. Once the ribbon comes out the other side, tie the ends into a knot, and close the bag by pulling the ribbon tight.

elegant red velvet clutch

Joan K. Morris

If you can sew a seam, you can add a hint of drama to any ensemble with this simple, yet sensuous clutch purse.

skill level

Easy

materials

Small piece of specialty fabric red velvet

Skein of silver embroidery floss

12 square beads

Thread

tools

Scissors

Ruler

Dressmakers pen

Large-eye embroidery needle

Sewing machine

Pencil

instructions

1 Cut the two pieces of velvet, each 10 x 18"/25 x 46cm.

2 Place the two pieces right sides together. Use the dressmakers pen to mark the center of one of the 10" edges. From the top corners, measure 6"/15cm down along both 18" side edges and mark. Draw diagonal lines from the marks along the side edges to the center mark on the 10"side, and cut to make the triangular flap at the top of the purse.

3 Thread the embroidery needle with three strands of silver floss, and knot the end. Take one of the pieces of velvet and, on the right side, measure in 1"/2.5cm from the point of the triangle. That's where you stitch down your first bead. Then place the remaining eleven beads 1" apart, referring to the photo as a guide.

4 With the silver floss, use a chain stitch to connect the beads, referring to the photo as a guide.

5 Place the two pieces of velvet right sides together. Thread your sewing machine with the red thread, and stitch all away around the edges, using a 1/2" seam allowance and leaving about a 3"/7.5cm opening along one side. Remember: it's difficult to keep the two layers of velvet together while sewing, so stitch slowly and keep lining up the layers as you go. Clip the corners. Use your fingers to press the seams open. (If you iron the seams open when working with velvet, you risk losing a lot of nap.)

6 Turn the bag right side out through the hole. Push out the corners with a pencil. Hand-stitch hole closed with red thread.

7 Lay the bag on the table so that the flap with the beads is facing you. Fold the bottom of the clutch up to the base of the triangular flap so that the main part of the purse measures 10 x 6 inches (25.4 x 15.2 cm). Machine-stitch the two sides as close to the edge as possible, making sure to catch all the edges.

8 Turn the bag inside side out and flip the flap over.

monogrammed floral pillow

Anna Griffin

Pillows make beautiful canvases to showcase and personalize your favorite embroidery designs and great special occasion gifts. For best results, look for pillows with a zipper or envelope construction so you can easily remove the fabric cover. If you're handy with a sewing machine (or have a sewing friend), you can also embroider directly onto fabric yardage and then make it into a pillow cover.

skill level

Intermediate

materials

Removable pillow cover

Small piece of tulle fabric

Sewing needle and thread

Small embroidery hoop

Monogram letter, reduced or enlarged to fit inside floral pattern*

Silk ribbon in two floral colors and two foliage colors**

Cotton embroidery floss in three colors, one for stem, one for monogram, and one for floral monogram accent

Embroidery needle

Small scissors

*Calligraphy books and the internet are good sources for monogram patterns.

**Chose colors that complement your pillow cover.

instructions

1 Wash the pillow cover, then press well.

2 Place the tulle over the embroidery pattern and trace the stitching outlines with an ink pen.

3 Trim the tulle, leaving about 1"/2.5cm of space around the design. Position the tulle on the pillow front and secure temporarily in place with loose bast-

ing stitches. Center the pattern area in the embroidery hoop.

4 Separate the floss into three threads and embroider the stem in an outline or whipped outline stitch.

5 Using silk ribbon, embroider the leaves with a ribbon stitch or padded straight stitch, then embroider the flowers with padded straight stitches.

6 Add French knots with silk ribbon in the flower centers and on the stems as decorative accents.

7 Transfer the monogram letter to the tulle and baste in place as directed in Step 3.

8 Embroider the letter with three strands of cotton floss using a combination of satin stitches (for wider areas) and outline stitches (for narrower areas).

9 Choose an area in the monogram to add a floral accent or two. Separate the floss into three strands, then embroider the flower(s) with a circle of small French knots. Add a single French knot in the center of each bloom using the stem color.

10 Remove the embroidery hoop and gently cut and tear away the tulle.

whimsical holiday napkins

Cynthia Preston

Picture this: Your guests whip out their holiday-embroidered napkins at the dinner table, and the gentle sound of tiny jingle bells fill the air. How much more festive can you get?

instructions

1 Fold the napkin hem over just enough so the existing hem stitches still show, and pin it in place parallel to the edge. (Hint: If you're working with silk, use silk pins instead of regular straight pins, to avoid leaving marks in the material.) Thread the darning needle with the metallic embroidery thread.

2 Use whip stitches or blanket stitches to hold the folded hem in place. Space the stitches evenly, about 1/2"/12mm apart. You can use the existing hem stitches as a guide; for example, on the napkins used in this project, there is one whip stitch for every five hem stitches. Make three stitches in each corner.

3 Open the jump rings with the needle-nose pliers and put a jingle bell on each. At each corner, attach the jingle bell to the middle stitch and close the ring.

4 Use the iron to press the napkin on the wrong side, and don't forget to always launder by hand.

NOTE: Although this project uses burgundy napkins with gold thread and bells, you can try other combinations— for instance, white napkins with silver embroidery thread and bells.

skill level
Easy

materials
Napkins

Gold metallic embroidery thread

4 small jump rings

4 small jingle bells

Pins

Darning needle

Needle-nose pliers

Iron and ironing board

embroidered cards

Why limit your embroidery embellishment to fabric? Handcrafted cards are fun to make and cherished by the receivers.

Terry Taylor

instructions

1 Trim the ribbon to the width of your card. Spray the back side and smooth in place with right side up.

2 Cut decorative shapes of the paper and arrange them over the ribbon, spacing as desired. Spray their back sides with adhesive and press smoothly in place.

3 Use a paper piercer to punch small holes at the top and bottom edges of the ribbon where you would like your running stitches to appear. You will need to pierce through all three layers: the card stock, the ribbon, and the decorative paper.

4 Separate the floss into three strands, then embroider the top and bottom edges of the ribbon, leaving the floss tails dangling at both ends.

5 Trim the floss tails to 1"/2.5cm, then fold them under to the inside of the card and tape in place.

6 Remove the adhesive backing from the rickrack, then press gently in place in the center of the ribbon. Trim the edges flush with the card.

skill level
Easy

materials
Blank cards

Spray adhesive

Grosgrain ribbon

Decorative paper

Adhesive-backed rickrack trim

Embroidery floss

Paper piercer

Clear tape

Embroidery needle

Scissors

applique hand towels

Brighten any room with customized applique hand towels. Chose colors and shapes that complement your decor, then have fun!

Kathy Cano Murillo

instructions

1 Cut a length of decorative trim to the width of your towel plus 1/2"/13mm. Attach the trim with machine stitching or fabric glue.

2 Embroider a row of chain stitches above the decorative trim in a contrasting color.

3 Cut out six pieces of felt about 1.5"/4cm at the widest point in the geometric shape of your choice, then cut out six more pieces of felt in contrasting colors about 1/2" smaller on all sides.

4 Position the smaller felt shapes on top of the larger shapes and pin in place in the embroidery panel area of the towel. Hold in place with straight pins.

5 Secure the felt shapes in place with contrasting colors of embroidery floss, referring to the photo as a guide.

6 Add large decorative cross stitches in the blank areas between the embroidered felt shapes.

skill level
Easy

materials
Kitchen towels with embroidery panel

Several colors of felt

Contrasting colors of cotton embroidery floss

Embroidery needle

Decorative trim

Fabric glue (optional)

Sewing pins

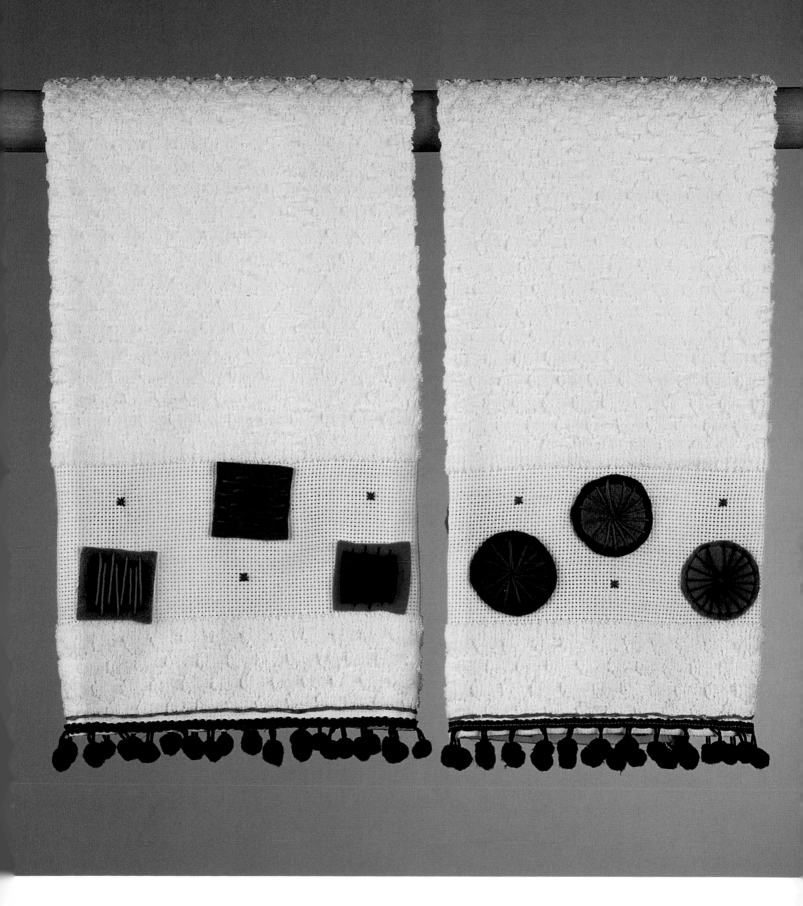

glitzy holiday sweater

Marylyn Hostetter

Why should knitters and crocheters have all the fun? Dozens of novelty yarns featuring everything from sparkles to chenilles to fluffy mohairs line the shelves, just waiting for a little attention from embroiders. Choose a large-eyed tapestry needle and a spectacular yarn, then embellish a plain sweater or blanket.

instructions

1 Photocopy the monogram letter of your choice, reducing or enlarging as desired.

2 Trace the monogram onto tissue paper, then position and pin it in place on the sweater. Tip: For a firmer working surface, place a magazine or sturdy piece of cardboard inside the sweater before pinning.

3 Embroider the monogram over the tissue paper in the stitch of your choice: the satin stitch and the chain stitch make good choices. Gently tear away the tissue paper.

4 Embellish the sleeves and neckline with a simple running stitch. If desired, leave the threads on the front side so they can be tied in bows.

variation

For a fun variation, embroider an initial letter and accent it with beads. A great selection of letters can be found in the scrapbooking aisle, as well is in calligraphy and typography books.

skill level
Easy

materials
Plain sweater

Metallic knitting/crochet yarn

Tapestry needle

Monogram letter

Tissue paper

Pencil

Sewing pins

embroidered greeting card

Kathy Cano Murillo

Although many people consider embroidery and craft painting as separate techniques, they complement each other beautifully and can be combined with great results.

instructions

1 Open the card and lay it flat, then gently pierce holes in paper around the edges that will form the front of the card in the running stitch locations. (See basics section for a review of the technique.)

2 Embroider the card in a running stitch. Tie off the threads on the back side and secure with a dab of glue.

3 Paint a rickrack pattern around the inside of the running stitch border. Allow the paint to completely dry, then add a thinner rickrack pattern over the first design in a second color. Set the card aside.

4 Use a craft knife to cut the cardboard into two 2"/5cm squares, then trim away the inside of the squares to leave a narrow frame border.

5 Paint the tops and sides of both frames. Allow the paint to completely dry, then glue the two frames together. Add accent dots in puff paint around the frame.

6 Trim the colored cardstock to a square that's slightly smaller than the frames. Decide on an embroidery pattern (an asymmetrical satin stitch star was used here) and pierce holes in the paper where the needle will go. Stitch the design, using the holes as a guide. Tie off the threads on the back side and secure with a dab of glue.

7 Place the cardboard frame face down and glue the right side of the embroidered square to the back side of the frame. Finger press and allow to completely dry.

8 Glue the craft jewel or bead to the center of your stitched design, then glue the finished frame to the center front of your card.

skill level
Easy

materials

Blank card

Small piece of cardstock in a solid color

Three colors of craft paint

One contrasting color of puff paint

Two contrasting colors of embroidery floss

Craft jewel or bead

Small piece of cardboard

Craft knife

Paper piercer

Embroidery needle

Craft glue

embroidered scrapbook elements

Kathy Cano Murillo

As diverse as they are, scrapbookers tend to have one thing in common: They passionately want their pages to be one-of-a-kind creations. Embroidering design elements for your scrapbooking pages is a simple, fun way to create unique page elements.

instructions

1 Fold down the long edges of the color copy in the location you want the photo to stop. Unfold the paper, place a ruler against the folded area, and tear gently to create a ragged edge. Repeat on the two shorter edges.

2 Repeat Step 1 with the decorative paper, allowing a 1/2"/12mm border around all sides.

3 Thread the needle with embroidery floss. Position the color copy in the center of the decorative paper, then gently pierce through both layers in the running stitch locations. (See basics section for a review of the technique.) Stitch the two papers together. Tie off the threads on the back side and secure with a dab of glue.

4 Separate the second color of embroidery floss into three strands and thread the needle.

Gently pierce the outside of the decorative paper in the chain stitch locations, echoing the torn shape of the paper. Embroider the chain stitches. Tie off the threads on the back side and secure with a dab of glue.

5 Trim the card stock to create a border of the desired size. Embroider the top and bottom edges with the same color floss you used to embroider the color copy, using the paper piercer to prepare the holes as you did in Steps 3 and 4.

6 Secure the embroidered photograph papers to the cardstock with adhesive foam squares, then position the entire element on a scrapbooking page.

NOTE: The same technique can be used to make handmade cards. Just double the width of the card stock and fold in half after embroidering.

skill level
Easy

materials
Color copy of a favorite photograph

Small sheet of card stock

Small sheet of decorative paper in a contrasting color

Two colors of embroidery floss

Ruler

Paper piercer

Embroidery needle

Craft glue

Adhesive foam squares

floral sampler

Fatema, Khadija, and Hajera
Habibur-Rahman

Bring the fresh colors and textures of the garden indoors.
This project combines silk ribbon embroidery and cross-stitch
on a ready-to-stitch afghan. The result is a comforting throw
that blooms year-round.

instructions

charts

There are symbols (usually numbers) displayed on Chart A and Chart B. The symbols are also found in the Legend for Chart A and the Legend for Chart B. The symbols represent the type of stitch and the number of plies or size of the ribbon used.

stitches

Chain stitch

Cross-stitch

Knotted Stitch

Lazy daisy stitch

Loop stitch

Ribbon stitch

Straight stitch

to start

Work the fringing instructions as directed on afghan label.

stitching

NOTE: Avoid transferring the pattern by tracing with a pencil or marker, as afghan material requires careful handling and should not be overworked.

1 Stitch a flower cart on each corner square. To locate the stitches accurately, start at the center of each square and count the squares as indicated on the Flower Cart Chart on page 303. Cross-stitch the wagons on the top left and bottom right corners, then stitch the wagon wheels and spikes on each wagon.

2 Stitch the flowers and foliage on each flower cart, referring to the chart on page 303 as a guide. Make sure that each knotted stitch is carefully centered in its loop stitch.

3 Stitch the flowers and foliage in colors of your choice, refer-

ring to the chart below as a gide. Make sure that each knotted stitch is carefully centered in its loop stitch.

protective backing

To protect the back side of your stitches and create a more finished look, cut a muslin square or rectangle to fit the stitch block areas of your afghan plus 1/4"/6mm on each side. Press under 1/4" on each side, then whipstitch the square in place.

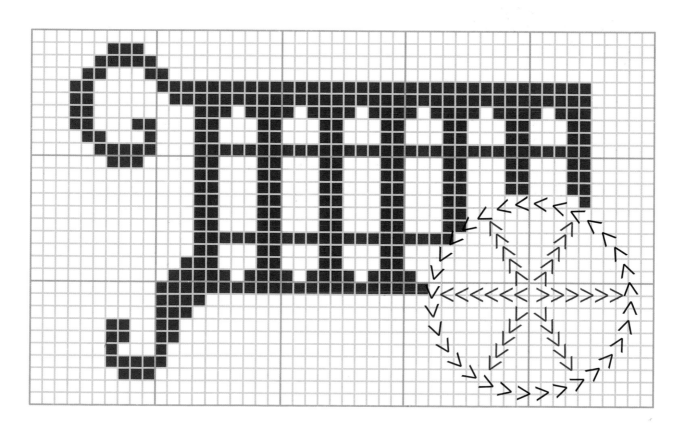

artful card

Kathy Cano Murillo

Raid the scrapbooking aisle to create this customized embroidered message card. The three-dimensional effect is created with adhesive foam squares. If you plan to send the card through the mail, ask the post office to hand-cancel the postage.

skill level
Easy

materials
Blank card

Metallic gold marker

2 small pieces of card-
stock in contrasting colors

Adhesive letters

Two colors of embroidery
floss

Ruler

Paper piercer

Embroidery needle

Adhesive foam squares

Craft glue

instructions

1 Fold a narrow edge down along the front side of your card. Unfold the paper, place a ruler against the folded area, and tear gently to create a ragged edge.

2 Lightly gild the torn edges of the paper with the metallic pen.

Cut a rectangle from one color of cardstock to fit on the center front of the card, then cut another rectangle that's slightly smaller than the first from the second piece of cardstock.

3 Gently pierce the outside edges of both rectangles with the paper piercer in the running stitch locations, then embroider each rectangle in a different color of floss. Tie off the threads on the back sides and secure with a dab of glue.

4 Spell out the word of your choice in stickers on the smaller rectangle. Add adhesive foam squares to the back side, then attach the smaller rectangle the larger one.

5 Glue the embroidered assemblage to the center front of the card. Allow the glue to dry undisturbed with a small book or other weight on top.

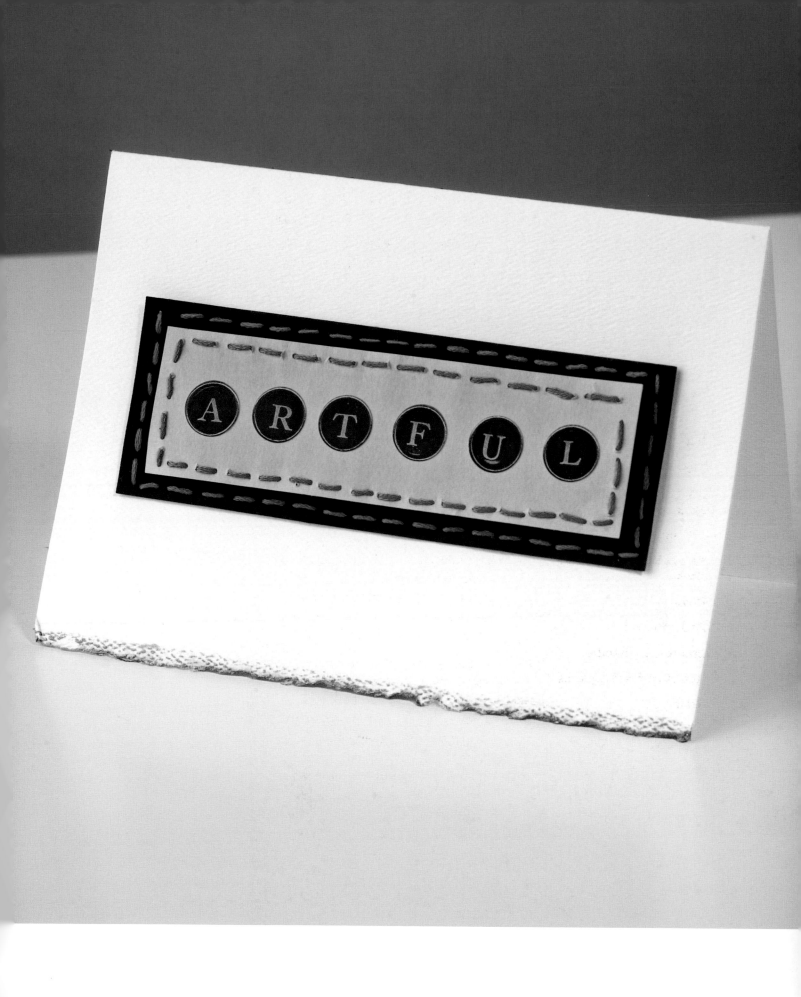

victorian hardanger wrist purses

Fatema, Khadija, and
Hajera Habibur-Rahman

This embroidered wrist purse makes an exquisite accessory, especially for dressy evening events. Using basic Hardanger stitches and techniques, even a beginner can create wearable artwork—reminiscent of a period when feminine charm flourished. Instructions are also included for the more challenging version shown on page xx.

skill level
Easy

finished measurements
Finished Wrist Purse measures 9 x 6 x 4"/23 x 15 x 10cm

materials
14 x 18"/35 x 45cm 25-count white needlework fabric

2 colors of Pearl Cotton embroidery floss

26 4mm crystal beads

Invisible sewing thread

Tapestry needle (size 24)

Embroidery scissors

Embroidery hoop

1/2 yard/.45m satin material for lining

Sewing needle and thread to match the evenweave fabric

instructions

PATTERN NOTE: Work the stitches in the color displayed on Chart A. For a review of basic Hardanger stitches, refer to the illustrations on pages 252–257.

stitching

1 Fold the fabric in half to form a 14 x 9"/35 x 22cm rectangle. Cut the fabric and zigzag the edge on the sewing machine to prevent fraying.

2 To determine the starting point, measure 1" (2.5cm) from the top center edge of the fabric. Referring to Chart A, work the buttonhole stitch in the first color at the starting point. Moving clockwise, continue working buttonhole stitches. Work the kloster blocks (except those in the vertical center diamonds) in the same color.

3 Referring to the chart on page 309, work the kloster blocks and eight- pointed star stitch in the vertical center diamonds in the second color.

4 Cut the threads at the ends of satin stitches where the stitches meet the fabric, referring to the dotted lines on the charts on page 308. Remember to cut in groups of four threads and to pull out the threads carefully.

5 Work the woven bars and square filet filling in the second color, referring to the chart on page 309 as a guide.

6 Thread a sewing needle and knot the end of the thread. To add beads, bring the needle from back to front, slip a crystal bead onto the needle, and center the bead. Secure on the back of the fabric by knotting the ends.

purse assembly

1 Trim the excess fabric around the top of buttonhole edge only, then trim the side and bottom edges, leaving a 1/2"/1cm seam allowance. Trace the shape of your trimmed Hardanger fabric onto a piece of needlework fabric, taking care to keep the top edges of the backing straight. Pin right sides together, and sew the sides and the bottom of the Hardanger purse. Turn right sides out.

2 Cut four pattern pieces from satin fabric, using the diagram on page 308 as a guide. Pin two right sides together, and sew the sides and bottom edges, leaving the top edges. Turn the right side out and press with an iron. Repeat with the remaining two pattern pieces, but do not turn the second lining right side out. Place the unturned satin lining inside the turned satin lining. Press lightly with an iron, then place the satin lining into the Hardanger purse.

3 Whipstitch the back of the top edge of the Hardanger purse to the back of the satin lining top edge. For the front

edge of purse, whipstitch the satin lining below the top Hardanger eyelet edge, leaving room for the wrist strap.

4 To make the purse's strap, cut a 13 x 4"/33 x 10cm strip of satin. Fold the strip in half lengthwise with right sides facing. Stitch the sides, leaving the top and bottom ends. Turn right sides out and press so the seam is positioned in the center back of the strap. Stitch both ends of the strap together.

5 Make an indention into the tip of the back of the Hardanger purse with your finger so the tip sinks inward, allowing the edges of the wrist strap to fit snugly inside. Whipstitch the strap to the Hardanger purse, then pull the wrist strap through the large middle eyelet. Finish all the raw edges.

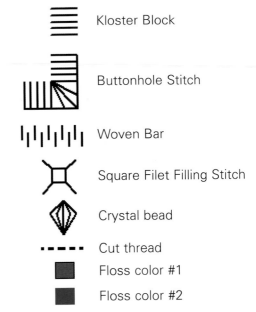

Kloster Block

Buttonhole Stitch

Woven Bar

Square Filet Filling Stitch

Crystal bead

Cut thread

Floss color #1

Floss color #2

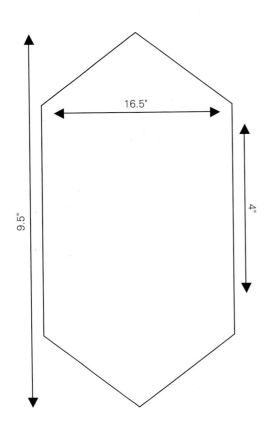

16.5"

9.5"

4"

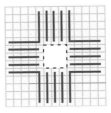

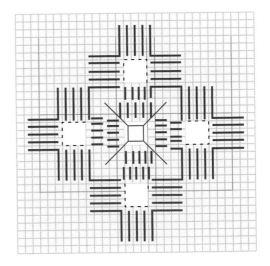

intermediate hardanger purse

Once you're comfortable with Hardanger techniques, this intermediate-level wrist purse should be your next project! The purse uses the same stitches as the beginning-level purse on page 306, but is worked on a finer linen (28 count). Square filet fillings fill the side diamonds, giving the stitch pattern a lacy look, and each eight-pointed star is accented with a crystal bead.

etceteras

contributing designers

index

acknowledgments

contributing designers

Rhonda Black dabbles in paper crafts such as card making and book binding, is an avid beader, and knits up a storm. Inspired by creative friends, great teachers, and a love of vibrant color, she lives happily in Dallas, Texas.

Stacey Budge is an art director at Lark Books. When she is not designing books, she can be found gardening and knitting at her home in Asheville, North Carolina.

Lisa Carnahan is the owner/designer of Lisa Knits, a line of original patterns, available in yarn shops nationwide. In addition to her own line, her freelance designs have appeared in publications such as Cast On, Knitter's, Knit It, Knit.1 and Interweave Press' "Christmas Stockings" and in the collections of Classic Elite, Fiber Trends, Berroco, and Lion Brand Yarns.

Cathy Carron is a knitwear designer, consultant, and owner of Pond Edge Bespoke Designs, a knit hat business based in New York and Connecticut. She lives in New York City with her husband and two daughters.

Anna Griffin never imagined her early love of crafting would lead to a career. Anna's elegant and sophisticated design style has captured the hearts of brides, crafters, and design savvy consumers everywhere. In her 17 years as a graphic designer, she has created numerous product lines inspired by the antique engravings, European textiles, and hand-painted botanicals from her personal archives. As an expert crafter, she can be seen regularly on QVC and DIY Scrapbooking. To Anna, everything old is new again as she loves to renovate old houses while living in Atlanta, GA.

Fatema, Khadija and **Hajera Habibur-Rahman** are a sister knitwear team who learned the art of needlework from their mother at very young ages. They have been needlework designers for over twelve years. Their most current publication is *Gorgeous Knitted Afghans: 33 Great Designs for Creative Knitters*, by Lark Books. Besides designing, Fatema spends her time reading books, researching about cultural textiles, and cooking Indian cuisine. In addition to needlework, Khadija loves making pastry, reading historical books, and shopping for just about anything. Hajera's hobbies include graphic art, sewing, and spending time with family and friends. She is a full time wife and mother and is currently an online computer technology instructor at Indiana University Purdue University. They all reside with their mother in a small farming town in Ohio.

Catherine Ham divides her time between homes in Austria and Greece. She is never without her knitting bag when traveling, and finds it starts conversations in the most unusual places. Catherine is the author of *25 Gorgeous Sweaters for the Brand-New Knitter* (Lark Books, 2000), and *Weekend Crafter Knitting: 20 Simple Stylish Wearables for Beginners*, (Lark Books, 2003).

Marilyn Hastings thinks through yarn from the fringe of downtown Asheville, NC. Yarn is the medium for her work in designing, free-lance technical editing of knit and crochet instructions, and her current quest for the secrets of a fine-fitting sweater that can be made in infinite variations while maintaining the fit.

Marylyn Hostetter lives in Sanford, Colorado, and has enjoyed a long history of needlecrafting. During her more active years, Marylyn once crocheted change purses for an entire girl scout troop of 16. Given her recent retirement, Marylyn now enjoys crewel embroidery and crochet at her own pace.

Glenda Larsen is an accountant by day, and a knitter and crocheter by night. She taught herself to crochet from an encyclopedia. She lives in the North Carolina mountains.

Cathy Maguire has been designing textiles and knitwear for Seventh Avenue since 1990. She has contributed knit and embroidery designs to several widely circulated knitting magazines such as *Vogue Knitting Magazine* and *knit.1*. Cathy teaches creative embroidery classes at the Fashion Institute of Technology.

Donna May is a self-taught crochet veteran of 40 years. Donna also works as a hands-on healer and a professional consulting astrologer. Though these disciplines may sound miles apart, she believes they are similar as each is about patterns, cycles or repetitions, creativity, and harmony.

Carrie McWithey is consumed by textures, colors, and good deals on yarn, (The yarn patch on her floor grows ever-so-close to her bed these days.) Also known by her business name, Hatgirl, Carrie has become the vessel through whom the goddess Crochetta works. Hatgirl items are sold across the country, and are also available direct from her website, www.hatgirlhats.com.

Marty Miller has been crocheting and creating her own patterns since she was a little girl. Using all kinds of yarns, she designs and makes afghans, sweaters, jackets, ponchos, toys, puppets, scarves, shawls, tote bags, and more. Her designs have appeared in magazines, books, and fashion shows, and in pattern collections of a major yarn company. She teaches crochet classes and workshops at a yarn shop in Greensboro, NC, and is a professional member and the Mentor Coordinator of the Crochet Guild of America (CGOA).

Joan K. Morris' artistic endeavors have led her down many successful creative paths. A childhood interest in sewing turned into professional costuming for motion pictures. After studying ceramics, Joan ran her own clay wind-chime business for 15 years. Since 1993, Joan's Asheville, North Carolina, coffee house, Vincent's Ear, has provided a vital meeting place for all varieties of artists and thinkers.

Kathy Cano Murillo, (aka The Crafty Chica), is book author, a national arts and crafts columnist, and an artist/designer specializing in Latino culture. She runs the website www.CraftyChica.com, where she shares her craftylicious ideas for all the world to see. She is married to Patrick Murillo, also an artist. They have two kids, three chihuahuas and live in the magical metropolitan desert of Phoenix, Arizona. She can be reached at kathymurillo@ hotmail.com.

Sally Poole lives in South Carolina, and has dabbled in many crafts over the years. Her mother taught her to sew and knit at an early age, and these skills she still uses when making clothes, doing whimsical appliqué quilts, or knitting wild and fancy socks.

Cindy Preston lives in a 1900 farmhouse in the cornfields of southeast Iowa where she once raised sheep. She lives there with her husband, John, a Midwest landscape painter. She spins, crochets, designs, and has 3 dogs and 4 cats. Her book *Too Cute Crochet for Babies and Toddlers* published by Lark Books, will be available in 2005.

Nanette M. Seale began creating her own crochet designs while making a baby sweater for my third child back in 1985. While crochet is her favorite sport, she also do cross stitch and plastic canvas. She has four children and a new grandchild, for whom she has "a whole new realm of ideas just waiting to be stitches."

index

acknowledgments

Almost every book is a miraculous blend of creative contributions from dozens of talented, hard-working people, and this one is no different. The following people deserve thanks and acknowledgment.

Carol Taylor, Chris Bryant, Deborah Morgenthal, Rhonda Black, Catherine Ham, Terry Taylor, and Stacey Budge shared advice and support;

Hilary Tyor, Rebecca Rosen, Kathleen Sams, Tim Sampson, and Rob Willie provided yarn samples and technical information;

E.B. Wade for photostyling the home dec projects;

Rosemary Kast and Duncan Rice prepared materials for designers;

Jeff Hamilton lifted, toted and painted;

Atkinson Luke Furniture Company and Diggin' Art of Asheville, North Carolina, loaned props;

And the following models made the projects look great: Lauren Abe, Kia Baden, Anna Barker, Jackie Dobrinska, Liam Evans, Mai Fon, Delia Grace Fowler, Emma Rose Galloway, Chad Hajek, Myra Hester, Sara House, Linwood Jaycocks, Emma Mann, Cel Naranjo, Skip Wade, Candice Kilgore, Emily Stokes, Margaret Rose Murphy, Skip Wade, and Jax the dog.